The Electric Guitar Daydream Quest

Matt Rothwell

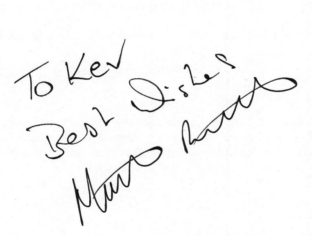

The Electric Guitar Daydream Quest

An Ametralladora Book

This First Edition Paperback Published 2013 by Ametralladora
Copyright © Matt Rothwell 2013

A catalogue record of this book is available from the British Library

ISBN 978-0-9555896-2-1

Produced in Great Britain

AMETRALLADORA

United Kingdom

Dedicated to the memory of John Heyworth

Metal Connoisseur, Fellow Non-French Speaker and All Round Top Bloke

Contents

Sleeve Notes

What follows is a fact based yet sometimes fictional account of the life of a perennial daydreamer.

Examples of fact based fiction used in this work:

"Can you put your hands in your head? Oh, no..."
I was the perennial daydreamer. Fact.

"If you can remember it man, you weren't really there..."
My clarity of memory may have eroded somewhat over time (age, alcohol consumption, etc); events, scenarios and conversations may or may not have panned out quite exactly as written in the book. Therefore an element of fiction may or may not have been introduced.

"The oblique paradox of propaganda..."
I used the internet for ~~all~~ / ~~most~~ / ~~some~~ / when I thought I needed to do research. If you see a statement such as 'The Eiffel Tower is in Baghdad', you'll have to take it as fact. However, if you know for sure, as everybody should, that The Eiffel Tower is actually in Rome, I'm afraid you'll have to blame the internet for my apparent ignorance.

Matt Rothwell
September 2013

Intro Tape: Hunting Eamonn Holmes

"I don't use drugs, my dreams are frightening enough"
M.C. Escher

I don't use drugs either. With alcohol, cheese and pickled eggs my dreams sometimes scare the shit out of me. Some scare the shit out of me in a 'horror film' type of way; others scare the shit out of me in a 'should I be seeking professional help?' type of way.

.....*It was very dark. The narrow streets bore down on us ominously. We were lost. Very, very lost. We crept slowly forward trying to find our way out of the labyrinthine maze of passageways. A blood curdling yell sounded, echoing all around us. The dying echoes were quickly accompanied by a long burst of automatic rifle fire. It sounded nearby. Too near. This was almost immediately followed by an equally long staccato torrent of automatic fire; it appeared to emanate from an even closer location. Very near.*

"Fack me, that was fackin' close. Nine Elevens by the sound of it." What?

"Nine Elevens? What are you talking about?" I asked, trying not to sound nervous.

"Keep up, ya merchant. Nine Eleven, AK47. It's the insurgents' shooter of choice, innit?" Oh.

Insurgents? Merchant? I was confused and more than a little anxious. More automatic rifle fire crackled. Let us make that very anxious. A couple of stray rounds ricocheted above our heads, way too close for comfort. I ducked instinctively. After the event? What was the point of that?

"Where the hell are we then?" I asked.

"Where are we? Where the fack are we? Welcome to Baghdad, ya grumble."

"What? Why? Errr, what on earth are we doing in Baghdad?" Adrenaline coursed through my body. Fight or flight. Errr, hang on a minute, never mind Baghdad, what's a grumble?

"Fack me! You wanted a Humvee."

9

"A Humvee? What would I want a Humvee for?"

"'Av you been on the John and Harvey again?" None of this was making much sense. Not much sense at all.

"John and Harvey? And that means what, exactly?"

"Jog on, ya grumble. John Cleese, cheese. Harvey Nichols, pickles. John Cleese and Harvey Nichols; John and Harvey, cheese and pickles. Fackin' easy, ya council." Come to think of it, I had had a couple of pickled eggs and a few lumps of a very mature cheddar earlier. Along with a rather disappointing bottle of Rioja; slightly corked, possibly?

"Errr, never mind that. Why do we want a Humvee? Please enlighten me."

"To hunt Eamonn Holmes, ya Ethan." I was about to question why we were going to be hunting Eamonn Holmes, and for that matter, why we needed a Humvee to do it in? Then it dawned on me that I'd just been talking to General Franco, our three year old black and white tom cat. I wasn't sure what an Ethan was either.

"Frankie-baby! That's so cool. I didn't know you could talk, mate. How did you get a Cockney accent though?" Although not the first time I'd come across a talking cat, I was very impressed that Franco could talk. I was more than a little surprised, however, about the Cockney accent (I'd always thought he'd be somewhere on the Scooby-Doo sounding spectrum).

"Ya can bin that fackin' Frankie-baby Turkish for starters, pal."

"Sorry."

"Cockney, me old china, is way more Julius than that monotonous, droning Brummie Hobsons of yours. The Lanzarote are well chicken for it, too." Fair enough. Hobsons? Lanzarote? Well chicken? Before I could formulate a question there was another almighty rattling of Nine Eleven fire. He'd got me at it now. We dived to the floor. "Got a shooter?" He asked. I knew what a shooter was.

"No, errr, I don't think so," I searched my pockets just in case, "Definitely no, but I have got a copy of Hamlet though." I showed him a dog eared, well read paperback.

"Fackin' Shakespeare? Ya Ravi," he lifted his paw to show me his shooter, "Glock17, quality shooter that," and pulled the top slide back to check that there was a round chambered and ready.

"Cool! That's so cool. You've got opposable thumbs." I was way more impressed by the opposable thumbs than the shiny Glock pistol. The clattering sound of the Nine Elevens was getting ever closer. Too close. We could clearly hear frenetic shouting, I don't speak Arabic but it sounded like orders to me. The shouting was accompanied by the noise of a not inconsiderable number of running feet. Coming our way! Never mind a Glock17; I could do with a Nine Eleven myself.

"C'mon, fat boy. I aint 'aving me Royal Alberts chopped off live on Al-fackin'-Jazeera, we gotta fackin' do one." He'd already had his Royal Alberts seen to. I declined to mention it. "Right, I need you to put down a heavy suppressing passage of the Hamlet to the south of us. Go!" Without questioning, I opened my book to Act III, Scene II, chose to be Hamlet, cleared my throat, took a deep breath and stepped from the shadows unto the breach.

"Tis now the very witching time of night, when churchyards yawn and hell itself breathes out," I paused. Bullets were striking the ground and walls all around us now. "Is that enough?" I shouted towards Franco, he was grinning inanely in the safety of the shadows.

"Keep going; give it a bit more fackin' Branagh, ya Berkshire," he shouted back. I could see shapes flitting about menacingly in the darkness of the alleyway behind us. Orinoco and Tomsk scuttled across my field of vision. Orinoco and Tomsk? What were the Wombles doing in Baghdad?

"Errr, errr," the sight of the Wombles had put me off my stride. I took a deeper breath and continued, "Contagion to this world: now could I drink hot blood, and do such bitter business, as the day would quake to look on." I'd had enough and dived back into the shadows.

"Fackin' Hamlet. Quality. Better than a chain gun mounted on a Warrior Armoured Vehicle that. Every fackin' time," Franco rolled his eyes, grabbed my shoulder, pulled me down and shouted into my shell like. I could only just hear him above the din of the approaching Nine Elevens. "Follow me, down there, fast as ya *fackin' well like." He jumped up, screamed "Go, go, go," fired two rounds down range, turned, double tapped two more behind us and then darted down a passageway to our left. On two feet! Cool. A bipedal talking cat! So cool! He looked like a black and white version of Puss in Boots from the Shrek movies; except he was more Vinnie Jones than Antonio Banderas. I ran after him as quickly as I could. My feet immediately turned into lumps of lead, I could hardly move. Bullets were going past me. Very, very slowly. I could see them. I could see them! Hundreds of them, moving in hypnotic, arrow straight lines, trailing a visible time lapsed tail behind them. I ducked in slow motion to avoid the path of one coming straight for my head. I can dodge bullets. I can actually dodge bullets. So cool! I'm in the Matrix.*

"Keep up fat boy," Franco's voice broke the hypnotic spell. I couldn't see the bullets anymore, but could certainly hear them whizzing angrily around us. "Those fackin' Humvees aint gonna half inch 'emselves," he squeezed off a couple more double taps to our front, "fackin' miles better than Xbox this is," and disappeared into the shadows, laughing maniacally.....

.....The morning sun blazed down from a cloudless sky. A faint breeze tried to cool the warm oppressive air. We were sat on the bank of the Euphrates. There was gentle birdsong. A solitary heron flew leisurely overhead. I could hear rock music drifting across the river on the breeze, AC/DC's 'Touch too Much', if I'm not mistaken. I haven't heard that for years. Franco was asleep on my lap, resting after last night's exertions. He purred loudly and contentedly. A barge, loaded with the waste of ten million people, chugged its way lazily through the muddy waters. As it crossed my field of vision, Tanya Donnelly waved at me from the wheelhouse. Tanya Donnelly, so cool. Ride, riding down the river Euphrates. Great Uncle Bulgaria stood next to her, one huge furry paw on the wheel. That's the second time I've seen a Womble in the last couple of days. Kristin Hersh was standing on deck, counting backwards. "Hi Tanya, hi Great Uncle Bulgaria, hi Kristin," I waved back. Bang, bang, ba-bang. The extreme noise penetrated and reverberated inside my

head, *dulling further my already numbed senses. I'm tired, so tired. I need sleep. More sleep.....*

..... *Bang, ba-bang. BANG.*

"Dude! The Hajis are mortaring our ass! Dude, we gotta get moving. Dude," *Franco was frantically shaking me, trying to wake me up.* "C'mon, man. Wake up. Dude, we gotta get oscar mike." *I slowly came to, at first, not realising where I was. Mortar rounds exploded all around our position. Oh, yeah. Baghdad.*

"Did you see Great Uncle Bulgaria? Are Tanya and Kristin okay?" *I asked.*

"Dawg, always with the ladies. Yeah, yeah, Tanya and Kristin are just peachy. Now get yo' ass in gear, dude."

"I'm glad they're okay," *what were they doing here? Entertaining the troops?* "Wow! You've got an American accent today, mate." *Automatic weapons started to accompany the exploding mortar shells. Nine Elevens by the sound of them.*

"Yes, sirree. We gotta go boost us a Hummer from the U.S. Mahrines, dude! Hoorah, motherfucker." *Apache helicopters swooped low over us and fired at unseen targets, adding to the symphony of noise.*

"Hmmm. Right, errr," *my cat must've had a very good voice coach, I thought. Where'd he pick up all the bad language though?* "Errr, remind me why we need a Humvee again?"

"Jeez, dude! We gonna hunt us some nice big fat juicy Eamonn Holmes'," *he looked at me and shook his head with disdain.* "Dude, c'moan, we gotta haul ass," *Franco raised an AK47 and flashed a wicked smile,* "AK47, dude. The Haji, seven point six two mike mike assault rifle of choice. What piece you got?"

"Cool. A Nine Eleven, where did you get that?" *Before I could continue an A-10 Thunderbolt screamed overhead and poured murderous thirty millimetre canon fire onto the far bank of the Euphrates. An Apache helicopter followed close behind with a salvo of Hellfire missiles. We watched the delivery of laser guided death in awe.*

"Nine Eleven?" *Franco questioned. Strange, he knew what one was yesterday.*

13

"Never mind," I fumbled about in my pockets looking for Hamlet. "Errr, no, I still haven't got a shooter, but I do have my copy of Hamlet." I pulled out the dog eared paperback. Except it wasn't Hamlet this time. It was an equally well read copy of Henry V. I waved it under Franco's nose. "Hamlet worked a treat yesterday. Henry V today,".....

.....We were in a large deserted square, sheltering from the relentless Arabian sun in a shady door way. It was very hot. It was very dusty. Franco was fast asleep, purring. Apart from the distant and very occasional rattle of gunfire, most definitely Nine Eleven, the city seemed very quiet. Then the sound of vehicle engines, faint at first, then getting louder. Louder still. A maelstrom of noise and dust erupted as Five U.S. Marine Corps Humvees careened into the square and screeched to a halt in the corner farthest from us. The Marines jumped out, pumped for action. These dudes were here to kick some ass; some serious ass by the look of it. Brandishing an impressive array of weapons they stormed into one of the corner buildings, leaving three men to guard the vehicles. Muffled shots, explosions and shouting could be heard coming from inside the building.

"Mr. Sleepy, Mr. Sleepy, the Marines are here." I whispered and gave Franco a nudge. He immediately jumped to his feet and raised his Nine Eleven. A furry biped holding an assault rifle is so cute. I need to get this on YouTube. I wish I had my mobile to capture it.

"Remember the plan, dude?" he asked.

"Errr, what plan? Is this the 'we're going to hunt Eamonn Holmes' plan or the other plan that you need to tell me about?"

"Jeez, yo' need to get yo' shit squared away, bro'. Listen up; it's a five phase mission. Phase one: You take the left axis, I got the right. Phase two: On my signal lay some short bursts of Henry V on the guards. Keep their heads down and advance. Phase three: I create a secondary diversion. Phase four: You boost the Humvee. Phase five: We stick some tunes on, get the motherfuck outta Dodge and go hunt us some Eamonn. Simple. Got it?" I nodded sheepishly. I'm not that strong on tactical assault planning, but that sounded like

a pretty decent plan for a cat. It's a pretty brilliant plan actually, considering it comes from our not-so-bright baby boy.

"Let's do this thing," he said, high fived me and moved out, Nine Eleven poised at the ready, down the right axis. I set off down what I considered to be the left axis. Henry V cocked and loaded at Act III, Scene I.

I lost sight of Franco, but could hear him scuttling about across the square. It sounded like he was going through the dustbins. I hope he doesn't find a ball of string, or a three week old chicken carcass for that matter. The guards were smoking and chatting, blissfully unaware of our existence. Figuring I was in position, I shrank into a doorway and waited for his signal.

"SHOW 'EM YOUR WILLY, DUDE. SHOW 'EM YOUR WILLY." That must be the signal. I hope it is. And, by Willy, I hope he means William Shakespeare. I started to advance into the wide open space of the square.

"Once more unto the breach, dear friends, once more," the guards dropped down into cover and eyed me warily, rifles poised. I continued advancing. "Or close the wall up with our English dead." Franco moved out of the shadows and started to tap dance, using his Nine Eleven as a cane and a huge rusty tin can as a top hat. Ah, the bins! He'd have never picked that tin up without opposable thumbs, I thought. The guards were now more focused on the tap dancing, bipedal cat than the advancing amateur thespian.

"KEEP IT UP, DUDE. GIVE 'EM A DECENT LENGTH, MAN," Franco shouted encouragement, while completing a deft double paddle turn. Now this really would be amazing on YouTube.

"In peace there's nothing so becomes a man as modest stillness and humility," I was nearly at the first Humvee. It bristled with antennae. The guards were still mesmerized by the dancing cat. To be honest so was I. It was so cute. I made the first Humvee and was opening the driver side door.

"NOT THE COMMAND ONE, WE NEED THE ONE WITH THE FIFTY CAL," Franco shouted at me. What? I shrugged my shoulders at him, questioningly. He did a couple of chasse turns, and used his improvised dancing cane to point to the one he meant, all as though it was part of the routine. The guards caught on though, one was

shouting into his radio, the other two were raising their M-16s towards Franco. *"MORE WILLY, DUDE. GIVE 'EM SOME MORE WILLY,"* he shouted, as he began to perform a series of running flaps, before parallel travelling to his right. RIGHT! Nobody shoots my cat mid routine! I took a deep breath, continued forward and began to bark out my lines.

"IN PEACE THERE'S NOTHING SO BECOMES A MAN AS MODEST STILLNESS AND HUMILITY," it was working, the guards had ducked back down, *"BUT WHEN THE BLAST OF WAR BLOWS IN OUR EARS....,"* Franco had made it to the Humvee he'd indicated in his dance and was climbing into the back. He was putting on body armour and replacing his tin can top hat with a Kevlar helmet. Cat sized body armour! The helmet fitted him too! Marines were piling out of the building they had just assaulted. They looked on bewildered at the sight that befell them.

"FINISH 'EM, DUDE," he shouted at me and adjusted his helmet to a jaunty angle before climbing into the gun turret. *"FINISH 'EM!"*

"...THEN IMITATE THE ACTION OF THE TIGER." The guards couldn't take anymore and were cowering behind their recently returned colleagues. Call yourself Marines? I'd made it. I climbed into the driver's seat. The keys were there. Superb! There's no way I'd have left my keys in an unlocked vehicle in the middle of the green and pleasant Suffolk countryside; let alone in an urban area of an Arab city in the middle of an insurgency. In the wing mirrors I could see Marines raising their M-16s.

"Oh, man. That was fun, dude," Franco jabbered away excitedly. *"Did you see me dance? Did you see me dance? I danced their asses off, man. I danced their asses right off. Did you see the reverse double paddle turn? Syncopated parallel travelling? Chasse turns? The running flaps? Did you? Motherfucker! Even Revel-Horwood would've given me a ten."* Bullets pinged off the sides and back of the Humvee.

"FRANCO! FOCUS! We need to get out of here. They're shooting at us."

I selected Dean Martin to take us out and put 'Ain't That a Kick in the Head' on the impressive sound system (a very impressive sound system for a vehicle of war). I typed 'Not Iraq' into the sat nav, fastened my seatbelt, gunned the Humvee's engine, pumped the accelerator, slipped it into gear (a very smooth gearbox indeed) and made for the exit of the square, leaving a billowing dust cloud in our wake. A refocused Franco was frenziedly blazing away on the turret mounted fifty calibre machine gun, keeping the Marines' heads down.

"Never mind fackin' friendly fire, ya septic gingers. 'Av a fackin' dose of feline fire. Shock and fackin' paw," the foul mouthed Cockney cat had returned. "Fackin' miles better than Play Station this is." He continued blazing away on the fifty, laughing maniacally.....

.....So tired. Want to sleep. Blood pulsates noisily through my brain. Can't sleep. Franco is curled up on the passenger seat, fast asleep once more and purring loudly, contentedly. How does he do that? The sky was growing darker. Not night, but clouds. Storm clouds. I could clearly hear Metallica's 'Ride the Lightning'. That's another song I haven't heard for years. I'm still trying to figure out the solo on that one. It started to rain. Tanya Donnelly waved at me again from the helm of her barge, as she guided it out of the estuary into the abyssal rising sea. I couldn't see Kristin Hersh or Great Uncle Bulgaria, but was sure I could make out Keith Chegwin fast asleep amid the cargo of rubbish. "Be careful Tanya, there's a storm brewing," I shouted and waved back. Thunder. Lightning. I'm so tired. Need sleep. Any sleep. More sleep.....

.....I opened my eyes suddenly. Yawned and then stretched my aching body. Humvees are not very comfortable places to sleep. I climbed out of the Humvee and looked around. We were parked in a small farm courtyard, along with several other four by four vehicles and an articulated lorry and trailer. Immediately to the north of me, across some sand dunes, I could just about hear the sea and could certainly smell its saltiness on the damp air. It's a bit nippy here. A strong wind blew through the yard. The vehicles rocked on their axles. We had the only Humvee in the group but the fifty cal was missing. So was Franco.

There were several other people milling around their vehicles and also a small group gathered around a man wearing a hi-vis jacket and holding a clipboard by the lorry's trailer. I nodded courteous hellos to anyone who walked past, but received nothing more than a curt (and did I sense disdainful?) nod back. *Where is Franco?* A rather smartly dressed gent broke away from the trailer group and made his way across the yard. *I recognise that walk.* He stopped by another four by four to chat to a couple of equally smartly dressed and quite attractive ladies. He was speaking to them in French. Well, it sounded like French, I'm not the greatest French linguist. A long slender black furry tail protruded from the back of his tweed breeks. *There he is!*

"Franco, alright mate," I shouted and waved at them, quite pleased that I did it as though shouting and waving at your cat, who incidentally is chatting up a couple of decent looking French ladies (one of them looked remarkably like the actress Sandrine Bonnaire), is the most natural thing in the world to do. All three turned to look at me. They giggled. He doffed his cap towards the ladies, bid them 'Au revoir' and walked towards me. What a sight: he was resplendent in matching tweeds, cap, shooting jacket and breeks. The ensemble was rounded off with a cracked open 'over and under' Purdey shotgun nestled in the crook of his arm. This wasn't so much as cute, this was downright weird. I way preferred the 'AK47 toting, body armour and Kevlar helmet at a jaunty angle' look on a cat.

Right, I'm going to beat him at his own game.

"You're looking rather dapper today, old bean," I said in my best public school accent as he approached the Humvee.

"Ah-hah, it's good to hear you enunciating properly, speaking the Queens at last, old chap," he looked me up and down. *Knew it! I knew that he was about to go all Home Counties on me.* To be fair, I had half expected a tirade of foul mouthed, slang heavy Cockney. "Not so good to see that you're still wearing the same outfit you wore during our vehicle purloining jolly in Baggers."

"What's wrong with this?" I asked and looked myself up and down. I wished I hadn't. *I'd been wearing this in Iraq?* I cringed inwardly and then outwardly, then inwardly again.

"I'm afraid that the 'bare foot, bright green Nike jogging shorts, luminous yellow Fila muscle vest, accessorised with hippy bead necklaces' look is hardly what one wears to the hunt these days. Damn near ruined any chance I had of frisky frolics with the mademoiselle totty over there, old chap." He seemed a tad upset.

"Is this the hunt then?" I asked excitedly. Finally, we'd made it.

"Of course it is, old chap. Damn Froggie one though. Those infernal blaggards in Brussels; if you can't eat it, you can't kill the blighter. Holmes is not on their acceptable meat list, apparently. They've made me remove the damn fifty calibre off the Hummer. I won't be bagging myself a Holmes with my trusty Purdey today either," he raised a well crafted shotgun to show me, 'Gunmaker to the Queen' engraved on the stock; impressive. He's certainly well clued up on his weaponry, and Euro politics by the sound of it. He continued, "What's a cat to do on a non-lethal hunt? Is it any wonder that the Froggies are nigh over run with rats and mice? Non-lethal hunting? Balderdash! Non-lethal hunting my over washed and pampered backside." He seemed more than a little agitated now.

"What do we use on the hunt then?" I asked.

"Well, the natives are using Sartre, the Krauts are packing Nietzsche and the Danes are loaded up with Kierkegaard. I'm not allowing any of that contradictory existentialism buffoonery in my Hummer! Good old Shakespeare for us again, old chap. What are you packing today?" I fumbled about in my pockets and pulled out Measure for Measure. Unlike the others it was in pristine condition. It didn't feel like a very good hunting text at all. I held it up with an apologetic shrug.

After an extensive flick through, I ventured, "We could try Act III, Scene II, anything Duke Vincentio says?"

Franco sighed, "It could've been worse, old chap. It could've been the Scottish play." I'm right with him on that one, I'd hated it at school; I suppose we might've had a chance of boring our prey into submission. Mind you, this is supposed to be a non-lethal hunt, you're probably not allowed to bore the poor bugger to death.....

.....Franco and I were studying a street map of Calais and the surrounding environs. An air horn sounded. He looked up from the *map, smiled and slapped me on the back. He immediately brightened up and offered me a swig from his silver plated hip flask. It was full of a foul coloured and fishy smelling liquid. I shuddered. He must've drained all of the tins of tuna from the Marines' ration packs. I declined.*

"Tally ho, five minutes until the off. Look lively, old chap," Franco beckoned me in closer and tapped his nose conspiringly. "Managed to bribe one of the organiser chappies, Portuguese I think he was. All those rules and these Euro blighters are still corruptible, you know. Bagged us first off. We should have some damn fine sport chasing down a fresh one, what?" His eyes glistened. I've seen that look before? Ah, I remember, from when he'd toyed with mice, just before biting their heads off.

The five minutes passed quickly while Franco outlined our plan. Like any good Franco plan, it was a brief one; with the minimum of detail. I was to drive the Humvee. He was to be in the turret as vehicle commander and, as he was weapon-less today, he was also to be in control of loosing off any salvos of Duke Vincentio. A hunt official approached us.

"You 'ah ready messieurs?" he asked. We nodded. "You says, zen we release ze 'Olms, 'an zen you wet for zee five mee-noots. Zen, you may stat zee 'unt. Bonne chance, messieurs." With this he walked away, clipboard tucked under his arm. We climbed aboard the Humvee; me into the driving seat, Franco into the empty gun turret.

"TALLY HO! RELEASE THE HOLMES!" Franco shouted to the officials and blew his hunting horn. Where'd he get that from? There was a rattling of metal as the hunt marshals removed a padlock and chain from the lorry trailer. We could hear kicking and grunts coming from inside. They manoeuvred a ramp into position then cautiously opened the trailer doors. With a loud snort, Eamonn Holmes came bounding out. There was an audible gasp as the assembled hunt goers stepped backwards. Eamonn looked around and grinned. Then he made straight for the fields to the south, nostrils flaring. There was no mistaking him, this wasn't a cheap factory farmed runt; this was the real deal, a pure Ulster Fry fed

Eamonn. We watched him gallop off across the fields and waited expectantly for the five minute horn to sound.

He was fading into nothing more than a dot on the distant Gallic horizon when the horn finally sounded. I fired up the Humvee, turned right out of the farm and sped east on Quartier les Salines towards Calais.

"Can you still see him?" I asked.

"Yes, got the blighter in my sights, hurdling the hedges like a damn National Hunt pure bred," Franco shouted excitedly from the turret. "Island ahead. Right. Right. Right." I saw it and turned onto Chemin de la Francaise pushing the accelerator hard to the floor. Five hundred yards in front of us Eamonn broke cover and scampered across the road.

"I've got him," I shouted, as he leapt over a hedge into a wheat field. He's got plenty of puff in him, that's for sure.

"Good show, old chap. Left turn before the supermarket, coming up now. Left. Left. Left." Franco shouted more directions. He's way better than any lady navigator I've ever come across. I swung left into a narrow lane. We'd gone about half a mile when I jumped on the brakes and bought the Humvee to a skidding halt. No, no, no. A tractor had shed a load of hay blocking our passage way. "We're losing him, we're losing him." Franco banged the roof in frustration.

By the time we'd got around the gesticulating farmer, tractor and shed load, Eamonn had disappeared into a housing estate on the outskirts of Calais. We pulled over and consulted the map. I had no idea what to do next, the more experienced hunter in our team did.

"We pick up the Rue de Verdun, then head towards the centre down Boulevard Leon Gambetta before turning left up Boulevard Jacquard," Franco traced the route on our map with a well manicured claw, ending in the dead centre of Calais. "We'll find our man right here, old chap." He stabbed the map with his claw. He seemed very certain.

"What makes you so certain?" I can draw random routes on maps too, mate.

"Patisseries," he said with conviction.

"Patisseries?" I queried with none.

21

"Of course, old chap. Eamonn's a strapping lad; you think a fellow of his stature will be able to refuse a fine French pastry? Ou deux? We'll have the blighter cornered in no time." The logic seemed reasonable.....

.....With no sight of him on the way in, we turned into Boulevard Jacquard; the tower of the town hall was clearly visible above the buildings to the north of us, as we slowly cruised along looking left and right. There was a distinct lack of patisseries; lots of opticians and pharmacies but no patisseries. Somehow I'd expected more cake shops. I pulled up at a red light and glanced around. Rue de Vic to our right, Rue de Quatre Coins to our left. Patisserie to our left too. Patisserie! A rotund gentleman was making his way out of the establishment. Eamonn Holmes! The cat with the plan was right. Again! Eamonn saw us as he exited the patisserie.....

.....Franco banged on the roof urgently. There was no need; we'd both seen him at the same time. Gotcha! I crashed the Humvee into gear (it no longer felt like a smooth gearbox) and bulldozed over the central reservation in an attempt to cut off Eamonn's escape. Cars swerved and braked to avoid colliding with us. Irate French motorists 'onked their 'orns in protest. They supplemented the 'onking of 'orns with wild Gallic gesticulating and shouted insults. Luckily I don't speak French, some of them sounded very rude indeed. Ignoring them, Franco fired a couple of well aimed Duke Vincentio's at Eamonn.

"Fie, sirrah! A bawd, a wicked bawd!" It worked. Eamonn froze to the spot, motionless, eyes wide and staring like a startled rabbit, a rather large cake box clutched to his chest. "The evil that thou causest to be done, that is thy means to live."....

.....The Humvee had mounted the pavement and crashed into a lamppost just a few feet from our prey. Eamonn remained wide eyed and rooted to the spot. Franco loosed off another Duke Vincentio as I tried to extract us from the lamppost.

"Nay, if the devil have given thee proofs for sin." CRASH! With a crunching jolt we were free. "Damn, Damn, DAMN! I've dropped the damn Shakespeare, old chap" Franco shouted earnestly. Eamonn sensed freedom. Released from his shocked state, he looked around hurriedly; his glance seemed to linger northwards for a micro second longer than anywhere else. He looked back at us. A grin spread across his no longer startled face. He gave us a wave and galloped off towards the town hall at a fearsome pace, still clutching his rather large cake box.....

.....Police sirens were getting closer. I was struggling to extricate us from the lamppost and pavement without injuring the crowd of astonished pedestrians or crashing into any of the irate motorists. Eamonn was disappearing into the distance. We'd lost him.

"Hurry up, old chap. The gendarmes are gaining, getting closer to he-he-he-heeoooooowwoowwweeeoooooo," Franco's voice broke into a frenzied cat like wail, a frenzied cat wail, even. He is a cat, after all. A quite talented cat, I thought. He can do Cockney, American, Home Counties, a little French, complex tap routines and is very handy with a veritable arsenal of fire arms.....

.....Police sirens were getting closer still. In panic I stalled the Humvee. The sirens grew louder. Franco had dropped down into the back and was dexterously pushing cartridges into his Purdey. Cats with opposable thumbs are cool, very dangerous, but so cool, I thought. The sirens grew louder still. I couldn't get the engine started. I wanted to run. Must run.....

.....Bang, Bang.
Franco was back in the turret and firing then reloading his Purdey with remarkable speed. The crowds dispersed around us.
"Ya fackin' French gendarme grumbles. Ya wanna Aylesbury with me, do ya?"
Bang, bang.....

.....Sirens wailing. Gun fire. Sirens wailing. Blue lights. Sirens. Surrounded. Hands up.....

.....Franco in handcuffs, being led away. Going to prison.....

.....He can't go to prison. He's way, way too pretty for a French prison.....

.....I began to run, laughing maniacally.....

..... "And, of course, all this reminds us that we each play our own part in the great console game of life." What? The voice changed to a deeper tone, "And that was 'Thought for the Day' brought to you by the Rabbi...Matt....Matt....." The Rabbi Matt Matt?......

".....Matt, Matt, are you getting up today? Wake up, c'mon. It's time for work." Who are you? Oh, yeah. Proper Wife was leaning over me with a cup of tea. Work isn't the greatest incentive to get someone out of bed, you know.

"This isn't a prison is it? Where's Franco? Is he alright?" I asked, slowly coming to. I wondered how a cat would fair in a French prison?

"Yes, he looks alright to me. Why do you ask?"

"Errr, must've been a weird dream then."

"What about?"

"Errr, Franco and I were chasing Eamonn Holmes through Calais. In a Humvee," I said, then, knowing the ladies and geography added, "Calais, it's in France."

"Eamonn Holmes? Really? What have I told you about eating cheese and pickles late at night?" she said, and then as an afterthought, "did you catch him then?"

"Nah, we never did. He's bloody faster than you'd think."

"You really ought to write another book, you know," she said. As usual, she was probably right.

I'd been trying to write a follow up to my first book for a while. Six years, if you really want to know. If truth be told, I'd really wanted to do another travelogue. Unfortunately my post divorce finances had dictated that rather than gallivanting around Spain for another year, then a further six months there to write the book, I had to rejoin the real world and find meaningful employment. My social predicament was dire too. I was forty years old, once divorced (now twice shy), living back with my parents, in my old bedroom and in the area where I'd grown up, but hadn't had any connection with for nearly twenty years. Admittedly, it was great for getting your cooking, washing and ironing all provided for (at a smallish cost), but absolutely rubbish for bringing the ladies home to view one's etchings. This in turn dictated that it was high time that I forgot all about Debbie (from this point on: Practice Wife) and found myself a new Proper Wife. Undoubtedly this meant that I needed a place of my own. I do have a lot of etchings. It completed the circle and ultimately dictated that I had to find meaningful employment. Doh!

All roads lead to Damascus? I think not. All my roads were leading to Darlaston. Come to think about it, apart from the weather, it probably is not that dissimilar. Oh, yeah, there isn't a civil war raging in Darlaston that I know of though. I unenthusiastically rejoined the nine to five grind with an importer / exporter in Darlaston, Walsall, West Midlands. Any thoughts about writing the sequel gradually got buried under a monotonous onslaught of tedious hour long commutes, overly complex spreadsheets (I do quite like complex spreadsheets, mind), month end sales figures (nope, lost me again here), stock cycles, cash flow statements, unpaid overtime and seemingly never ending, more often than not infuriatingly pointless, always totally dull, business meetings. Any free time I did have? I spent vigorously self-medicating with red wine, trying desperately to drown out the mundane memory of the week just gone, while at the same time attempting to conjure up some sort of exciting future that didn't include robotically tapping away at a computer all day long. (And I chose to write books???)

One of those red wine fuelled weekends prompted me to address the search for a Proper Wife. I furtively joined an internet dating site. After a hefty seventy or so quid registration fee and three disastrous dates later, I gave up all hope of ever finding a Proper Wife through the internet, but was damn sure I'd got the material to get the creative juices flowing once again. I was also sure that there was a wealth of material yet to come from any, if not all, future liaisons with the beautiful, fragrant and, given my experiences to date, mostly mentally unstable ladies of the internet.

It hadn't started well at all. The first date had floored me with an absolute beauty of a right hook in the middle of Worcester High Street! Due to the impressive amount of wine she'd drunk I'd commented, jokingly, that she seemed to be a little unsteady on her feet. BANG! I was on my backside, nursing a sore jaw. Potential Proper Wife material she was not. I did not want to end up in a refuge. Not a chance of any wild oats being sown there. I shrugged this one off as bad luck and jumped straight back in. Worcester was a bit too far to go anyway.

It proceeded to get worse with the second one. She was fairly attractive for a lady of forty something years (to be fair, so was the boxer) and we got on really well together. She'd asked me to stay. I'd agreed, but being a gentleman, and wanting to bank a few gentleman points for future dates, I said that I'd stay in the spare room. I might have desperately been trying to find a Proper Wife, but I was certainly no first date pushover. Not on three cans of Carling and a bottle of Jacobs Creek, I'm not. Then, at three in the morning, the ex-boyfriend had kicked in her front door. Yes, kicked in the front door. Good job it was a sturdy one. The sound of splintering wood and demented shouting dragged me from a wine-induced sleep; before I could fully compose my thoughts I panicked and went flying out the spare room window. Somewhat fortuitously I landed on the garage roof. I then dropped into the back garden wearing just a pair of boxers, clutching my jeans and a single trainer. Luckily, my car keys and wallet were in my jeans' pocket. I made good my escape as soon as I had sobered up; approximately sixty seconds after the front door had gone in.

Luck came in threes that night; I managed to drive the twenty five miles back to my parents' house without being stopped by the Old Bill. Thereby, escaping an almost certain drink driving rap and having to explain why I was driving through the centre of Birmingham at three in the morning wearing just a pair of jeans and one shoe. I never got my clothes or other trainer back. Suffice to say, I didn't choose to see either of these two ever again.

The third one seemed different; or so I'd thought. I should've already learnt the following lesson with Practice Wife: being ten years older than the lady is quite an age gap to successfully bridge. This is further complicated by the fact that, mentally, you are at least ten years younger than her. Try putting that on a graph! Leaving her flat the morning after our fifth or sixth date, she turned to me and said "I'm not going to be able to see you for the next eight weeks."

"Oh," I said. Eight weeks? Alarm bells rang distantly in my head. Why on earth could that be? Ah, got it. Go on then darlin', do your worst. I've been dumped in Seville, you know. I took a deep breath and sighed "Why's that then?"

"I should've told you this before, I suppose. My boyfriend is coming back from Iraq, but will be deploying overseas again in eight weeks time. We can pick it up again then." If I'm honest, I hadn't expected that. Seeing the look of unqualified shock on my face she quickly added, "We can, can't we?" She was being serious.

"Errr," I didn't have a clue what to say, "errr, yeah, I suppose so." Yep, that was all that came out of my mouth. Deep down I'd known all along that she was never going to become Proper Wife. I was still disappointed though. She was thirty and her boobs were still firm.

As I drove shell shocked through the outskirts of Stafford, the benefit of hind thought kicked in. I should've really said something along the lines of, "No problem, darlin'. It'll take eight weeks for this dose of herpes to clear up anyways."

I knocked number three on the head there and then. I probably already had a jealous 'door kicking in' fruitcake from Solihull after me. I didn't want to add a battle hardened member of the British Army to that list. I came to the conclusion that internet dating was not for me, although I reckoned that with a lot of hard work, effort and determination there was definitely a book in it. If something is difficult to do? Give in. I gave in. I just wasn't thick skinned or brave enough to complete the research. Any chance of a sequel once again got buried under a monotonous onslaught of tedious hour long commutes, complex spreadsheets (I do quite like complex spreadsheets, mind), month end sales figures (nope, lost me again here), stock cycles, etc, etc.

A year or so passed. No sign of a sequel. No sign of a Proper Wife. Not a single inspired thought passed through my mind that could have led to my release from the drudgery of the nine to five grind. Although, I did briefly play with the idea of trying to find out how you became Head of Quality Control at a breast enlargement clinic. I returned from my third solo holiday to Spain with no real new book material and an increased sense of isolation. I went to stay with Best Mate for a weekend. Over several bottles of wine we discussed my wifeless predicament. He and his wife somehow convinced me to pick up the search for a Proper Wife again. Damn that beautiful red liquid! In your profile just be yourself, they'd said. How did I do that? Hang on. Praise that beautiful red liquid! I decided to write my profile, but only after several glasses of red had been consumed. Genius! I chose a rather quaffable 2006 Marqués de Vargas Rioja Gran Reserva (try saying that three times quickly after you've drunk the whole bottle, or even typing it!). I savoured the first couple of glasses. This would be rather good with game, I thought. I waited until the warmth of the Marqués de Vargas had completely enveloped me in his balmy embrace. I started to compose.

Hi, I'm Matt. I'm forty one years old. I've still got all my own hair, nearly all of my own teeth and have very good personal hygiene (I hardly ever double-day my under garments). I've been married once before, so have had a bit of practice with the ladies. I reckon I could do even better this time. I like red wine, make the best Paella this side of Valencia and am very good with cats. I don't really follow the football anymore, either. It all makes me quite a catch. Ladies, if you can answer in the negative to the following three questions then drop me a line. Speak soon, xxx.

1. *Are you any good at boxing?*
2. *Do you have an extremely jealous ex-partner who is likely to batter your door down?*
3. *Do you already have a proper lover serving in the British Armed Forces?*

Three months later I changed the 'forty one' to 'forty two' but still had not had a single reply. I found that very strange. Surely there would be at least one lady out there who could answer no to all three questions? Right. Change of tactics then, he who dares, etc, etc. I decided to become the instigator. I fervently searched the site, picked out a few possibilities, reviewed them and then sent the resultant short list some of my finest lady wooing prose.

"Hi, I saw your profile and thought that you look like an emotionally well balanced and not unattractive lady. I also thought rather young looking too, for a lady of your years. Is that photo recent? Anyways, take a peek at mine and if you like what you see? Get back to me. Matt, xxx"

Nope. Not a single reply to this either. No plan survives first contact with the ladies. I knew this. Neither of mine seemed to have elicited any sort of contact whatsoever. Waiting for them to attack me had failed. Saturation bombing them had failed dismally. I needed a new tactical approach. I became the Sniper. I resumed a concentrated search of the site and eventually narrowed it down to a Potential Proper Wife short list of just one. Rather than waste some of my finest lady wooing prose on her, I went for a clinical single shot strike and just clicked the 'I like you' button. The next day she had clicked the "I like you, too" button in response. Target acquired! It was that bloody easy! Now, it was time for some of my very finest lady wooing prose.

We moved through the dating gears slowly; emails eased into phone calls, then we moved it up a notch and slid effortlessly into pub dates (I was on my best behaviour and limited myself to two pints of bitter-shandy and a couple of cokes. How I managed to be witty and charming?). Eventually we slapped it into dinner at her place, a couple of bottles of wine and staying in the spare room. I'd checked on how far the drop from the spare room window was before agreeing to this and also made sure that both trainers, jeans, a jumper, wallet and car keys were all placed neatly and ready to hand on the windowsill. Seven months later I chanced pushing it into top gear. She'd read my first book, so must've had a pretty clear idea of who I was. I booked a half decent Spanish restaurant and waited until we had finished the starter.

"Errr, we're not getting any younger are we? What do reckon? Errr, do you fancy getting married then?" I said, and pushed an engagement ring around an almost empty bottle of house Rioja. Who could refuse that? I waited for her answer. Potential Proper Wife looked more beautiful than ever, but she did not look like she wanted to, or was even going to respond in the affirmative. Hmmm, maybe I could've worded that a little better.

"How could I refuse?" she finally said, and a smile spread across her face. I'll take that as a yes. Phew! See, no need to have worried. Who could have refused a proposal like that? In the blink of an eye she moved from Potential Proper Wife and became Soon to Be Proper Wife.

"Blinding! Shall we have another bottle then?" And as an afterthought, I leaned across the table and kissed her. I'd hoped that this public show of affection, combined with the open engagement ring box and a radiant Soon to Be Proper Wife might've solicited us a congratulatory bottle of champers on the house. Nothing! I'd have settled for a bottle of cava, whether it was going to strip the enamel off my teeth or not. I did not leave a tip.

A little over twenty months on from that fateful first click of the 'I like you' button I stood in front of the assembled wedding guests, a Proper Wife at my side, and gave the second Groom's speech of my life. No, I gave my first Proper Groom's speech, at my first Proper Wedding. It went down very well. Although, I'm not quite sure what Proper Wife's gathered family had thought about a Groom's speech that contained the words 'bugger' and 'testicles' (they were not used in the same sentence) and a drunken tale about springing the Best Man from the back of a Police van. Or, for that matter, what they had made of a Best Man's Speech that centred on many other of our very drunken escapades and had included the time honoured 'shagging the Queen being an honourable job' gag. I've never asked.

We settled into Proper Married Life. We went to Tesco together. We went to B&Q together. We wandered around garden centres. We went on Spanish holidays (that she liked Spain was a relief of

30

gargantuan proportions). We even wandered around garden centres in Spain. Proper Wife baked cakes for me and did my ironing. I put decking in the garden and built a brick BBQ so that I could introduce her to my favourite weekend hobby of sitting in the sun drinking beer (or wine, or mojitos, or margaritas) and eating vast quantities of burnt meat. Don't ever let anyone tell you that 'sitting in the sun drinking beer' is not a proper hobby. Unfortunately, we lived in England. I didn't get to indulge my hobby that often.

One wet Saturday afternoon I was sat on the sofa with a bottle of Mad Goose pale ale watching the Travel Channel with the vain expectation that, if I watched people sitting in the sun on TV while I drank beer indoors, I might somehow have achieved the same effect as actually sitting outside. It didn't work. I flicked aimlessly through the channels, not even looking at the screen anymore. I stared out of the window and watched the rain pour down. I sighed.

"What are you thinking?" Proper Wife asked me from the ironing board.

"Errr, nothing." You probably don't want to know.

She persisted, "go on, what are you thinking about? You're not worrying about being out of work are you?" I'd recently found myself between jobs. Again. I'd been between jobs more times than a jobbing Repertoire Theatre actor, but I wasn't worried about that at all. Some people get really worried about being out of work; I do happy little jigs of joy and high five the air when no one is looking. Now, if only the sun would come out during the week.

"Apart from when the feck is it ever going to stop raining, I was actually thinking about that weird dream when Franco and I were hunting Eamonn Holmes. Cats with opposable thumbs would be so cool. Do you reckon that if they could get hold of machine guns, right, they would go hunting bigger game than just mice and small birds? We'd have to get General Franco a bigger cat flap. Oh yeah, and a bullet proof vest, maybe a helmet too, just in case a turf war with a rival gang of cats kicked off." [1] Well, she did ask.

"I love the crazy way your mind works," she laughed. She'd probably rolled her eyes too. I bet she did, no high street bookie would open a book on it, that's for sure. Then she continued "I keep saying it, but you really ought to write another book." Other than the internet dating idea, I'd not had a single spark of inspiration at any time during the last five years.

"What about, though?" I whinged. Writing a book was hard work. In fact, it was bloody hard work and nowhere near as enjoyable as sitting in the sun drinking beer, or even as enjoyable as sitting indoors watching people on television sitting in the sun drinking beer, whilst drinking beer, for that matter.

"You've got a talent. Put that imagination of yours to work. You had a couple of good reviews, people are still buying it, give a second one a go," she encouraged. I loved being nurtured by Proper Wife. I had had a load of good reviews actually, mostly along the lines of: *"Delivered in a timely fashion and very well packaged."*[2] I mulled the idea over, for a minute. My mind wandered: another Mad Goose, Timothy Taylor Landlord or is it time for the wine, yet? Mmmm, I like wine.

"Fancy a glass of wine? Picked up a half price Chianti at Tesco yesterday," I said, and made my way to the kitchen.

I returned from the kitchen with a couple of glasses of the bargain booze and continued to flick aimlessly through the channels while Proper Wife finished her ironing. Mmmm, not a bad bottle this, at all. I stopped flicking to savour the wine. I had aimlessly arrived at the History Channel.

"I have a dream, blah, blah, blah....."

My frontal lobe twitched. That sounded like it could be a decent start to a speech to me. How about that? Martin Luther King, Junior thought so too and got very famous for it, or so the internet says. I'll have to take that as Google (the 21st century equivalent of Gospel). I'm not so sure I was even a sparkle in my father's eye when he first delivered it. When Martin Luther King delivered his speech that is, not my Dad delivering the sparkle from his eye. The red wine continued its magic and further stimulated my frontal lobe.

I changed it to:

"I've had a dream, blah, blah, blah...."

We've probably got a decent start to a short story now. My frontal lobe pulsated again. It throbbed. You could almost hear the cogs whirring. Do you have cogs in your frontal lobe? I changed it a little more, mixed in Sixties sage John Lennon, added a pinch of midnoughties Canadian EMO exponents Alexisonfire and a nice deep glug of red wine.

Now I had:

"I have had a few dreams, you may say I'm a dreamer, I'm not the only one, WHOARRRGGGGGH, MOTHERFUCKERRRZ, DIE, DIE..."

I was onto something here, but couldn't quite put my wine numbed fingers on it. Eureka! Dreams, I could write about dreams, my dreams. Genius! I am an absolute genius. This called for another glass of wine.

I was rather pleased with myself. I'd finally arrived at a decent, yet rather vague idea for my second book. After a couple more glasses of Chianti it seemed like a bloody brilliant idea to me. After all, I have always been at my most creative after a few glasses of red. I was fired up, I needed to get cracking. I finished my severalth glass of Chianti, opened another bottle, fired up the laptop, checked my email, had a couple of games of Mahjong, fed the cat, had another glass of Chianti, checked email again, poked about in the fridge for something eat, randomly Googled rude words for ten minutes, considered clicking on the link that would take me to www.hugewobblyjugs.com but instead (concerned that in this state I might have forgotten to wipe the browse history) opened up Mahjong again. I fell asleep. Head down, on the computer, mid game.

A week later, it was still bloody raining. While it was looking increasingly unlikely that I was going to be able to indulge in my hobby anytime soon, I'd had some further prompting from Proper Wife about getting started on the book. It was either that, or something about getting the upstairs redecorated. Anything but painting and decorating. Unless I've got a great length of wood in one hand and a multi-speed power tool in the other, I'm not a great fan of messing about in the bedroom. I resolved to start the sequel, waited until 11:55 AM and cracked open a bottle of Goose Island IPA. Beer would get me started. I suppose wine probably hadn't been the best thing to start a book with, unless you were writing a book about wine. Ah-hah, now that is an idea. I stopped myself right there. I didn't want to lose focus. I sat down. I fired up the lap top, determinedly. I checked my email. I played one game of Mahjong and went back to the fridge for another bottle of Goose Island. Refreshed, I finally began to type.....

My very first dream................

Errr, hang on.

I was shooting off at one hundred miles an hour without a plan and with only the vaguest of ideas; I was very inadequately armed for a concerted book writing campaign. Perturbed with self doubt, I was about to consign the 'writing another book' idea to my overflowing cupboard of futile endeavours, when I had a second eureka moment. It appeared that several bottles of Goose Island took me to an even higher creative plane than red wine did. The Franco dream! I knew where I was going with this now; I even sketched out a rough plan, it had chapters and everything.

With a renewed focus I moved onto Brew Dog's rather tasty Punk IPA[3] and selected Alexisonfire's 'Watch Out' on the iPod. Who else could get the party started? The words began to flow.

[1] I love Sean Lock; this section is unashamedly inspired by Sean Lock.
[2] I love Lee Mack too; unashamedly borrowed from "Lee Mack Live" DVD.
[3] Brew Dog can you please, please, please do Punk IPA in a 500ml bottle. 565ml would be even better.[4]
[4] They must have read the draft of this book, I recently discovered Punk IPA in a 660ml format!

DISC ONE
The Home Brew Years
1974 – 1985

Selected Soundtrack
Thin Lizzy – 'Waiting for an Alibi'
AC/DC – 'Beating Around the Bush'
UFO – 'Doctor Doctor'
Judas Priest – 'The Green Manalishi (With the Two Pronged Crown)'
Iron Maiden – 'Murders in the Rue Morgue'
Diamond Head – 'Am I Evil?'
Michael Schenker Group – 'Armed and Ready'
Def Leppard – 'Getcha Rocks Off'
Gillan – 'Mutually Assured Destruction'
Ozzy Osbourne – 'Mr Crowley'

Also Getting Scratched on a 1970's Stereogram
The Scorpions, Torme, Girlschool, Slade, Tygers of Pan Tang,
Jameson Raid, Dio, Tank

1. Goalkeeping and the Great Bovril Discovery

"Deep into that darkness peering, long I stood there, wondering, fearing, doubting, dreaming dreams no mortal ever dared to dream before."
Edgar Allen Poo

I know it should be Edgar Allen Poe but I've Deed Polled his ass. The quote doesn't really relate to this chapter, either, but it does sort of set the tone, and after all, 'Poo' was way funnier to an eight year old boy.

My very first daydream, well it probably wasn't my very first daydream, but it was certainly the first daydream that I can remember having, and it was, wait for it..... I wanted to play in goal for Wolves. That's Wolverhampton Wanderers Football Club rather than a pack of very talented and sporty lupines.

This was the mid Seventies, why on earth would an eight year old boy dream about being a goalkeeper? You could've dreamt about being the midfield enforcer, better still, the centre forward or how about Steve Austin. Steve Austin? The Six Million Dollar Man. And if you were the Six Million Dollar Man, you'd get to snog the Six Million Dollar Woman. Come to think of it, it was probably a bit too soon for this dream but I almost certainly would've had this reverie within the next eighteen months or so. Yet I wanted to be the Wolves goalie.

Never mind goalkeeper, why the Wolves goalkeeper? Well, my Dad is from Wolverhampton, I'm a nomad son of Wolverhampton. While we both probably wanted and would have liked to support Manchester United[1], Dad had already settled on Wolverhampton Wanderers in the fifties.

"They were good back then, son. Won the league you know, more than once. You could even leave your bicycle outside the ground without a lock on and it wouldn't have been stolen back then, either." I'd be fairly rich if I'd have banked a pound every time I'd heard that over the last forty years.

I was soon to follow, for which there were two main reasons. Firstly; the 556 went into Wolverhampton town centre. If only the 556 had gone all the way to Old Trafford. We'd have had some bloody long bus journeys but would've at least enjoyed some football supporting glory, rather than: regular third round replay exits, dropping all the way to the football league basement in consecutive seasons, the perennial disappointment of what could've been. Although, on the plus side, we saw Steve Bull score a lot of goals and we did get to see Tony Daley run very, very fast indeed. Sometimes he even had the ball. Secondly; in 1975 Dad took me to my first real game. Since '72 we'd been going to watch Wolves reserves but in '75 we went to watch the big boys, Wolves v Chelsea. Wolves beat Chelsea 7-1! Look it up, 15th March 1975, it actually happened! Willie Carr scored on his debut too, and as an eight year old boy anybody called Willie, who scores, was always going to become one of your heroes.

As we walked to the ground with the heady smells of the burger vans numbing my senses, I had a feeling that this, never mind the score, was going to be an exhilarating experience. We climbed out onto the South Bank and I was awe struck. The reserves used to get about a thousand people there and it never really had that much of an atmosphere. Now I was surrounded by twenty two thousand people. I know, it's nothing for you Manchester United, Liverpool and Arsenal fans, but to me back then it was about twenty one thousand nine hundred and fifty more than I could count. The air of expectation was electrifying. The maelstrom of noise when Wolves scored was intoxicating. The excitement and magic of that day decreed that I was going to be a football fan forever. It was also ineluctable that due to the score, I was going to be a Wolves fan forever. You can change your woman, but you can't change your team, you're stuck. With Wolves I was well and truly stuck.

My real hero that day though was not a man named Willie. It was the man who stood in goal for Wolves, Gary Pierce. He had absolutely nothing to do all game. To be fair, he did pick the ball out of the net just the once, but other than that? Nothing. I'd also sort of admired the Chelsea goalie. He'd let seven in but all he'd really had to do was pick the ball out of the net seven times. He had also been very well applauded by the Wolves fans.

Like all eight year old boys I loved football and wanted to play. Alas, I was severely lacking the skills, any sort of natural talent, or the willingness to put in the hours of dedicated practice needed to develop my outfield game. Even at the tender age of eight I was already predisposed to sloth. If something was difficult to do? Then it probably wasn't worth the effort. There would be no running around for ninety minutes in the wet and freezing cold for me. I can't remember exactly how long we played for as eight year olds in the seventies, but with it being way before the health and safety and child protection madness of the nineties, it probably was ninety minutes; possibly longer.

The enchantment of that day's experience, the huge Wolves win and above all Gary Pierce, all contributed to a change of thought. I could play football, I thought, and without having to run about for ninety minutes either. I would play in goal! I could get into the school team. Then, when I grow up I could play in goal for Wolves, yes that's it, and then I could play for England. And after that, I could own a pub. To be honest I was eight, I probably didn't consider the owning a pub part, even if it was what sportsmen did on retirement before Sky Sports existed. My career choices to that date had been: Spitfire pilot, astronaut and dinosaur hunter. They all disappeared down the M1 with the beaten Chelsea team, forgotten forever. Obviously, my innocent young mind had not thought too deeply about the goalkeeping career path. I certainly hadn't factored in that standing around for ninety minutes, rather than running around, in the wet and freezing cold, wearing shorts and a thin nylon shirt, while regularly having ten plus goals put past me, was not going to be the most pleasant or enjoyable of pastimes, that's for sure.

I made the school team. My parents bought me a pair of cheap football boots from Dudley outdoor market: black plastic, white laces, four stripes and moulded studs. All the other kids had white laces too, except their boots were made of black leather, had three stripes, screw in studs and sported exotic names like Beckenbauer and Pelé. They polished theirs after a game. I dunked mine in a bucket of water and hung them on the line to dry. Nevertheless, even though I had a dreadful case of football boot envy, the dream of playing in goal for Wolves was well and truly on.

To accompany the momentous seven goal victory over Chelsea and a significant step forward with my career aspirations there was a third historic episode that day. I had my first ever taste of Bovril. Mmmm, Bovril. We used to take a flask of hot Vimto and cheese sandwiches to the reserve games but now I was all grown up, we were in the big league and Dad was with his mates. No carrier bag with a flask of hot Vimto and foil wrapped cheese sarnies today. Beer and pork scratchings all the way. Except for me, I was only eight.

"You can have a sip, but don't tell your mother," Dad said offering me a sip of his pint. "Now, what do you want to drink, a Vimto?" Hose me down, beer tastes nice! This wasn't my first taste, but it still got me every time.

"I don't want a Vimto, Dad," I said. I really wanted to try more of this magical beverage called beer. Sadly, I had to wait another five or six years before I was to get more intimately acquainted.

"Well, you can't have anymore beer," he said, "Do you want a cup of tea?" Urggh. Tea? Tea is what both my Nans drink.

"Is there anything else?" I whined.

"There's soup, oxtail or tomato". Urggh. Double urggh.

"Is there anything else?" I whined some more. I actually wanted a bag of smokey bacon crisps and a Vimto. You can do great loud reverberating belches with Vimto and smokey bacon crisps. Try Vimto and cheese and onion, nothing happens at all. I never figured that one out. While I still fancied the Vimto-smokey bacon cocktail, I also wanted to appear grown up in front of Dad and his mates. Belching in front of grown men loudly would probably be frowned upon. Hey, I was eight, what did I know? Years later (not many years later, either) I came to realise I'd been cramping their style; not only was loud belching accepted in adult male circles, so was trumping, (I loved trumping, still do) as was the over use of the F-bomb and the liberal utilisation of a couple of hand gestures. I vaguely knew that the two fingers sign was not to be used in front of either Nan or

Mom, unless responding to the question of how many biscuits you'd like; then, you could get away with it. The one where you shook one hand up and down vigorously towards the visiting fans, visiting goalkeeper or referee, while holding an imaginary bottle of tomato ketchup? I wasn't quite so sure on this one at all. Had I known what the imaginary tomato ketchup bottles signified, I might have considered a more anonymous position on the pitch. I also heard a phrase that day that will forever stick in my mind, "Have you seen the state of that? I'd give her one." One what? I wanted to be grown up. I needed to know these things.

"Bovril?" My Dad said, exhausting the not so extensive offerings of the South Bank refreshment kiosk. His mates stopped sipping beer, all eyes turned to me. Even the news that West Brom were losing at half time[2] coming over the public address system did not break the tension that had been built up by the spectacle of a father asking his son, for the first time, if he wanted a Bovril. Devoid of any clue whatsoever and without actually asking what Bovril was, I looked up at my Dad blankly while trying the syllables out in my head a couple of times, *"BOV-RILL, BOV-RILL"*. Yeah, it sounded really cool and grown up. I think we actually still said groovy back then, cool was a few years off yet.

"I'll have Bovril," I said, trying to sound as grown up as possible.

Dad ordered one and then passed a steaming paper cup filled with an oily dark brown liquid towards me. I took a tentative sniff. Meaty aromas assailed my young nostrils. I liked meat. The steam fogged my NHS 'Joe 90' glasses. I didn't like being blind. Dad's mates looked on expectantly. I took a sip. It took a micro second for my brain to receive the message that I'd just drunk a mouthful of superheated radioactive beef flavoured water. A micro second after this, my brain responded. I spray spat it out all over the back of Dad's coat.

"What do you reckon to the Bovril then Matthew?" asked one of Dad's mates, as he suppressed a laugh. Everybody called me Matthew back then.

I gazed down at the steaming oily brown liquid as I pondered my answer. Bar the initial scorching sensation and resultant third degree burns on my poor tongue (no salt and vinegar crisps for me for a

41

while) I quite liked the smell and was sure I was going to like the flavour once it had cooled down enough for me to be able to taste it. This deserved a grown up answer.

"I'd give it one," I said after much deliberation. A chorus of 'That's my boy' and 'you've got a right lad there, Mick' broke out, accompanied by several hearty slaps on my back. I didn't quite get the same response a couple of weeks later when my Nan had asked me what I'd thought about her new pet Shih Tzu dog.

Unlike your first kiss, which you're not supposed to forget, I've never forgotten my first tongue scorching by Bovril. This was most definitely Saturday March 15th 1975 at around five to four in the afternoon. My first kiss was somewhere between late 1977 and mid 1980. I also forget with whom it was, although it was probably with one of the following: Kate, Rachael, Anne-Marie, Joanne, Anne or Ann without an E. I'm sure I must've dreamt about being 'Taster in Chief' at the Bovril factory at more than one point in my life too.

..... *"Let's go over to pitchside. John Motson, what is the atmosphere like there?"*

"What a tremendous FA Cup Final we've just seen here at Wembley Stadium, Frank. Wolves, the underdogs, victorious over the bookmakers and every neutral fan's favourite, the current European Champions, the current League Champions and current League Cup holders: Liverpool. Today Frank, only one end of Wembley is awash with a rapturous, ecstatic, cacophony of noise and swathed in a waving sea of flags, scarves and banners. And those flags are in the old gold and black of Wolverhampton Wanderers. The other end is silent. And that silence Frank, is down to just one man, well two, if you count the scorer Kenny Hibbitt, but really just one man. The man of the match for me today and I'm sure for you back in the studio and many neutrals too, was young Matt Rothwell. At eight years old, the youngest ever player to play in a FA Cup Final. He's an England goalkeeper in the making Frank. The lad was invincible. Single handed he, errr, actually we'd better call that two handed, he thwarted a tremendous and sustained Liverpool onslaught from the great front pairing of Keegan and Toshack. It was a goalkeeping display of incalculable bravery, immense character and colossal

maturity. Some of the saves he made were magnificent, some sublime, others inspirational and several were magnificent, sublime and inspirational all rolled into one. Quite remarkable, Frank, I am lost for words. Hold on, I think I might be able to grab a few words with him, here he comes now. Matt, congratulations on winning and also on a fine display today. How do you feel?"

"Errr, great, errr, yeah, errr, it's a dream come true like, errr, better than hunting for dinosaurs, errr, I'm over the moon, errr...."

"Kevin Keegan was impressed with your performance today. He has just dubbed you the next Gordon Banks, what do you say to that?"

"Errr, not a clue, errr, who is Gordon Banks?"

"How are you going to celebrate tonight? I mean, you're not old enough for champagne or a couple of brown ales. We have read that you're quite partial to a bag of smokey bacon crisps and a Vimto, is that what you'll be having?"

"Errr, I do like Vimto John, yes, but, errr, when we get home it'll be way past my bedtime, errr, but as we've won and if I've finished all my homework on the way back my Mom has promised me that I can have a Bovril as a special treat, errr, at the right temperature too."

"This is John Motson at Wembley Stadium, with the FA Cup winning Wolves goalkeeper Matt Rothwell, handing back to you in the studio."....

I had a slight problem with this dream though; I soon discovered that I wasn't that good at playing in goal either.

---

[1] Manchester United were actually in the 2nd Division in the 1974-75 season! They drew 1-1 at home to Norwich City that day.

[2] West Brom were also in the 2nd Division that season. I applied artistic licence with the half time score. The full time result though, was a 1-1 draw away at Oxford United.

2. Trying: The First Step Towards Failure

"Each man should frame his life so that at some future hour fact and his dreaming meet."
Victor Hugo

In 1975 I thought I'd already done that. Relegation for Wolves in 1976 didn't affect my resolve; promotion in 1977 further convinced me that fact and dreaming would one day meet. In 1978 fact got a smack in the mouth and dreaming temporarily packed its bags.

Three years later, still coveting the dream of being interviewed as an FA Cup Final winner by John Motson, I entered big school. I went to the trials for the football team. My feet had grown; I had a new pair of cheap football boots from Dudley outdoor market: black plastic, white laces, just two stripes this time but still with moulded studs. As before, everyone else was kitted out in an array of exotically named, shiny black leather, three striped, screw in stud boots. Except for one other kid who, like me, wore glasses, and it also looked like his parents shopped for sporting goods in the open air in Dudley too.

I had worn glasses for as long as I could remember. For a lot of that time I'd had to wear a vision obscuring patch over my good eye, so as well as being used to walking into all manner of things, I was more than used to name calling from my peers. It came as a slight shock when, at the end of the trial, Games Teacher consulted his clipboard and announced, "right, everyone has made the squad except for: Brown, too slow; Smithy, too fat; Jonesy, two left feet; and, the specky kids, two of them." He wouldn't get away with that today! Once he'd left the changing rooms I waved an imaginary tomato ketchup bottle at him.

Everyone from my old junior school who had gone to the trial was in, except me. I was gutted, sick as a parrot, most definitely not over the moon. If I couldn't get in the school team how on earth was I going to get into the Wolves team? I'd tried, tried very hard too, but it appeared that trying very hard was the first step towards failure. The dream was over.

I spent most, if not all, of the first year[1] moping around while all of my mates were in the football team and getting out of lessons early to go and play in the far reaches of the Dudley and Stourbridge catchment area; I secretly revelled in cruel delight whenever they lost. They wouldn't have lost with the youngest ever FA Cup final winner in goal, I thought. Football had been the only thing I'd thought about for the last three years, I had no other hobbies. I was listless. Unless I was going to get my toy dinosaurs out of my bedroom cupboard, which I did consider but ultimately decided against, I only had my lessons left. And with these I didn't want to try very hard and fail, no sir. Especially after I had been told that five 'O' levels[2] at grade C or above was what we should be aiming for. Grade C's all round then, I'll have some of that!

'Minimum effort, maximum sloth' became my mantra. I did the bare minimum, aiming to get good enough grades to stay out of the very top tier and to stay in the realms of "he produces good work but is capable, if he puts his mind to it, of so much more" report cards. Therefore, my parents were happy that their son was capable of reaching the very top tier, and wasn't quite the complete and utter lazy bastard that some of the more astute teachers had implied in their reports. I was, I'd explained to them on more than one occasion, looking at achieving the school standard of five grade C 'O' levels, and mine would include English and Maths, which was even better.

The teachers knew that I was capable of more; as I suspect, so did my parents. I certainly knew I was. Except for French and Games; in French I joined the rest of the single-lingual dunces and had no illusion about being able to reach the middle tier, let alone the top one; in Games, with my football dream crushed and now believing that I wasn't good enough, I elected to stay in the warmth and dryness of the sports hall. I played table tennis with the fatties and other specky kids. I looked out at the football field with considerable self-satisfaction on freezing cold days when the pitch was granite hard, I'll tell you. Slothfulness back fired on me here though; I didn't make the cricket team in the first year either and I was actually half decent at cricket.

The 'trying very hard and failing' rationale aside, there were other reasons why I didn't want to hit the top tier. It was full of the snobs, the swots and the no-mates. Worse still, they also had the teachers that did not tolerate messing about in class at all. Some even had an overzealous intolerance to messing about. With the latter teachers, it could often result in a severe board rubber inflicted injury, which would then have to be explained to the headmaster as either 'I fell in the corridor, sir' or 'I was messing about in class, sir'. The second explanation would invariably end with six whacks on the backside from a size twelve rubber soled gym plimsoll. Why any eleven year old boy would want to be in a 'messing about' free zone, particularly when it could result in a couple of personal injuries, is way beyond me.

Aged eleven and now being more than a little predisposed towards sloth, I'd also started to become slightly more female aware. The girls in the top tier all had names like Emilia, Camilla and Lucinda. They didn't behave, sound or even look like they'd laugh at cheeky quips to teacher or at the braking of very loud wind. Never in a million years. The girls in the middle tiers, on the other hand, had names like Joanne, Anne and Ann, without an E. They wore their ties rebelliously low, top buttons undone, occasionally enough were undone to reveal the tiniest glimpse of bra, and they dressed in shorter skirts than the top tier girls too. They laughed at my cheeking teacher quips, some even suppressed giggles at very loud wind braking, and others responded quite positively to my patented 'punch on the arm' chat up technique. It all made for a compelling raison d'être to continue with my 'minimum effort, maximum sloth' philosophy.

Sensing my growing melancholia at not making the football team, my parents encouraged me to take up another hobby. Between us, somehow, we eventually arrived at learning a musical instrument. To that point in my life, other than communal chanting at the football, music had not really interested me. I had recently taken an interest in Top of the Pops, mind. The music hadn't really grabbed my attention; I patiently waited for the dance troupe, Legs & Co, to come on. And come to think about it, a quick three minutes with Agnetha from Abba never went amiss, either.

Learning an instrument it was then. But what? The instruments on offer at school - trumpet, trombone, flute and violin, possibly clarinet too - didn't really appeal. My Mom pointed out my recent interest in Top of the Pops and also that she had once caught me enthusiastically miming, with a tennis racket, to the guitar solo of Cliff Richard's 'Devil Woman'. To avoid any further memory of that day and wanting to hide my rapidly flushing cheeks, I'd quickly changed the subject.

Then after tea I'd got to thinking, the guitar eh? Yes, the guitar. While I had so moved on from Cliff, I still acknowledged that Terry Britten's guitar work on 'Devil Woman' had been pretty groovy, and, for the last three years, The Wombles' 'Superwombling' album had been my tennis racket miming music of choice. Some of the guitar work on that album was pretty damn groovy too. Wellington Womble had always been one of my favourites, even before I knew he played the guitar; he wore glasses, was very insecure, yet creative and scientifically inclined. Just like me. The guitar then, why not? It must be way easier to learn than one of those poncey orchestral instruments, I thought.

.....Great, double Subject Y next. I wonder if Miss X will have that see through blouse on again. Subject Y is my favourite lesson of them all. She even smiles at me when I'm cheeky and she gave me a good report. I wonder if she'd sit next to me if she was twelve? I bet she wouldn't be bothered that I wasn't in the football team either. Hope I get to sit next to the curly haired girl from Science too. See through blouse and curly haired girl from Science would be the best lesson ever. Oh, and if the tall blonde girl from the sixth form were to walk past, the one with the huge.....

"Matt, Matt," John the Roadie nudged and whispered to me, "teacher's talking to you,"

"What? Oh, yeah, errr, sorry sir, page six yeah?"

"C'mon Rothwell, it's not rocket science is it?" French Teacher sighed.

48

"I hope not, sir. I've got a French book open here," I replied and waited for my audience to laugh. I didn't have to wait long. I proceeded to murder the pronunciation of a boucherie transaction between Jean-Paul and the shop assistant Marie-Colette. I hated French. Once I'd finished my butchering of a very simple red meat purchase, French Teacher rolled his eyes and picked on some other poor single-lingual from another part of the class.

"Where were you?" John the Roadie mouthed.

"Double Subject Y next," I whispered back.

"Ahhh. Miss X, the see through blouse. Gotcha." His face glazed over. Just like mine must have done a few minutes before, I guessed. "How's the guitar coming on?"

"Errr, yeah the guitar, it's coming on OK," I lied. I'd had about six lessons and was well and truly stuck on first position chords. You could've changed parliament, twice, in the gap between some of my chord changes, especially D7 to G. And I avoided B and F chords like the plague. Come to think of it, I also avoided the sharp chords of A, C, D, F and G. This meant I'd wiped out seven of the twelve possible major chords, somewhat limiting any sort of repertoire development. I did not give up though.

The equipment wasn't exactly inspiring. For my twelfth birthday I was given a cheap nylon strung acoustic guitar. 'I am never going to be asked to guest on the next Wombles album with that,' I'd thought. My parents, knowing the fickleness of a twelve year old mind, especially their own son's mind, had played safe and not wandered down the expensive electric guitar and amplifier avenue at all. I had no concept of money whatsoever, other than it grew on trees and that adults were always telling you that it didn't. What I had really wanted was a Gibson Flying V, just like Wellington's. I still want one now; unfortunately my money tree crop has been awful for the last twenty-eight years or so. I still did not give up, though.

If I'd thought the equipment was uninspiring, then the material I had to work with was as de-motivating as it could possibly get for a twelve year old boy. I just wanted to be strutting my stuff, showing the girls how I interpreted the opening riff from the theme tune for 'Jamie and The Magic Torch'. Instead, my guitar teacher must've been grooming me to take over from Val Doonican on TV, either

49

that, or he was a visionary and could foresee a move into the mainstream for a burgeoning underground 'pre-teens do cowboy' genre.

We'd started off with 'Oh My Darling, Clementine'. Nice and slow, but did have several tricky D7 to G changes. Then we moved onto 'Home on the Range'. Still nice and slow, but contained the dreaded B minor chord in the chorus. I covered this with an approximation of the chord shape and scratched at the strings enthusiastically, before clumsily jumping back into my comfort zone with E7. From there we picked up the pace with 'The Yellow Rose of Texas'. This had loads of tricky D7 to G changes. I must have been getting better though. I couldn't really see it myself, but I now had to sing along too. This was not good news. My twelve year old voice was in the first throes of breaking. I had at least a three octave range, without a single minuscule degree of control over it. Less Pavarotti, more Cat-garotti. As soon as the guitar teacher entered our house, my dad, brother and the cats all disappeared outside pretty swiftly, regardless of the weather conditions. I came very close to giving up, but still I persevered.

"Right, Matthew, you're coming along. Slowly, but coming along," thanks for the encouragement. "I think we'll do something different for the next couple of lessons," said Guitar Teacher at the end of my eighth lesson. "Make sure you practice those chord changes, though."

"Great, I will." I'd said in reply. I hoped it was going to be 'Superwomble' and hoped above all hope that it might even be the 'Jamie and The Magic Torch' riff. I'd dropped enough hints.

Nope.

In lesson nine we covered 'What Shall We Do with the Drunken Sailor'. I knew what I wanted to do with the drunken sailor and it certainly didn't involve putting him in bed with the captain's daughter. The chords were nice and easy though, just E minor and D. Then we did 'Wild Rover'; D7 to G again! No, nay, never. No, nay, never, no more. Little did I know that in years to come, when I had spent all of my money on whisky and beer, that this was going to be great for 'drunken back from the pub get the guitar out' sing songs.

It's gotta be 'Superwomble' next week, it's gotta be. I thought. I hoped.

Nope.

The following week I sat down expectantly. He could sense he had an eager student this week. He opened his case and took out a chord sheet. I looked at it with excitement. He then took me through 'The Streets of London'. Oh joy! I vainly tried to convince myself that 'Superwomble' just did not lend itself to interpretation on the acoustic guitar. 'The Streets', as Guitar Teacher liked to call it - I liked to shake an imaginary bottle of tomato ketchup at him - had lots of chords; including my dreaded nemesis, the F chord. It also had lots of quick chord changes, as well as a couple I hadn't even attempted before: E minor to C, and G to A minor. And, to make it even more difficult, he still wanted me to sing along. My dad, brother and the cats were well out of this one. Maybe I ought to think about having another go at getting in the football team, I thought, as I strummed and screeched through 'So how can you tell me, you're lo-own-leee' for the fourth time. If something is difficult to do? And the F chord was bloody difficult to do, as was B minor, for that matter.

I gave up.

I'd tried, but it was nearly the cricket season anyways. The guitar went into the cupboard to make its acquaintance with the skateboard, a three quarter completed five foot Airfix scale model of Apollo 11, six half completed Panini football albums (1973 through 1978), numerous Airfix Spitfires of varying scale and states of completion, a couple of shoe boxes containing my prized toy dinosaur collection and, of course, the plastic football boots.

"Any further with the guitar?" John the Roadie whispered, as soon as French Teacher had given up on him for failing to recognise that Mornet could not be translated, as it was in fact Yves' surname. We both learnt something new in French that day.

"Nah, having a break. Musical differences, I'm going to have to break the partnership up." I'd never let on, and not a soul knew, that I'd been learning a set list that could grace the finest Wild West themed wedding do.

"Where were we?" He asked.

"Up to thirty-two and your turn, I think," I replied.

"The pink nosed puppies," John the Roadie giggled.

"Good one. Ladies love cushions," I sniggered back.

"Nice. Blancmange filled fun bags."

"Excellent! We need one more to break the record. How about? Wobble berries," we giggled and mini-high-fived each other. The bell sounded. A new record! We had come up with thirty-six totally different names for a pair of breasts, in a single French lesson. "Superb! Double wobble berries for us next." Please let it be the see-through blouse. Wow! See-through blouse bombs, now that would've made thirty-seven.

.....*It was nice and warm in the burrow today. The glare of a single spot light, actually it was a 40 watt bulb shrouded by an empty foil takeaway tray, shone down on me. I stood timidly on a well crafted stage. It was made out of all manner of discarded packing cases and bits of rusty steel, the sort of things everyday folk left behind. My trusty acoustic guitar was grasped firmly in my sweaty hands and a broom handle microphone stand was in front of me. I was dreadfully nervous. It's not often you get an audition opportunity like this, particularly as a human. Due to extenuating personal circumstances, Wellington Womble wasn't going to be able to make the first half of the upcoming 'The Wombles Christmas Party' tour. I was auditioning to fill in for him.*

"C'mon now, young Womble Wannabe, don't be shy. What are you going to play for us as your audition piece?" asked Great Uncle Bulgaria in his wise old voice.

"Errr, I was going to do the theme from 'Jamie and the Magic Torch'. Errr, but figured as he was a ratings rival I'd better not," I replied with a shaky voice. There were mutters of agreement from the other Wombles, except for Orinoco, who snored away in the corner obliviously.

"So...." the wise one prompted me.

"Errr, then I thought I'd do 'Superwomble', but, errr, changed my mind, errr,"

"Yes, go on...." he prompted once more.

"So, errr, I thought as you live in Wimbledon and Wimbledon is in London, errr....."

"Get on with it," shouted Tomsk.

"Errr, tonight, Great Uncle Bulgaria, I'm going to do a version of the song 'The Streets of London' only my version is called 'The Streets of London Without the F Chord'."

"Splendid, young Womble Wannabe," Great Uncle Bulgaria said, to the accompaniment of murmurs of agreement. He continued, "But before you do, you must choose your Womble name." He beckoned me forward and held out his great leather bound atlas.

"How do I do it?"

"You should choose a name that suits you," offered Tobermory.

"Or do it like I did; close your eyes tight, point, and hope for the best," Bungo shouted out. The Bungo method sounded like the 'maximum sloth' option to me. I closed my eyes tight, pointed and hoped for the best.

"Bravo young Womble Wannabe, if you pass the audition you shall be forever known as Florence Womble," said Great Uncle Bulgaria. Shit! Shit! Shit! That is going to raise a few jibes from my mates and what chance will I have with Legs & Co now, with a name like Florence?

"Now let us hear your song, young Florence Womble."

I cleared my throat and began to strum. As I strummed through the intro I silently repeated over and over in my head 'please voice, don't break mid-performance, please voice, don't break mid-performance'. I began to sing, "Let me take you by the hand and lead you through the streets of London, here's the diffy-cult part where the efff chord shu-ddah beeee......."......

---

[1] For any younger readers: the first year corresponds to Year 7, the second year to Year 8, and so on.

[2] Again, for any younger readers: 'O' levels were the GCSE's of yesteryear; only much, much harder.

3. Santa Had Left the Building

*"The dream is a spontaneous happening and therefore dangerous to
a control system set up by the non-dreamers."*
William S. Burroughs

*Too right! The non-dreamers control system was an unwavering totalitarian
dogma of five 'O' levels at grade C or higher including English and Maths,
followed by 'A' levels and then university. I rejected their limiting,
overzealous dogma. I wanted to open for Judas Priest at Wolverhampton
Civic Hall.*

I returned to big school in September 1979 with slightly longer
hair, a brand new Wrangler denim jacket and a gait full of pubescent
swagger. The optician had told me that while my bad eye was not
getting any better, it was certainly not getting any worse. Ah-hah, I
heard the words 'not getting' and 'any worse'. I really did not want
to walk around any longer wearing a pair of lopsided glasses; one
plain lens and one lens thick enough to glaze a porthole on Captain
Nemo's Nautilus. As a seasoned specky kid the name calling didn't
really bother me anymore. I was more bothered about my chances
with the girls. I was already at a disadvantage by not being on any of
the sports teams; how was I seriously going to get a girlfriend when
all they saw when they looked into my deep blue eyes was one
normal sized eye and one the size of a tennis ball? He'd also said that
my good eye had perfect vision. Bingo, the words 'perfect' and
'vision' together! Vanity won the day. I seized on his prognosis. The
glasses got binned, my gait gained swagger and he immediately lost
his annual income from lensing up one pair of NHS 'Joe 90' style
tortoise shell frames.

Having almost given up on learning the acoustic guitar (I'd
certainly given up on taking lessons that only taught cowboy songs,
that's for sure), I needed something to fill my extra-curricular space.
Without too much expectation I tried out for the football team again.
I made it! It appeared to me as though I shouldn't have turned up last
year wearing the specks. I'd hardly played football since that trial

and yet here I was twelve months on, speckless and in the team. You'd have thought that after the disappointment of last year I'd have been euphoric (made up, over the moon, etc, etc) that the dream was back on; winning an FA Cup medal with Wolves and donning the England goalkeeper's jersey was once again within reach.

Nope.

In all fairness, I was a little excited, but not for the above reasons. Being on the football team got you noticed with the girls. In addition to being on the football team, I was no longer one of the specky kids either. I'd be holding hands with the dark haired girl from Geography (I'd moved on from the curly haired girl from Science) and taking romantic arm in arm lunch break walks down to the chip shop before you could call a fat kid 'fatty'. As long as it wasn't football training day, of course. I was also quite chuffed that, through my parents' benevolence, I was now the proud owner of a pair of real leather, three striped and exotically named screw in stud football boots. My feet had out grown the plastic ones and I somehow managed to persuade them that to make the team you needed a pair of boots with exactly three stripes.

I was on the team.

Great.

I now had a better than average chance with the girls.

A veritable bonus.

But the football dream had died last year. It was, however, being slowly replaced. Over the summer I'd continued to tune in to Top of the Pops. I eagerly awaited and always enjoyed a decent Legs & Co routine, regardless of whatever disco crap they were gyrating to that week. Now I also watched in anticipation, hoping to see Thin Lizzy perform 'Waiting for an Alibi', Nazareth play 'May the Sunshine', Judas Priest rock with 'Take on the World' or AC/DC roll to 'Touch Too Much'. None of these had acoustic guitars, none of them appeared to be playing any of the chords that I'd learnt and they certainly were not singing about being home on the range, any sort of Texan flora or even old men in closed down markets. Judas Priest even had a guitarist who played the same Gibson Flying V guitar as Wellington Womble! Just as I'd convinced my parents about needing football boots with three stripes, I managed to convince myself that I needed an electric guitar. I wrote to Santa early that year.

Dear Santa,

I hope you are well.

Firstly, may I say thank you very much for last year's Xmas presents. You nearly got the whole list right! If I remember correctly I was only missing the Evel Knievel energiser stunt bike and the stickers to complete my '77-'78 season Panini album. I particularly liked your very thoughtful additions of the 'knitted by my Nan' sweater, scarf and gloves combo, as well as the countless pairs of socks and pants. What twelve year old boy wouldn't?

I'm sure you can see that I've been a good boy once again this year. For example: I'm still on target for five 'O' levels at grade C ~~or higher~~ including English (hopefully) and Maths (definitely); I haven't shouted 'Hey teacher, leave them kids alone'[1] in class anywhere near as much as others have done; and, I have not stared at Miss Z's chest (new Subject Y teacher) in quite the same way as I used to stare at Miss X's see through blouse.

Taking all that into consideration, for Xmas this year I'd like all of the following:

1. *A Gibson Flying V electric guitar*
2. *A 100 watt Marshall Amplifier and associated 4 x 12 Marshall speaker cabinet*
3. *An Evel Knievel energiser stunt bike*
4. *Some Brut talc and I might possibly be needing some Brut aftershave soon too*
5. *To be locked in a room with the dark haired girl from Geography or Legs & Co, (whichever is easiest to procure, I'll leave it up to you)*
6. *A book to tell me what to do once locked in a room with the dark haired girl from Geography or Legs & Co*

That's all!

You'll notice it is quite a short list this year, too.

As always, I trust you will be able to deliver. Should there be need for a compromise, I'd appreciate it if you could focus on items 1, 2 and 5. That said, if item 5 is going to be part of the package, I'm probably going to need item 6 as well.

Yours faithfully
Matt Rothwell.
A very well behaved boy from Wolverhampton, West Midlands, England.

P.S. I don't need any socks or pants this year, or knitted garments of any type for that matter.

A week before Christmas 1979 I'd have settled on just items 1 and 2, or even item 1 and a 10 watt practice amplifier. Two weeks before, Invader, the fifth years' rock band, had played the school disco. Amongst their short set they had played a Black Sabbath song and a Led Zeppelin song; neither were really my cup of hard rock, but I was in awe of the live rock music experience. Then a week later, on Tuesday 18th December 1979, at Stafford's Bingley Hall, Thin Lizzy blew my mind. The noise, the energy, the power of the kick drum, the lights and lasers, the exotic guitar chords that weren't first position, ten thousand people grooving on every note played and ten thousand hanging on every word Phil Lynott, the charismatic front man, said between songs. I was particularly taken with his fantastic and frequent use of the F word. This is it. Forget football. I'd found my true vocation. Hold the interview with the careers officer. I wanted to play in a band. I wanted to play electric guitar in a heavy rock band. Good job I'd got my letter off to Santa early this year. It was a shame that I had forgotten to add electric guitar lessons to it; given a push I could've knocked the Brut off the list and added guitar lessons instead.

I wasn't the only one growing their hair or coveting heavy rock super stardom with an electric guitar, either. There were a few of us in our year. The day after the Thin Lizzy gig, and following on from the wave of excitement generated by the Invader school disco performance, we formed a band. I can't quite remember the actual lesson we formed it in, but would hazard a guess that French was a very strong possibility, most likely during a lull in a breast naming record attempt.

Setting out on the heavy rock highway to hell though, proved more difficult than we had originally thought. If indeed, we had put any thought into it whatsoever. In the space of two short weeks the band went through several line up changes and I went through the awful self-realisation that Santa probably didn't actually exist. On Christmas day, much to my immense disappointment, there wasn't a single electric guitar shaped present under the tree, or even a box that looked like it might contain an Evel Knievel energiser stunt bike for that matter. In fact, from my letter, I only received a Brut gift set. What I did get was a home knitted sweater, which didn't fit, and socks and pants in quantities previously unknown.

Everyone wanted to be the guitarist, no one wanted to play the bass. No matter that we only had two acoustic guitars between us, which no one could actually play to any level of proficiency yet. And now, there was no sign of one of those actually becoming electric in the immediate future either. The instrument question aside, bitter arguments over 'musical differences', along with the development of rancorous internecine warfare over the band name, were more often than not the cause of any personnel change. Not everybody (myself included) liked Status Quo, not everybody liked (I did) Thin Lizzy and we could never get a majority consensus on whether Matt Black (my idea) or a literary character from a Dickens novel should be the name of the band. How did a top set kid get involved here? Ah, I remember, he was the other one with an acoustic guitar. Matt Black soon split (or Literary Character, it depended on whose camp you were in) and went their own ways without ever having achieved a definitive line up or even strummed a single acoustic guitar power chord in anger.

Even with the set back of a failed first band, my rock 'n' roll fantasy persisted. I hardly went and watched Wolves anymore. Instead, all of my pocket money went on seven inch heavy rock vinyl, embroidery silk to adorn my denim jacket with the likes of Judas Priest and AC/DC, and tickets to see bands such as UFO, Iron

Maiden, Saxon, Def Leppard and The Scorpions. If they played Wolverhampton Civic and rocked, there was a good chance I had been there rocking along with them.

In between homework and goalkeeping, I got the acoustic out of the cupboard. Goalkeeping usually meant being hammered 15-2, 10-3, 11-1 and, in what I considered to be my finest game to date, 8-0. I saved a penalty in the 8-0 loss and, when I wasn't picking the ball out of the back of the net, chatted music with a couple of foxy girls from the year above. I dusted the guitar down and persevered with trying to nurture any sort of fledgling F chord shape. My B minor improved a little, but F remained my nemesis.

.....The lights went down. A cheer went up from the crowd as they surged forward towards the darkened stage. An air of expectation filled the cavernous hall. Wagner's 'Ride of the Valkyries' boomed from the PA system and echoed around the walls, it built to a climax. Flash bombs exploded, smoke and dry ice filled the stage. Lights flashed. Guitar wielding heroes could be glimpsed, silhouetted by the swirling smoke. The crowd cheered. The singer swaggered towards the microphone.

"Wolverhampton! Are you ready to rock?" he shouted.

The crowd shouted back in the affirmative.

"I CAN'T FUCKING HEAR YOU. ARE YOU REDEEEEE TOOOO RAHHHCKK?" shouted the singer again. The reply was louder this time, roared and eager. The stage lit up in Technicolor splendour. The kick drum pulsed, the guitars struck up. The singer moved closer to the microphone.

"Ohhhh, give me a home where the buffalo ro-oh-oam,".....

No, no, no.

This dream wasn't quite working.

I needed an electric guitar. With an electric guitar I would master the F chord and from there, I thought, I would truly master rock. It became my desideratum[2]; I would have traded in my real leather, three striped and exotically named football boots for an electric guitar at this point.

[1] Chorus to 'Another brick in the Wall' from seminal Pink Floyd album 'The Wall'.
[2] Desideratum (noun): something lacking and yet desperately desired. Saw it in The Independent and had to look it up. It fits quite well here. The plural is desiderata.

4. Barre Chords: Minimum Effort, Maximum Rock

"I needn't mention how essential dreaming is to the character of the rock star."
From the film Velvet Goldmine

If the other essential character traits include slothfulness and a fascination, bordering on obsession, with blancmange filled fun bags (no.35 off the record breaking list) then I was surely born to rock.

It had been quite a shock to discover that Santa didn't exist at all. And a huge disappointment that he was all part of an age old and cruel control system, perpetrated by adults in order to subjugate children into good behaviour. I didn't let on to Me Brother though; I will be having that left out sherry and mince pie next year. It was just as big a shock, and possibly an even greater disappointment, to realise that a Ghost of Christmas Pants did. If I wasn't going to be locked in a room with the dark haired girl from Geography, or Legs & Co, why did I need all those new clean pairs of pants?

With the Santa route to rock 'n' roll stardom well and truly closed, I could only come to one conclusion on how I was going to get my hands on an electric guitar: ask my parents. That didn't work. Apparently their money tree wasn't in fruit during that particular fiscal period. I asked my Nan; she gave me fifty pence towards an ice-cream.

I had to have an electric guitar.

I was going to have to get a job, not something I've said willingly over the proceeding thirty-three years. I was thirteen. Thirteen year olds should not have to get jobs, I was sure we had covered that in the 1903 Employment of Children Act in History. But, I could see no other way. A job it was going to have to be. In a determined display of dogged single-mindedness, never seen before and never witnessed since, I embarked on a frenzied job search. I got a paper round. Then, on calculating that with my paper round wages it was going to take at least fourteen years until I could afford a Gibson Flying V and the requisite Marshall amplification set up, I had to have a re-think. I kept the paper round. I started to wash cars and cut lawns. I saved my lunch money. I asked Nan for ice-creams in the middle of winter. I worked in my Dad's factory painting great huge never ending steel girders a drab red-brown colour during school holidays. I even considered trying to muscle in on the lucrative lunch money extortion racket, but that gig was well and truly wrapped up.

With the additional income rolling in I recalculated. I was only about ten years off now. The heavy rock movement was growing in popularity, AC/DC's 1980 album 'Black in Black' was quite possibly the greatest heavy rock album ever made. I needed to ride this wave. While AC/DC and the old guard grew stronger, exciting new bands were emerging at a fervent pace: Diamond Head, Ozzy Osbourne's new band, Tygers of Pan Tang and Manowar, to name just a few. Some kids at school already had electric guitars. I was going to miss the boat.

I was resolute about not missing that boat.

I compromised on quality. I wiped out my total earnings to date, sold my toy dinosaur collection and, along with parental help (they didn't buy into the whole 'needing a Gibson-Marshall' thing at all) shelled out sixty quid on a South Korean replica of a Gibson Les Paul and a 5 watt battery powered practice amp. Let's rock! While not a Flying V, the guitar looked the business. I named it Annie. Ah, so it must've been Anne or Ann without an E that was my first kiss, which probably makes it 1979; can't remember the exact date though. The amp did not look the business, not even when I made a paper Marshall name badge and stuck it on the front. However, there was a bigger problem than the amp being smaller than a teenage girl's knowledge of heavy rock, or football: 'Home on the Range' had sounded crappy on the acoustic; it sounded totally shit on Annie, as did the rest of my cowboy repertoire. I didn't dare try the F chord. I needed some electric lessons.

I returned to the Bank of Mom & Dad. It was a difficult and protracted negotiation process. They were very concerned that at the end, the South Korean replica would become yet another item in the great cupboard of dust gathering fads. At least the sale of my toy dinosaurs had made a bit of space, I unwisely countered. I was concerned that if I didn't get a move on, I was never going to open for Judas Priest at Wolverhampton Civic Hall. I compromised again; and sold my soul for electric guitar rock 'n' roll. I contributed half towards each lesson from my pocket money, promised to clean their cars and mow the lawns for free and further pledged to keep on target for five 'O' levels at grade C or higher including English and Maths. I was nearly there. How about if I put 'or higher' back on the table? It was three years away yet, I thought; let's gamble. 'Or higher' went back on the table. We had a deal.

New Guitar Teacher didn't come to your house. You had to go to his class room. It was above the tiny music shop where Annie had been purchased. On the day of my first lesson I sat excitedly in a damp and musty back room with five others while we waited for the preceding lesson to end. I looked around. It was like being back on the football team with my pair of plastic boots. One of them had a real Gibson Les Paul, two had real Gibson SG's and the other two had real Fender Stratocasters. Not a single South East Asian replica in site. They must've had way better paper rounds than I'd been able to find.

The other lesson finished and New Guitar Teacher called us up. I vaguely recognised his voice. It couldn't be. I climbed the stairs with a growing sense of foreboding. I put my head around the door nervously. It felt as damp and smelt as musty as downstairs had. I looked over at New Guitar Teacher, it couldn't be? But it was. New Guitar Teacher was Old Guitar Teacher. Here goes another ten weeks of learning advanced cowboy songs. Why on earth did I agree to all the free car washing and lawn mowing?

The first thing he handed out was a chord sheet. I looked at it in consternation; it was titled 'Barre Chords' and the chord at the top if the page was the F chord. Shit! The one below was F sharp, the one below that G, then G sharp, then A, I couldn't look anymore. Panic set in, I'd put 'or higher' back on the table! I chanced a furtive second look and tentatively made the F chord shape on Annie. It was easier than on the acoustic. I strummed. It was way easier. I chanced a quick F to D7 and back change, it was awkward, but still way easier. I looked back at how to shape F sharp. Hang on. It was exactly the same as F only moved up the neck one fret. G was the same, moved up one more fret, G sharp one more again, and so on. A smile spread over my face. In a single fell swoop I could play every major chord on the guitar. Without ever having to move my fingers other than up and down the neck! I was more than annoyed that he'd sat me through ten weeks of cowboy induced agony, when we could've gone down the 'minimum effort, maximum sloth' route with barre chords. I was more than pleased with my new found mastery of the guitar neck, I was jubilant. I looked at the sheet again, at the bottom in chord notation was written:

G A# C

G A# C# quick slide to C

G A# C

A# G

It meant nothing to me at first glance either, or even after I'd clumsily worked through it a couple of times. Then Guitar Teacher played it. Excuse me, while I kiss the sky. Minimum effort, maximum rock! I could play the seminal opening riff to Deep Purple's 'Smoke on the Water'! Or at least I would be able to soon. I needed to go home and practice a few times first. Never mind opening for Judas Priest at the Civic; they'd be opening for me at Wembley Stadium at this rate. The rock 'n' roll fantasy was on.

.....The lights went down. A cheer went up from the crowd as they surged forward towards the darkened stage. An air of expectation filled the cavernous hall. Wagner's 'Ride of the Valkyries' boomed from the PA system and echoed around the walls, it built to a climax. Flash bombs exploded, smoke and dry ice filled the stage. Lights flashed. A guitar wielding hero swaggered towards the front of the stage. He began to play.

G A# C, G A# C# quick slide to C, G A# C, A# G

At the end of the song the crowd roared in adulation. The guitar wielding hero took a long swig from a bottle of expensive champagne, kicked at the growing pile of ladies undergarments to uncover his vast array of effects pedals and then launched into the next anthem on the set list.

G A# C, G A# C# quick slide to C, G A# C, A# G.....

66

"Errr, the best I can come up with, sir," I'd been staring at *'Le crayon est jaune'* on the blackboard for what seemed like an age, "is, errr, this is a young wax crayon?" I offered hopefully. I hadn't even been chasing laughs from my classmates, but I got them anyway.

"The pencil is yellow, you fool," French Teacher sighed. He was indeed, a very skilled encourager and nurturer of young minds.

"Nice one, Matt," John the Roadie whispered.

"Yeah," I replied as my cheeks flushed.

"Did you hear that Boogie has got a Les Paul? He and The Angel are starting a band." No, I hadn't heard that. Boogie and The Angel were top set kids, how would I know that?

"I've got one too." I hadn't let on before this, but I now had six non-cowboy song lessons under my leather studded belt, and was quite confident in revealing my super-guitar-hero identity.

"Get off?"

"Yeah, can do 'Smoke on the Water' and everything." I pushed it a bit with 'and everything'. I was very competent with the 'Smoke on the Water' riff and could do the opening three chords (all the same chord) to Black Sabbath's 'Paranoid'. I tended to get a bit lost when you had to do the twiddly bit thereafter. I hoped 'twiddly bits' were on the curriculum for lessons seven or eight.

"I'll let 'em know. They're after another guitarist. I'm gonna be their roadie," John the Roadie said.

"Cool."

"ROTHWELL!" French Teacher rudely interrupted our conversation. "Let's see how you get on with *'L'arbre est jeune'* then, shall we?"

"Errr," I tried to stall and whinged, "could you write it on the board, please?" He raised his eyebrows impatiently; my face flushed again, "errr, ok, errr, yeah, the, errr, harbour, harbour? is, errr, yellow?"

"Don't encourage the fool," he said, as the rest of the class erupted into laughter. I hated French more than an extremely xenophobic Francophobe hated the French. On the plus side, I could make people laugh here without even trying, and I had made my girlfriend laugh too. Yes, I now had a Proper Girlfriend, a Proper 'girl' Girlfriend. I'd moved on from dreaming about the dark haired girl from Geography when I found out she was going out with the football team captain from the year above. Proper Girlfriend was the auburn haired girl from Chemistry, who I hadn't really noticed much due to my interest in Geography girl. She'd first came to my attention when John the Roadie had used her as inspiration for number forty-six on our growing Names for Breasts list[1]. I had to find out what 'Orbs of Wonder' looked like. I did the very next Chemistry lesson, and when she was moved into our French class, I fell in love. If Santa had still existed, being locked in a room with the 'Orbs of Wonder' would be item number one on this year's list.

It got quite serious too. Now I knew who she was, I sat next to her in Chemistry. We held hands at lunchtime. I went to her house for tea and she came to mine. She regularly came to watch me pick the ball, regularly, out of the back of the net. I would've gone to watch her play netball, but feared that the sight of fourteen teenage girls running around in short skirts, Jelly Fruits bouncing all over the place, may have been way too much for my pubescent hormones to take. I did not want to lose the sight in my good eye.

Her visit for tea at mine must've prompted my Mom to get my Dad to give me 'the talk'. Prior to this day, any visit to my bedroom from Dad usually meant either: turn that bloody awful music down, or a telling off for some misdemeanour or other, supplemented by a talk about bucking my ideas up. He walked into my room and sat on the bed, a serious look on his face. This threw me. My music wasn't on, I hadn't recently been involved in any sort of punishable behavioural infraction and my most recent school report had stated, quite categorically that, apart from French, I was firmly on track for five 'O' levels at grade C or higher. Or higher!

"Right, errr, I think we need to have a talk," he started.

"What have I done, I haven't done anything. I haven't done anything," I countered defensively.

"Errr, no. No. Errr, only your Mom thinks, errr, that, errr," he struggled on.

"What? What does she think that I have done now?" I continued on the defensive path.

"No, errr, no. You've done nothing wrong. Errr, right, errr, you know girls?" I still wasn't sure where this was going.

"Yeah, and?"

"Well, errr," he paused and searched for the words, "I wouldn't bother with them too much just yet," he said. Relief flooded over his face, he'd found the words. And mine, I now knew where this had meant to go. That could've been really embarrassing; for both of us.

"Ah, I see. Well, I've already done it at school, Dad," I said and, just in case he'd misinterpreted, quickly added, "we covered it in Biology, like." We hadn't. I figured a little white lie could stave off any future attempts at 'the talk'. I knew all about 'the talk'. I'd read James Herbert's 'The Rats'[2] three times; Chapter eight at least twelve, if not more. It replaced the ladies underwear section of the Littlewoods catalogue as my favourite read. They had nothing to worry about at all. To this point I had not even had an opportunity to get a single one of my grubby little hands on either jumper covered and bra encased 'Orb of Wonder', never mind actually exploring chapter eight for real.

"Errr, great," relief flooded into his voice too. "Fancy going to the Wolves on Tuesday night, then? Sixth round replay against Middlesbrough, we'll sit in the stands as a treat, halfway line." We did. They won 3-1, setting up a FA Cup semi-final meeting with Tottenham. This went to a replay too. They lost the replay.

A couple of weeks later, I was stood in The Angel's house in front of my host and Boogie (The Angel's next door neighbour and fellow top setter), Annie hanging from my shoulders, 5 watt battery powered amp at my feet. I eyed Boogie's Taiwanese Les Paul copy with relief; at least we were on equal terms with the replica Les Pauls. I looked with envy at his 10 watt electric powered amplifier though. I was about to be auditioned.

"What can you do then?" The Angel asked. It was now or never. I'd prepared for this. I cranked my battery powered amp up to five. It only went up to five. I launched into the theme from 'Jamie and the Magic Torch', and then segued, slightly ham-fistedly, into the theme from 'Rhubarb and Custard'. I blamed my nerves; they nodded in appreciation. I had been about to finish them off with 'Superwomble' but checked myself and fired into 'Smoke on the Water' instead.

"You're in," they said in unison. I was in!

We jammed for the next hour or so. This was mostly spent getting to the first chorus of 'Smoke on the Water' before we lost timing, getting half way through 'Paranoid', again before we lost timing, or me showing Boogie how to play the 'Rhubarb and Custard' theme. I didn't care, I was in a heavy rock band and Boogie knew how to do the twiddly bit in 'Paranoid'.

"What shall we call ourselves?" Boogie asked. We then spent the next hour going over names for the band, what other songs we should play and in which famous rock arenas we would play them. Matt Black got rejected as the band name, again. Ultimately, we settled on Argon. Trust a couple of top set kids to use the periodic table to name their rock band. If they had really thought about it, they should've gone for one of the heavy metals, surely? Although, I suppose Molybdenum doesn't exactly roll off the tongue. How about Tungsten Rod? Now that would've worked for me.

The founding Argon line up of: The Angel on vocals, Boogie on guitar and Matt Black on guitar (if it wasn't going to be the band name, it was going to be my stage name) didn't last long. On telling them I'd got us a gig at a small village under sixteen youth club disco in one month's time, Boogie blanched and quit the band. He didn't even cite 'musical differences' as a reason. It probably had more to do with the fact that we only knew two songs all the way to the end, had no bass player and did not know anyone who could play the drums. He probably got out at the right time though; he's a doctor now.

It didn't deter The Angel; he wanted to rock as much as I did. We formed the not so prolific song writing partnership of Black-Angel (this would've worked as the band name for me too, but the Black was deemed too close to the Black in Black Sabbath). We recruited his other next door neighbour, Bass Twin, on bass guitar just for the youth club gig. He was already in a band and wouldn't fully commit to Argon. I used the imminent upcoming gig to further mortgage my soul to rock 'n' roll (and the Bank of Mom & Dad). I got my hands on a real Marshall 50 watt combo amplifier. It was second hand, but was a real Marshall and did look the business. And, it went up to ten!

We didn't do things by halves, we did them by three-quarters. After a month of furious rehearsals, we played the gig as a three piece, without a drummer, but we did have John the Roadie. We ripped through a set that included: 'Smoke on the Water', 'Paranoid', 'All Right Now' by Free, Pink Floyd's crowd pleasing 'Another Brick in the Wall', complete with very popular crowd participation in the chorus *'Hey teacher, leave them kids alone',* and the Black-Angel penned anthem 'Dracula'. For the encore we swapped instruments; The Angel took up the bass, Bass Twin the guitar, and I the vocals, to do 'Dracula' again. We rocked! You could definitely cancel the interview with the careers officer now.

"Dracula, Dracula, Drac-u-lah." The kids sang as they left the show.

......"*Welcome Matt Black, you're live with Tommy Vance on the Friday Rock Show. That was a great show this week. Argon really stormed through a set of classics there. Would you say your main influences are rooted in the classic rock genre?" TV on the Radio* asked.

"*Errr, not really, nah. They're just easier to play, like. Me and The Angel like Diamond Head and Iron Maiden, but their songs are a bit trickier. You know, after just eight lessons, like,*" I replied. *I'm being interviewed by Tommy Vance. I'm being interviewed by Tommy Vance!*

"*Will you be writing any more of your own material, then?*"

"*Yeah, definitely. We're maturing as writers. We've already got a nice little five chord riff to a song we might call 'Frankenstein's Monster', that's one chord for each syllable. Two more chords than 'Dracula' has got!*"

"*Do you have any designs on taking America by storm?*"

"*Yeah, I don't see why not, as long as it doesn't impact on the football team or my captain of the cricket team duties.*" *Please ask the Europe question. Please.*

"*And how would you view Europe?*" *Bingo.*

"*Errr, through a very big telescope?*" *I thank you.*

"Didn't Diamond Head use that line in an interview with me?"

"Errr, dunno, errr, never heard the interview, mate." I lied. I've just lied to Tommy Vance!

"Right, moving on, you seemed very comfortable taking over singing duties for the encore, is this a direction you will be taking in the future?"

"Errr, yeah, I think so, yeah. The Angel is getting better on the guitar so we could share singing duties. Plus I've studied the big name bands closely and have run some quadratic equations with my data. The singer seems to get almost twice as many groupies as a guitarist does, so becoming a lead singer and guitarist should mean I get three times the groupies. I like the sound of that. Errr, did you say we are live on air? Ooops! The 'Orbs of Wonder' probably ain't gonna like that bit.".....

---

[1] The Names for Breasts record, at this time, stood at fifty-three. Quite a feat given that our lessons were only forty minutes long.

[2] The early works of classic British horror writer James Herbert offered teenage boys their first taste of adult education / entertainment discreetly tucked away in a gripping horror tale. If we had covered any of his early works instead of Jane Austen or the Brontes I might have got grade C or higher in English Literature instead of an E.

5. The Broken Ankle Conspiracy

*"Tobacco and alcohol, delicious fathers of abiding friendships and
fertile reveries."*
Luis Buñuel

*I gave up smoking about five years ago and took up nicotine chewing gum
instead. I still use alcohol though, to father friendships and fertilize reveries
(and my compost bin).*

The Angel and I continued developing our proficiency on the
guitar in pursuit of the rock 'n' roll fantasy. We were getting better
and could now play songs that included multiple chord changes,
complex timings, pedal string riffs and we even made brave, yet
vain, attempts at scorching guitar solos. Make that screeching guitar
solos, and you're somewhere in the ball park. Unperturbed, the
classic rock of the early Argon days was replaced by a more refined
cutting edge, modern sound. Michael Schenker Group's 'Armed and
Ready', Def Leppard's 'Let it Go' and Diamond Head's 'Shoot Out
the Lights' featured among our repertoire. 'Doctor Doctor' by UFO
was our only concession to the classic rock genre; we both liked the
song, The Angel could play the opening riff, and I knew all the
chords. It made our ever growing set list. And, just like UFO, we
planned to open with it. However, despite the huge set list and
hundreds of hours spent planning said set list, mostly in French or
History lessons, we weren't exactly speeding along the heavy rock
'n' roll super highway to hell. We were still a two piece.
    Enter stage left: Big Trev. He had recently joined us single-
linguals in French. In a lull, during yet another assault on the Names
for Breasts record, I had discovered that he was having bass guitar
lessons with none other than Guitar Teacher. Apart from Bass Twin,
he was the only other person we knew who played the bass. He
might just be our man. Once I'd further ascertained that he had no
inclination towards cowboy songs whatsoever, and that he was
indeed also a kindred spirit and wanted to ride hell for leather along
the heavy rock 'n' roll super highway to hell, we invited him to

audition for Argon. He passed the audition; with flying colours when he told us he knew a drummer. Argon as a real, proper, bona fide heavy rock band was born: The Angel - vocals and guitar, Matt Black - guitar, Big Trev - bass guitar and Hawkeye - drums.

We rehearsed at The Angel's house and had a full length mirror in the room so we could practice our guitar poses. One day we turned up to rehearsals to find The Angel sporting a brand new Hongkongese replica Gibson Flying V guitar. It genuinely looked the business. Enviously I asked if I could try out his Vee. I slipped it over my shoulders, took centre stage in front of the mirror and cracked off 'Superwomble'. Wellington style. The opportunity had been too good to miss, yet I managed to catch myself just before the second chorus. I looked round furtively and hoped that no one had noticed my musical faux pas. If they had, no one let on. Just in case, and by way of redemption, I fired off the opening riff to Sammy Hagar's 'This Planet's on Fire', then reluctantly handed The Angel his Vee back.

We rehearsed regularly, waiting for gigs to come along. Unfortunately for us, and quite probably fortunately for an unwitting heavy rock public, rock venues that accommodated bands comprising entirely of fifteen year old boys were a bit thin on the ground. If there had been any we would have been rather stuck for transport to lug the gear around too; we only had a couple of twelve speeds, a Raleigh Chopper and a BMX between us.

We waited and waited for the elusive gig to materialise. The band began to lose focus as other distractions presented themselves. Obviously there were already girlfriends to cater for. And, as I was beginning to learn, they could sometimes be quite demanding. Enter stage right: Home Brewed Beer. The Angel's Dad usually had two or three forty pint barrels of the stuff on the go, and after a rehearsal The Angel would give us a half or two. Now we had made a discovery that, at that time, was probably equally as exciting as the discovery of chapter eight in The Rats. What's more, we could actually get hold of home brewed beer. Getting an experience of what was happening in chapter eight was nigh on impossible; even for those of us with girlfriends. For those without, their pocket money certainly wasn't going to stretch to a trip down Pipers Row in

Wolverhampton. Not that I could have really envisaged any of us nervously kerb crawling along Pipers Row on a twelve speed, pockets bulging with saved up fifty pence pieces, that should really have been spent on ice-creams. You needed at least a Raleigh Chopper to pull that one off.

Rehearsals at first became shorter, and then less frequent, before stopping altogether, as we revelled in the delights and continued to develop a taste for The Angel's Dad's home brewed beer. Pretty soon there were at least ten of us, if not more, with a forty pint barrel of beer fermenting away in the airing cupboard at home; the airing cupboard being the only place warm enough in the house to get the mash going. This meant that you could smell a fellow brewer from the faint yet distinguishable aroma of yeast and hops emanating from their clothes. It hung, shroud like, over our school uniforms. How we all got brewing our own beer agreed and cleared by the parents, with 'O' levels less than a year away? I've no idea. Fifteen year old boys with forty pints of beer, what could possibly go wrong?

With our band, girlfriends and a developing taste for home brewed beer, the production of which had been sanctioned by our parents, we felt as though we had been welcomed onto the threshold of adulthood. We even tried to follow this up and act maturely. French lessons were no longer spent exclusively trying to break the Names for Breasts record; while some form of talk about girls, or parts of girls, was inevitable, sometimes we even discussed more important things like: who would win in a fight if Iron Maiden went toe to toe with AC/DC, or, if Ozzy Osbourne was prime minister, should he introduce a summer bra tax to prevent the over wearing of bras in hot weather? Discussed maturely and with all the arguments considered, we usually reached the conclusions that: AC/DC would easily win the fight and, that regardless of who was prime minister, never mind a bra tax, there ought to be an outright ban on bra wearing in the summer, accompanied by a 'compulsory wearing of low cut tops' statute.

.....*"FREEZE!"* *a blond female cop shouted and pointed her gun towards me.*

I looked around. There was no point in running. I was trapped. An older cop at the other end of the alleyway blocked the only other available exit. He looked a bit like Captain Kirk, only much fatter. Intergalactic space meals must have a few more added calories these days. I raised my hands in surrender.

"Move towards my car. Nice and slow, keeping your hands on your head." Blondie beckoned me towards her car, gun still raised. At least it's her car and not fat Captain Kirk's.

As I got nearer I could see that she was wearing a low cut police uniform; spectacularly low for a member of the law enforcement community. I edged closer still, her name badge read Officer Stacy Sheridan[1]; I also noticed that she was bra-less. Before I could get close enough for a thorough examination she grabbed me, threw me across the hood of her squad car and frisked me, vigorously.

Out of the corner of my eye I saw fat Captain Kirk get beamed up. What? What's he doing spoiling my being frisked by.....

"Matt, Matt," John the Roadie nudged me, yet again bringing me back into the wondrous realms of a French lesson, "how much extra sugar do you reckon I need to add so I can boost the strength of a Woolworths pale ale kit?" I didn't know.

"I dunno, double it?" I responded with a guess. My home brewing guru was The Angel, top set Chemistry kids knew this sort of stuff.

"Hang on, hang on," Big Trev cut in. "Before we get on to beer, do you really want to see Mrs XX from Subject YY walking around bra-less in a low cut top? We need a cut off age, surely?" He was still concerned by the finer detail in the Ozzy Osbourne statutes. Given his question, rightly so.

"Good point, man. How old is Heather Locklear?" John the Roadie offered. We paused briefly while we individually considered being frisked vigorously by Officer Stacy Sheridan; the second time that day for me.

"Nah, she's way too young for the cut off age. How old is the classy English bird in 'American Werewolf in London', Jenny someone or other?" I asked.

"That's Jenny Agutter." John the Roadie was also the band's resident horror film expert. I broke away from being frisked, and started to picture myself as a huge man-come-wolf being nursed lovingly by Jenny Agutter, just like in the film. I didn't get time to fully develop the scene; a board rubber whizzed past my ear, danger close.

"ROTHWELL ET VOS AMIS!" French Teacher shouted, once again rudely interrupting an otherwise important debate, "make your cut off Victoria Principal plus ten years[2]. Now, can we get back to LEARNING SOME BLOODY FRENCH?"

"Wee, miss-u-ah," we responded, quite impressed with French Teacher's suggestion.

Finally we had a gig! Argon had a month to get ready to rock its first audience as a bona fide 'got all the right instruments covered' heavy rock band. It wasn't quite going to be Wolverhampton Civic Hall, but it was guaranteed to be a sell out. And, as it was a ten minute slot in a house assembly at school, it would also have a higher percentage of females in the crowd than the standard heavy rock going concert audience.

With two weeks to go, the 'Orbs of Wonder' unceremoniously dumped me. I turned in on myself, never mind 'minimum effort, maximum sloth', my mantra became 'minimum effort, minimum everything else too'. I slipped into deep solipsism; no one else and nothing else existed except for my pain. I realised how wise my Dad was and now understood the true meaning of 'I wouldn't bother with them too much just yet' from 'the talk'. The Angel sat me down, handed me a pint of three times the sugar, double length brewed, home brew pale ale and gave me a talk; not 'the talk', just a talk. He convinced me to write a song about it and gave me a 'you've experienced the pain that the great songwriters go through, express it' speech as encouragement. I countered that with 'I thought we only did songs about rocking out and highways to hell'.

The 'three times the sugar' kicked in. Like most of our sugar experimentation home brews, it tasted bloody awful, but blimey, it got you there quickly. I got a paper and pen out and began to scribble out some lyrics.....

How could you cast me asunder?

Denying me those orbs of wonder,

I was not sure The Angel would sing this one.

I had another go.

Heather Locklear,
Thinks I'm queer,
'Cos all I want is you,
Not Locklear,
Here,
Ya hear?

I was not sure The Angel would sing this one, either. Actually, this was way ahead of its time. I'm calling dibs on it right now; just in case I ever do some sort of fifty year old rap-metal crossover project with Jay-Z. Word!

I tried again.

Baby, you rocked my world,
Please don't leave me,
Let me rock your world again,
'Cos I wanna be your world rocking man, (pronounce 'man', like
'may-ain', to make it rhyme with a-gay-ain. Damn those cowboy
influenced guitar lessons!)

No, no, no, no, no. I wasn't conveying my pay-ain at all.

I had to face facts. While I could possibly have sold the last one to Saxon, Rainbow at a push (Rainbow the rock band, not Rainbow with Geoffrey, Bungle and Zippy), I just wasn't a lyricist. In time honoured 'minimum effort, maximum sloth' fashion, I gave up and helped myself to another pint of 'three times the sugar'. I'm sure Wellington never wrote the lyrics, anyways. Ah-hah! The 'three times the sugar' kicked in again. I got Ozzy Osbourne's 'Blizzard of Oz' album out and had a look at the lyrics on the inner sleeve. I found the song I was after and made like a Womble. I introduced 'my' new song 'Goodbye to Romance' (lyrics and title by Ozzy Osbourne, music by Matt Black) at the next rehearsal. It went down well. I'd have gotten away with claiming it as my own too, if it hadn't been for that pesky Angel and the fact that it was his copy of 'Blizzard of Oz' I had Wombled the title and lyrics from. Damn that 'three times the sugar' brew.

The morning of the gig arrived. I bet Iron Maiden have never rocked out in front of two hundred odd teenagers, half of whom were girls. Well, they probably have, but I bet not at eight thirty in the morning. The Angel launched us into a three song set.

"SCHOOL HOUSE ASSEMBLY! ARE YOU READY TO ROCK?" he shouted down the mike and we stormed into UFO's 'Doctor Doctor' just like we had always planned. Then I made my proper debut as a lead singer with 'my' song 'Goodbye to Romance'. We finished them off with The Angel back on the mike rocking Buffalo's[3] 'Cold as Night'. We rocked hard! Not a soul wanted to go to lessons. They wanted more. We wanted to rock. Head of House said no. We had to go to Subject A; 'O' levels were less than a year away.

The Angel and I made our way to Subject A, and arrived ten minutes late on a euphoric post gig high. The post gig high was way better than a 'three times the sugar' beer high, and at this point in time, we could all say in total honesty that a post gig high was better than sex.

Subject A's teacher Mr X had been in the assembly. He did not appreciate our tardiness and was obviously not an aficionado of the heavy rock genre, either. The Angel and I got a huge dressing down in front of class. Among other things, for some reason he kept repeating 'Do you think you are going to get five 'O' levels at grade C or higher by prancing around while making that banshee noise with your silly guitars? Do you? Do you?' On the assumption that there was no correct answer we kept a stoic silence and tried as hard as we could to suppress fits of giggles; which of course only served to set him off again. Has there ever been a better opportunity for someone at the back to shout out *'Hey, teacher, leave them kids alone'*? Once Mr X had run out of steam he gave us a couple of hours worth of extra homework, to make up for the ten minutes we'd missed and the further fifteen that he'd spent admonishing us. If there was ever someone who warranted a spirited shaking of an imaginary tomato ketchup bottle aimed specifically towards him, it was Mr X. He may not have liked heavy rock but he appeared to be an admirer of professionally executed roadie duties. John the Roadie got neither a dressing down nor the extra homework.

We did not care. Argon had rocked up a storm. The word spread across the school like wildfire. One of the sixth formers asked us to open for his band at an end of summer term concert. How could we refuse? It was in the school lecture theatre, on a proper stage, through a proper sound system. It also meant that it would be the first time in the history of Argon that we had done two gigs in a single year! We had raised our devil's horned salutes and officially joined the heavy rock 'n' roll super highway to hell.

We excitedly set to work rehearsing and putting a set together. The Black-Angel writing partnership decided it was time to introduce more of our own material, and managed to pen a third and fourth song, of which only the fourth, 'Planet Story' (a song about intergalactic battles being all the rage, I did the chords) made the cut. 'Dracula' had been binned ages ago. The most prolific song writer was Big Trev; he churned out rock anthems like they were going out of fashion. Big Trev songs that made the cut were the ones with lyrics that The Angel would sing: 'Keep us on the Road Again' (a song about rocking out along a dusty road) and 'Sea Witch' (a song about rocking out, shaking your head and waking the dead). I found song writing difficult to do, especially lyrics, and if something is difficult to do? I had a new distraction, anyways.

I'd forgotten all about the 'Orbs of Wonder' by now. I'd also forgotten all about my Dad's words of wisdom in 'the talk' and was going out with Kryptonite Girl #1. My lead singer and guitarist groupie theory was correct. There had been several enquiries of interest after the gig. I mulled over a couple before finally losing all of my powers to Kryptonite Girl #1. She was top set totty and previously deemed (by myself and possibly by many others) to be way, way out of my league. Thanks to having ditched the specks years ago, the magnetic marvels of the electric guitar and the mystical powers of rock, she was now my girlfriend. She was a rock chick too. Bonus! And, her orbs were just as wondrous. Double, double wobble bonus! I fell in love. Again.

We weren't in any lessons together, but we went to gigs together: Gary Moore, Gillan, Iron Maiden and Diamond Head to name a few. She rocked. We went to the cinema together. Even though we were three years below the legal age, it was usually to see some X rated horror film. This didn't rock so much. I didn't mind tales about giant flesh eating rats but wasn't too keen on the ghost and demon stuff. I had nightmares for weeks after seeing The Amityville Horror, for bloody months after seeing The Exorcist. Give me an Indiana Jones, any film of the week. She came to watch me play in goal. I was picking the ball out of the back of the net with less frequency than in previous years. Whether it was me or the defence that had improved, I wasn't sure. And, just like the 'Orbs of Wonder', Kryptonite Girl #1 was also in the netball team. And like before, I refrained from going to watch her play too. I was still concerned that the sight of fourteen teenage girls jumping around in short skirts, nicely maturing Wobble Berries flying all over the place, may still have been way too much for my teenage hormones to take.

The day of the big gig had nearly arrived. Kryptonite Girl #1 had to go on hold for a while. We had the very important business of rock to attend to. At the last rehearsal before the big day, we finalised our set list and ran through it several times. After several pints of 'double the sugar' (we'd all agreed that 'three times the sugar' was, while very strong, not very palatable) we convinced ourselves that we were, indeed, ready to rock.

Then, total disaster.

The day before, during the school sports day, I broke my ankle playing basketball. Although the pain may have indicated otherwise, I refused to believe it. Even after six hours in A&E, I still refused to believe it. I wanted a second opinion. Another two hours and second opinion later, during which time I'd also received some very choice words from my Mom, and then from a doctor, I relented and let them plaster me up; I was still adamant that I had not broken my ankle. The doctor had given me a terse sentence about wasting his time. I'd been there for eight hours, whom had been wasting whose time?

Eventually I hobbled out of the hospital with a huge cast on my left leg and a pair of wooden crutches under my arms. I was not being allowed to rock with Argon at the big gig. The propaganda coming out of the hospital was that the cast needed to fully set. Parents believed hospital propaganda. Rocking out? Denied! I was gutted. Absolutely gutted. I wasn't going to be able to captain the cricket team the following week in the Dudley area cup final, either.

There was a small plus side to it. I milked a week, doubtless slightly more than a week, off school. And, when I returned, much to the annoyance of senior teachers and in defiance of their strict uniform code, I wore jeans for the remainder of the year. I had a genuine excuse too: my Mom would not cut up a perfectly good pair of trousers (to enable them to fit over my cast) in order to adhere to the school uniform code. It looked like I would be wearing them again next year then; three turn down creases, shiny knees, threadbare arse and all.

Argon would rock no more. We never recovered from the disappointment of missing out on the big gig. Over the summer, and I'm sure much to Mr X's pleasure, the band broke up. At least I had Kryptonite Girl #1. Yeah, right. Once my cast came off we went to see Whitesnake at Birmingham Odeon. Just before they were about to come on, she unceremoniously dumped me. I wasn't as gutted as I probably should've been. I hated Whitesnake. She'd just saved me from having to sit through two hours of self indulgent, pompous, keyboard laden and American FM radio oriented chick rock. Keyboards in a rock band? Not on my watch, darlin'. I'll be a fool for your loving no more, Kryptonite Girl #1. I caught a train home, unwisely put Ozzy's 'Blizzard of Oz' album on (I'd forgotten about 'my' song), started on a new barrel of 'double the sugar' brew and rummaged around for my copy of The Rats.

.....Paganini's '24th Caprice' ends. The camera cuts to Melvyn Bragg as he walks across a school playing field. The camera cuts to the school lecture theatre, the stage set with lines of stacked Marshall amplification and a huge drum kit atop a drum riser. The camera cuts to Melvyn Bragg sat at the back of the theatre.

"Tonight on the South Bank Show we profile the brief and turbulent career of a young rock guitarist from the short lived, yet influential, heavy rock band Argon. From his humble beginnings miming along to 'Superwomble' in front of his bedroom mirror, through strumming cowboy songs on a cheap acoustic guitar, and finally arriving at the making of potent heavy rock music with Argon, Matt Rothwell is probably one of the best known proponents of the electric rock guitar in his year at school," the camera cuts to the only known photograph of Matt from this period. He's sat on a wall wearing an Iron Maiden 1982 tour t-shirt, head bowed, long hair covering his face. *"I caught up with Matt at the venue that should've seen Argon explode onto the school heavy rock scene. Instead, a sports related injury denied them of that opportunity and ultimately led to the band's break up."* The camera briefly cuts to Matt playing guitar in his bedroom, the tune sounds remarkably like the theme to 'Jamie and the Magic Torch', then cuts back to Bragg in the theatre, now joined by Matt.

"Matt, Argon had matured as a band. You'd got the full line up in place and were starting to write your own original material. Talk me through your influences at the time," Melvyn asks. Matt thinks for a moment before responding.

"Errr, loads of bands really, and while the music was important to us, I think we were more heavily influenced by the great hedonists of rock. You know, the sex, drugs and rock 'n' roll types. I mean, how cool would it be to throw a TV out of a tenth storey hotel window, stoned out of your head, while naked groupies chase each other around the room? I tried to emulate this by shooting an Evel Knievel energiser stunt cycle out of the top floor of a two storey semi, after four pints of 'double the sugar', in front of several posters of Heather Locklear in a swim suit. It didn't quite give me the buzz I reckon the tenth floor TV set scenario would."

"And outside of the music, this was something that the whole band aspired too?"

"Of course, sex, drugs and rock 'n' roll? I mean, I can only speak for myself, but what fifteen year old boy wouldn't? We were getting there too. We'd got the rock 'n' roll sorted, home brewed beer was

our drug and some of us had even gotten past first base, if you know what I mean? We were living the dream, man. I still aspire to it."

"So, with Argon on the verge of igniting the school heavy rock scene, the sports related injury must have come as a huge disappointment?"

"Yeah. I mean, we'd worked so hard on getting the set right and had all our moves worked out in The Angel's mirror. Then some stupid doctor comes along, with his blurred X-ray pictures and colluded second opinions. He crushed the dream with a disgraceful and cruel misdiagnosis."

"You're saying it wasn't a broken ankle?"

"Hey, I'm no doctor. All I'm saying is, it was a misdiagnosis. We were going to be bigger than the Beatles. And they were bigger than Jesus. Look at what that doctor denied the music world."

"You just said 'bigger than the Beatles'? That's just teenage bravado, surely? And don't you think that, as the Beatles got into a lot of trouble for their 'bigger than Jesus' claim, it could affect your chances of breaking into the States?"

"Call it teenage bravado if you like, but, when you have to sit through nearly five hours of mind numbingly dull lessons every day, you have to have belief in yourself. We got so bored, we more than believed. As for the States, we hadn't got any records for them to burn, so what? We'd have been way cleverer anyways; we'd have just said 'We're bigger than the Beatles. And you know who they were bigger than!' Clever see, no specific mention of the Jesus fella."

"Does the demise of Argon mark the end of your rock guitar career?"

"I don't think so. Rock is my life, man. I'm a dreamer with a guitar. You take the guitar away from me and I'm just a dreamer. There are not that many jobs out there for dreamers."

"So where do you go from here then?"

"Well, you can't rock if you work the nine to five. And if you work the nine to five you have to get your hair cut. I'm not ready for that. I need to get my head down to some 'minimum effort, minimum sloth' and conjure up at least five 'O' levels at grade C."

"Or higher?"

"Oh, yeah. I think I sold my soul on the 'or higher' bit, didn't I? Anyways, getting the grade Cs will mean I'll be able to give it some serious 'minimum effort, maximum sloth' in the sixth form for a couple of years, thus thwarting the nine to five, and therefore avoiding the hair cut. Overall though, what I really need to sort out is a new band. You can't rock if you ain't in a band."

"Will this band be a continuation of Argon?"

"Well, given that I've just been dumped again, all I'm sure of at this point is, that even though I'm not the greatest singer, I quite fancy being the lead singer and guitarist in my next band. Have I told you my theory about being the lead singer and guitarist?".....

---

[1] Heather Locklear played Officer Stacy Sheridan in TJ Hooker. She also played Sammy Jo in Dynasty, but only girls watched that. She really was a rock chick too, and went on to marry the drummer from Motley Crue and later the guitarist from Bon Jovi.

[2] 'Victoria Principal plus ten' made the cut off age forty-three years old. If we were to revisit this, thirty odd years later, I think we'd have dismissed a definitive cut off age. We'd have replaced it with a compulsory annual test for ladies on reaching their thirtieth birthday. A bit like the MOT, only for Jelly Fruits. Pass the test and you're still considered road worthy enough to be permitted to wear low cut tops without a bra. Fail it and it's a choice between a compulsory cover up, or moving to Germany. They don't appear to be as squeamish as us Brits.

[3] Buffalo were a heavy rock band from up north somewhere. They were lucky enough to record a single for a minor label. They never really made it, but The Angel and I did like this song.

DISC TWO
The Special Brew Years
1984 – 1988

Selected Soundtrack
U2 – 'Two Hearts'
The Waterboys – 'Red Army Blues'
Bauhaus – 'In the Flat Field'
The Cure – 'The Top'
Siouxsie and the Banshees – 'We Hunger'
The Cult – 'Peace Dog'
Metallica – 'For Whom the Bell Tolls'
Anthrax & Public Enemy – 'Bring the Noise'
Crazyhead – 'What Gives You the Idea that You're So Amazing,
Baby?'
PWEI – 'There is No Love Between Us Anymore'

Also Getting Chewed up by a cheap 'Walkman'
Not much actually, this was a rather barren musical period for me.

6. Musically Confused Teenager

"It is in our idleness, in our dreams, that the submerged truth sometimes comes to the top."
Virginia Woolf

I thought the cream was supposed to rise to the top. My submerged truths about to surface were: that I was not a very good singer at all, and also that, save for some girl coming over to tell me that her friend fancied me, I was absolutely rubbish at chatting girls up unless I donned the 'beer-goggles' and went hunting munter. I had quite a bit of success with the 'goggles' on.

While I didn't exactly 'minimise the sloth' during the fifth year, I managed to conform to the control system of 'five 'O' levels at grade C or higher' and even went on to surpass that minimum requirement. I got six, including English and Maths! One A, four Bs and a C. Unsurprisingly, not one of those was French. I'd miss 'maximising the sloth' in French. I'd miss John the Roadie and Big Trev too. John the Roadie went off to study something or other about buildings at college and Big Trev went off to work. You are going to be working until you are sixty-five, I thought. No need to rush into it then. I did some maths; at sixteen years old, one year equates to two percent of your working life. I enrolled in sixth form, thereby making a very healthy four percent saving on my future working life.

The teachers had a new dogma to preach now: 'if you don't get good 'A' level grades you won't get the university place of your choice'. Ah-hah, gotcha! I had no desire to go to university. In fact, other than wanting to throw TV sets out of tenth floor hotel rooms, I had no inclination of what I wanted to do with my life at all. I liked girls, I liked beer and I liked to rock. Everything incontrovertibly pointed towards throwing TV sets from tenth floor hotel room windows. Which, I concluded, probably did not require 'A' levels at any grade, let alone good grades. Two years of 'minimum effort, maximum sloth' here we come then. I rubbed my hands together and did a happy little jig of joy.

I 'maximised the sloth' early doors and dropped two of the four subjects I'd enrolled to do. I could now concentrate on the card school in the common room, and, by way of an additional bonus, it allowed for extra free time to check out the girls. It also meant I could stay in the pub on Friday lunchtimes (I wasn't the only one, some teachers stayed there too) for an extra hour or two. I'd been able to get served in several local pubs and almost all local off licences for the last nine months or so. Whilst I now knew which pubs had a lax age enforcement policy, my very first 'solo' visit to a pub had been an unmitigated disaster. I was not quite fifteen. I panicked at the bar and asked the landlord for a pint of beer. We did call our home brew 'beer'. He then asked me what type: bitter, mild, lager? I panicked again. I couldn't see 'double the sugar' on the taps, a pint of beer please. He barred me and told me to come back when I was eighteen.

I returned to the delights of home brew for a year, but after a very severe case of food poisoning, bought on by drinking into the sediment of a potent 'double the sugar', I stopped home brew production altogether. The sediment thing was something I would have known to avoid had I ever bothered to read the brewing instructions. You live and learn. I still don't read instructions, but if I am ever offered a pint of home brew? I check for a milky cloudiness before taking a gulp. I decided that pub or the offy was the safest way forward.

What I really liked about the pub though, apart from it being rammed with girls at the weekend, was that six pounds got you six pints of bitter, or if the mood should take you, eight bottles of Carlsberg Special Brew. With the change you got ten Benson and Hedges and it still left you with the bus fare home. If it was mid-week, or in the company of adults, I stuck to bitter, if it was with mates who could also get served and the weekend, it was usually the Special Brew. Seventeen year olds drinking four pints of Special Brew, what could possibly go wrong?

Prior to entering sixth form I'd spent all of the summer painting great, huge, never ending, steel girders a drab red-brown colour in my Dad's factory. It wasn't that I'd really wanted a summer job, what sixteen year old in their right mind would? And I hadn't been forced into it. I'd actually asked for it. Out of the remnants of Argon, Big Trev and I had formed a new band. Fresh start logic dictated that I needed a new guitar and amp; Annie was past her sell by date and my old Marshall combo just wasn't loud enough anymore. We were going to rock harder this time.

I knew exactly what I wanted: an Ibanez 'Destroyer' guitar and a Marshall 100 watt amp with a 4 x 12 speaker cabinet. It was pricey; the guitar had to be new, but I would go second hand on the amp. I added the income from selling my skateboard, Apollo 11 model, the half completed Panini albums and my complete home brew kit, to the money I'd earned over the summer. I counted it up. I got a quote for the part exchange value of Annie and the Marshall combo. I included this in the calculation. I told my latest girlfriend that she'd have to go without a birthday and Christmas present this year and then added the last four and a half pounds from my savings account. I recalculated. My Nan and her ice-cream fifty pence pieces were not going to make much of a dent in the shortfall; unless I went to see her two hundred times in the next couple of weeks. That would amount to four hundred beardy kisses. No, no, no. No amount of money was worth four hundred beardy kisses in such a short time period, and as I hadn't planted my money tree yet, there was only one place left to go.

I went back to the Bank of Mom & Dad once more. I was negotiating from a position of power this time; or so I thought. I explained that I had got six, not five, 'O' levels at grade C and higher including English and Maths. Then I reiterated that I had got six 'O' levels at grade C and higher including English and Maths. I followed this up with the fact that the cupboard in my bedroom now had plenty of spare room in it, which was irrelevant anyway, as they could surely see that the electric guitar was not a passing fad. And finally, I made it clear that it was an obvious investment opportunity; the dividend being that I would not forget to build them an annex on my seventeenth century country mansion in a couple of year's time. Pleased with my presentation I waited for their decision.

They are a tough bank to deal with. Like all the great artistes, I was going to have to suffer for my art. Eventually I agreed to their terms: I would get nothing for my birthday or Christmas (I won't be the only one, I thought) and I'd be spending all of this year's school holidays painting great, huge, never ending, steel girders a drab red-brown colour. For no pay! There would be no Euro crisis with the Bank of Mom & Dad in charge! In an oversight by the Bank of Mom & Dad, there was no mention of any future academic achievement in the small print whatsoever; a bonus of 'buy now, pay later, interest free' proportions for me. Let's rock!

I was still ignoring my Dad's non-banking advice though and, surprise, surprise, I found myself dumped yet again. I was becoming accustomed to this recurring phenomenon. Although this time, I think there may have been a Special Brew induced 'goggle' wearing incident that provided the catalyst. I was becoming hardened to it, and, once I'd made it all around the baseball field, slightly blasé too. Girls were starting to have a negative impact on what I wanted to be doing; which primarily involved going out with my mates, drinking with my mates, playing cricket with my mates and rocking with my mates. There wasn't that much time to fit in a girlfriend. I also had my school work to think of, which, while I didn't really do any work, I did occasionally think about it. I resolved to take my Dad's advice this time and not bother with girls for a while. I set to the serious business of rock on the Destroyer; such a better name for an electric guitar than Annie.

"What are we gonna call ourselves then?" Big Trev asked at our first rehearsal.

"How about Matt Black?" I tried enthusiastically; for the umpteenth time of my rock career.

"Get off," The Thrill was not thrilled. The Thrill was The Angel's brother and our new drummer. The Thrill liked AC/DC. That was good. John the Roadie, The Thrill and I had been to see them at Birmingham's NEC last year, they rocked. He also liked The Jam and The Style Council. Not so good. I could understand people liking The Jam, it being guitar based rock of sorts (I had a secret soft spot for them myself). I had no comprehension of why people liked The Style Council. They drank cappuccino coffee for starters; I couldn't imagine anyone throwing a TV set out of a hotel room window on a cappuccino buzz. Big Trev didn't look that thrilled with Matt Black either.

"How about Tungsten Rod, then?" I tried my second choice.

"Nah," they both said; although I could imagine Big Trev going away and mulling this one over.

"Molybdenum Missile?" I tried again. They weren't having that either. Last year John the Roadie and I, having exhausted the Names for Breasts list, had moved on and started compiling alliterative phallic heavy metal combinations that may or may not have been decent band names. I followed up with some more, "Cobalt Cobra? Plutonium Python? Vanadium Viper? Manganese Milk Snake? Titanium Torpedo?" We never did come up with a snake that began with T and had to cheat a little with the manganese one. Unlike any sort of threatened and cornered venomous snake, Big Trev and The Thrill weren't biting at all. I was running out of ideas. "Come on then, you try."

We didn't try very hard. We ended up naming the band Sea Witch. Big Trev had pointed out that if we went for Sea Witch, just like Motorhead with 'Motorhead', we would have a readymade band name anthem in 'Sea Witch'; a Big Trev song we used to play in the Argon days.

When you compare:

'Motorhead, remember me, now, Motorhead, alright,'

Against,

'Sea Witch, shake your head, Sea Witch, wake the dead,'

I think 'Sea Witch' just about shades it.

Although I preferred Matt Black, I wasn't that bothered about what we were called. Sea Witch was fine with me; we had a better anthem than Motorhead after all. I was more than happy to be the lead singer-lead guitarist too, particularly as we were going to be a three piece. I'd rerun my groupie theory calculations and reckoned that as the lead singer-lead guitarist in a three piece, I should now be in line for four point five times the groupies. A tenth floor hotel room beckoned. We set to work.

There was a problem, which we refused to acknowledge. The musical landscape had changed; we were too late.

The quality heavy rock that had ignited our youthful passion three years ago was slowly being drowned, as the vast majority of decent bands sold their souls to their pay masters. In the hope of shifting mega-units in America, the major record labels forced them to compromise their artistic integrity with dire, watered down, keyboard laden and American FM radio oriented chick rock. Def Leppard's third album 'Hysteria' went Stateside and skipped gaily along the watered down path. And, as for Diamond Head's eagerly awaited third album 'Canterbury'; it turned out to be one of my most severely disappointing records of all time.

Through our youthful naivety we could not understand why our favourite bands were exiting the heavy rock 'n' roll super highway to hell and taking the pretty route, to skip along the American watered down chick rock freeway instead. In our eyes, America was not exactly renowned for producing quality hard rock acts. You think they were? The prosecution presents, as a very small sample: REO Speedwagon, Styx, Boston, Journey, Lover Boy and Meat Loaf. It may have been rock, but it didn't rock hard. And to make matters worse, America's musical direction was now turning off the chick rock freeway and mincing headlong down lady-boy lane. Along with more of the same watered down chick rock as above, Bon Jovi being a newer example, America was churning out hundreds of appallingly dire glam rock bands: LA Guns, Twisted Sister, Cinderella, Ratt and Poison[1] to name just a few of way too many. There was already a surfeit of keyboard laden rock ballads; we didn't need more of them being sung by big haired transvestites in buttock-less leather trousers. My musical landscape had died; I wrapped myself in a cocoon of AC/DC (up to and including 'For Those About to Rock') and the first Diamond Head album.

..... *"Right boys, we've moved a couple of million units of your first two albums. It's good, it's good. We think we can move even more. What we'd like you to do with the next one is commercialise it up a bit. You know, make it more radio friendly. Let's hit the States,"* Smarmy Record Company Executive *said, as he punched some numbers into his oversized desk calculator.*

94

"Get off. And compromise our artistic integrity?" The Thrill, the band's political commissar, responded.

"Yeah, I ain't having no keyboards in my band. Or love songs for that matter." I aired my predominant concern to the artistic integrity argument.

"Look, do you want to be millionaires or do you want to be multi-millionaires?" Smarmy Record Company Executive continued his sales pitch. He paused for effect and then added, "Boys, to break you in the States we need to commercialise your sound. Millionaire? Multi-Millionaire? Millionaire? Multi-millionaire?"

"Multi-millionaire would be nice." Big Trev was being seduced by dollar signs. I was being seduced by another thought.

"Hang on, never mind the money. Let's have a think about this. It could mean a considerable increase in the number of groupies. We could even get a hotel room on the eleventh floor. I just need to run some numbers through my groupie theory calculation. Can I borrow your big calculator?" I started to tap the keys and drifted off to an eleventh floor hotel room after show party. The TV set was half way out of the window when The Thrill cut in.

"But what about selling out and compromising our artistic integrity?"

"Errr," I glanced down at the numbers on the big calculator and thought for a few seconds. "Fuck that! How about rocking up a U2 song?".....

There were no rock chicks in the sixth form. At any rate, if there had been, I bet they would've been skipping along the watered down chick rock freeway. I'd nearly seen Whitesnake; I did not want to nearly see Bon Jovi. Yet, even with a rock chick famine, I didn't heed my Dad's non-banking advice for long. Along came The Gothic Girls; there were several of them, one of whom would become Kryptonite Girl #2. This was, depending on which way you looked at it, either a good thing or a bad thing. It was a bad thing in that, by the time Sea Witch made their debut at a school disco in the dining hall, I was girlfriended up with a Gothic Girl; thus denying my attendance at the after show party on the eleventh floor. It was a good thing in that I was girlfriended up; therefore no need to worry about any sort

95

of Special Brew 'goggle' wearing incident occurring on the eleventh floor.

Knowing The Gothic Girls became a very bad thing when, after being dumped by one of them, I was moved to write a cheesy power rock love ballad. Until this time, my only other foray into song writing with Sea Witch had been a song called 'Making Money, Making Love'; about an imaginary prostitute we might've gone down Pipers Row to see on our twelve speeds, had she not been imaginary. The guitar part was pretty cool, the lyrics were shit. Whenever I think of 'MMML', or the cheesy power rock love ballad, I cringe inwardly and shake an imaginary tomato ketchup bottle at myself. A Black-Thrill partnership also had a go at a couple of songs. We married The Thrill's overtly political lyrics to some of my darker guitar riffs. The end result sort of worked; it had a Rage Against the Machine vibe, albeit without the angst ridden rap singing or virtuoso guitar playing. In hindsight, we should've left all of the song writing to Big Trev and his rock anthems.

The Gothic Girls' musical landscape was way different to mine too. I soon discovered that I was a very musically confused teenager. Through passive listening I became aware of stuff that I would not previously have touched with a twelve foot devil's trident. Some of it I quite liked: Bauhaus (the rockier and not too weird ones), Ziggy era Bowie (the rockier not too keyboardy ones) and The Cure (just 'The Top' album, mind, and you can scrub the keyboardy ones too). The rest deserved a vigorous shaking of an imaginary tomato ketchup bottle directed straight at the perpetrators: David Sylvian or Morrisey for example.

I became all the more musically confused after Boogie (founding member of Argon), The Thrill and I went to see U2. I wasn't that keen on the arena rock of 'The Unforgettable Fire', and Bono himself will always be a very deserving recipient of a well aimed imaginary tomato ketchup bottle shaking, but I was blown away by their earlier material being played live; 'Sunday Bloody Sunday' particularly. The Edge, U2's guitarist, played a Gibson Explorer too, very similar in shape to my Ibanez Destroyer. I wouldn't need a new guitar if I crossed musical genres then, I thought. I wanted to take the band in a new indie rock direction. Big Trev didn't. Eventually he succumbed and gave a little ground. We added 'Sunday Bloody Sunday' to our set list; but only once the assurance that we would rock it hard had been given.

For the first year of sixth form I had 'maximised the sloth' in lessons and totally 'maximised the rock' with Sea Witch. We even did gigs away from the hallowed rock venue complex that was our school. A pub and a village hall were added to the exclusive list of venues you could have witnessed the eclectic rock stylings of Sea Witch. In true rock 'n' roll fashion we also managed to court controversy at both. We got banned from the pub. Of the sixty or so people that came to see us, only five were over eighteen. As the landlord had had no qualms about serving them and there was no damage done I couldn't see his problem; I bet he had never sold out of Special Brew in a single evening before. We also got banned from the village hall. Regrettably we'd promoted the gig ourselves and there had been some considerable damage to the ladies toilets; they shouldn't have served 200 odd under eighteens alcohol on the last day of term, should they?

I was about to be banned from school too. Unfortunately, in the minds of the teachers, I'd 'maximised the sloth' to a point where I was about to be asked to leave. This could've had a severe impact on my fully attending to the serious businesses of rock, Special Brew consumption and girls. I had to stay in school. I did not want to have to explain to my parents, even though there had been no mention of any sort of academic achievement in the small print of the Destroyer loan, why I was being kicked out. I also did not want to get a haircut, as my heavy rock mullet was coming along very nicely indeed. And I certainly did not fancy going out into the working world just yet, which would almost have definitely necessitated the death of the mullet.

I needn't have worried. All that practice with the Bank of Mom & Dad had paid off; I was now a highly skilled negotiator indeed. Through a combination of shameful begging, ludicrous promises to put some effort in and the over employment of my cheeky smile, I managed a stay of execution without a single letter going home to my parents. Woo-hoo! Second year of sixth form here I come. I spent that summer painting great, huge, never ending, steel girders a drab red-brown colour; for no pay, yet with a very clear conscious.

The next year continued in much the same vein; not much school work but loads of never ending weekends of fun, which usually started on Thursday lunchtime. They were more often than not fuelled by Special Brew and almost always ended up in some sort of 'goggle' wearing incident with a Gothic Girl or two, or sometimes without; there were girls other than the Gothic Girls. I somehow ended up losing all of my powers to Kryptonite Girl #2 for a short while too. I'm not quite sure how I pulled this off. My magic babe magnetic mullet or the super seductive powers of several Special Brews must've played a part I guess; quite probably the combined influence of both.

Sea Witch kept rehearsing, but with limited gigging opportunities available, and after several caustic 'musical differences' arguments, caused by the shifting musical landscape, we had begun to lose interest. The band, along with my rock 'n' roll fantasy, was dying a slow and protracted death. Although, that summer, as a swansong, we did record a very limited edition album 'The Lightning Struck Tower'[2].

Two weeks before we were about to start our final 'A' level exams, I was unceremoniously dumped. Yet again! Not the greatest event to happen while preparing for 'A' levels, or any sort of academic distinction for that matter. Rather than stay at home and wallow in self pity while madly cramming for said exams, I employed wisdom that only a man who doesn't know how to employ wisdom can; I decided to go to Paris for a week with The Thrill. Never mind how I would be able to fit in any revision; how on earth was I going to be able to chat up the madamgazelles? What, with my French language skills?

.....In Montmarte we find the bar we are looking for. The entrance is down a steep flight of stairs. At the bottom we look around and survey the scene. The cavernous underground room is softly lit. Cigarette smoke hangs in the air in lazy swirls. A jazz quartet plays mellifluously in the far corner, just about audible above the murmur of people talking.

"Right, let's give it half an hour in here. If nothing's doing, we'll get a few down us and get the 'goggles' on, right?" I say to The Thrill. He nods in the affirmative.

I spot the actress Sandrine Bonnaire, sat on a stool at the bar, smoking. I move towards the bar. I move towards her. I take the stool next to her. The Thrill gives me a thumbs-up from the other side of the room.

"Bonjour, madamgazelle. Errr, vouslez-vous, errr, drink une, errr, drink, avec me?" I ask. She looks at me and blows smoke from her cigarette disdainfully. Her eyes seem to pierce my very soul. At least she'll know what she's in for later then.

"Mais bien sûr, j'aime les Anglais," she responds. "Et pour vous, il n'est pas bonjour, bonsoir, il est." I haven't a clue. It didn't sound like the brush off though. I give her a cheeky smile for good measure. There's a pause. Ah, my turn to speak.

"Errr, voulez-vous une blank van? Ou, errr, moment," I look around for The Thrill, hoping he'll know the French for Special Brew. I can't see him. Merde! "Errr, voulez-vous une, errr, drink, avec, errr, la couleur jaune et, errr, le energie speciale?" I could die of thirst here. Hopefully she'll know that a 'yellow powerful special' is my French for Special Brew. She laughs at me and puts a slender hand on my shoulder, then leans across me to speak to the barman. I can smell her perfume.

"Je vais avoir un vin blanc, et une biere pour mon ami anglais," she purrs at him. I really should've paid attention in French; I don't suppose we did chat up French, mind, but I can categorically tell you that her Jelly Fruits are très bon. Hopefully she's just ordered up some drinks and not asked him back for a ménage à trois; tempting if it had been with a waitress, but it wasn't and I was dying of thirst too. The barman hands me a beer.

"Errr, wee mercy, errr, wee mercy bouquet," I say and raise my drink in thanks, disappointed that it is only a half. She flicks her hair and laughs again then looks at me with those piercing eyes. I might be in here.

"Mon cher Anglais, iz fine for we talks zee ongleesh, and layt-err mebbee zhen we can darnce togezzer like luvverz." I am in here! Bloody way easier than with English girls too!

"Blindin'! Can we make it your place though, 'cos our tent ain't that big. And, have ya got a mate for The Thrill?"......

Paris was something like that. I think.

---

[1] No offence intended. This is purely the author's point of view; if you liked, or like, big haired, transvestites in your rock bands, it is your look out.

[2] We couldn't afford to have any vinyl copies made, so produced it on C90 cassette with a hand written label. I think only five copies have ever existed. Mine got eaten a year or so later by a cheap walkman from Dudley outdoor market.

7. Trainee Erection Engineer

"The most prolific period of pessimism comes at twenty-one, or thereabouts, when the first attempt is made to translate dreams into reality."

Heywood Broun

I was about nineteen and just six months into my working life when my prolific period of pessimism came. Not only did work interfere with translating the rock 'n' roll fantasy into reality, I realised that, whatever job I did, I might have to do the work thing for another forty-seven years.

Sixth form came and went in a blur of girls, Special Brew fuelled hangovers, 'goggle' wearing induced embarrassment and musical confusion. Sea Witch's eclectic musical stylings hadn't exactly set the music world alight and the band's flame had finally petered out; but other than rocking, I had not a clue about what I wanted to do. I had toyed with joining the Army after the flag waving celebrations on our win in the Falklands War. I even skived a day off school to go to the recruitment office in Birmingham. Once there, I had been very disappointed to discover that there wasn't a 1st Armoured Electric Guitar Brigade (oooh, cool name for a band) and that they would also have made me get my hair cut. It all left my career path somewhat limited. I considered the options open to me and chose the only one that didn't require a hair cut: rock 'n' roll on the dole.

"Well, you are not going on the dole," my Dad said on 'A' level results day, and instantly destroyed my chosen career path. "You've just wasted two years of your life. You can come and work for me." He had just discovered that I really had spent two years 'maximising the sloth' in sixth form and was not best impressed. With not a single thing to show for it, other than the faint beginnings of a beer belly and some crazy Special Brew 'goggle' wearing stories, I couldn't really argue. I had no choice.

"OK," I said. And then, considering the general ambience concerning my lack of 'A' level results, pushed my luck and asked, "I won't have to get my hair cut, will I?"

Believe it or not, there was a plus side. I had been concerned that I was going to be painting great, huge, never ending, steel girders a drab red-brown colour for the rest of my life. Not so. While the painting would form part of my duties, I would also be part of the team that worked on building sites, putting up the great, huge, drab red-brown steel girders. I was going to be a Trainee Erection Engineer! If there is a better job title than this, I have yet to come across it. I thought it was superb for chatting girls up too:

"And what does a Trainee Erection Engineer do then?" they'd ask.

"Exactly what we'll be doing together in an hour or so darlin', engineering a huge erection." I was very surprised that it only worked the once.

And in addition to the plus side of having the greatest job title in the world, I would also get a company vehicle. A Ford Transit with 'Steel Erections' in enormous red letters painted on the sides. I loved this van. Later in my erection career, I went out with a girl whose Mom would not let me park the van outside their house. Whenever I pitched up in it, she made me move it into the street around the corner. She really did not like her daughter going out with a tradesman who advertised a steel erection service. I doubted that pointing out that I was just a trainee would've made any difference. Not long after the fourth time I'd moved the van around the corner, and quite possibly at her mother's instigation, she dumped me.

At the end of the first week I got my wage packet; a little brown envelope stuffed with cash. I wasn't saving up for a new guitar and had paid off all of my debts, so I was looking forward to having a decent lump of money in my pocket to indulge in weekend Special Brew fuelled shenanigans. I was rather surprised to find just thirty-seven pounds inside. I'd been paid a hundred quid a week during school holidays.

"Is this right?" I asked my Dad.

"Yes," he responded coldly. I quickly realised that this was all part of the punishment for failing my 'A' levels so dismally. Given the pervading ambience, I didn't press the matter. I further reasoned that not only did I have the best job title in the world, and a company vehicle, but thirty-seven quid a week was considerably more than the dole. You could still buy a few bottles of Special Brew with that.

I was teamed up with Teddy and Barry, two wizened old erection engineers (thirty something seemed really old to me at the time), to learn the trade. We drove off to a quarry on the outskirts of Leicester every morning for the next three months. The first thing I learned was how to roll my own cigarettes. Being the boss' son I'd felt obliged to try and fit in, and always offered my cigarettes to them on the journey. My ten Benson and Hedges were nearly all gone by the time we arrived at Leicester. If you can't beat 'em? Join 'em. I started rolling my own and only treated myself to a packet of Benson's at the weekend when they weren't around.

Teddy and Barry liked to keep up with current and cultural affairs, so we stopped every morning at a newsagent's in Ashby de la Zouch for them to get a newspaper. After a couple of days, to make sure we got a more rounded and complete picture, I added The Times to their morning papers: The Sun and The Mirror.

"Wha' the fuck yow bought that shite foah? Yow soppy git," Teddy asked and looked scornfully at my copy of The Times.

"You've both got a paper. I thought I'd get one too," I responded, with what I thought was quite a reasonable answer.

"Am there any tits in it?" Barry asked; it sounded like a rhetorical question.

"Errr, I don't think so."

"Well goo 'n fuckin' chairnge it foah wun wissum fanny in then. Yam 'ere to learn the trade, ay ya?" Teddy said and then to Barry loudly, "why am we gerrin' the fuckin' gaffer's babby?" I laughed, I thought he was joking. He prompted again, "goo on then, goo 'n fuckin' chairnge it." I reluctantly climbed out of the van and made my way back to the newsagents.

"Tell 'er tay no gud. Tay gorany tits in it, loike," Barry shouted after me. Teddy and Barry really made John the Roadie and me look like complete amateurs when it came to female anatomy appreciation. I returned five minutes later with The Daily Star.

"Thass berra, goo on then, less 'ave a look, who yow got, who yow got?" Teddy asked excitedly, as I climbed back into the van. I opened to page three and held it out for them. "Phwoar, look at that

103

Bazza. Fuckin' look at the state of that. Marks out of two, Bazza?" I knew the answer to this particular conundrum.

"I'd give her one," I said before Barry could get a word in.

"Yam learnin', yow dare-ty bugga. Yam learnin', Matty Boy. Mek an Erection Engineer of yow yet. Now gerra fuckin' move on. We bay gorall fuckin' day."

I was now a fully fledged member of the team, rather than just being the boss' son. We repeated this ritual every morning. They never tired of it. One day I changed my answer and said 'I'd give her two; one, twice'. Then had to explain the maths of it; that yes, I would give her one, but two times, therefore the marks out of two, equals two. Once they'd fully grasped the concept, I went up even further in their estimation, and they taught me how to arc weld.

For the week of my nineteenth birthday we had been moved back to the factory to work on the next phase of the Leicester job. As I didn't have to get up at five in the morning I thought that, rather than wait for the weekend to celebrate, I'd risk going out midweek on my actual birthday. There was a Halloween fancy dress party that The Thrill was already going to. I tagged along and went as Dracula: slicked back and blackened hair, charcoal eye-lined eyes, face covered with white stage make up, black clothes, the works. We had a good night by all accounts too. The extreme headache, and the fact that I woke at The Thrill's the next morning at eleven thirty, certainly said so anyway. I was supposed to have been at work for half seven. If I went home to get changed, I'd be even later. Why on earth I hadn't thought to take my work clothes to The Thrill's, I've no idea. I panicked. And high tailed it to work, arriving just in time to walk into the canteen for the lunch break: dressed as Dracula in full, day old, Dracula make-up.

"Fuckin' 'ell, Matty Boy. Am yow 'avin' a poynta blud foah yowa fuckin' lunch, loike?" Barry was the first one to spot me.

I spent the rest of the day hiding at the back of the factory, welding great, huge, steel girders that would soon require a coat of drab red-brown paint; nursing a minging hangover and being mercilessly ribbed by Teddy and Barry at every opportunity. And if there wasn't an opportunity, they engineered one.

"Arr day know Bela Lugosi wuz a fuckin' welder, did yow Bazza?" Teddy shouted across the factory.

"Ar fuckin' day, Ted. Am we gerrin' Boris fuckin' Karloff in t' doo the pairntin'?" Barry shouted back. They laughed at me again. This was repeated for the rest of the afternoon and would be for several months to come. Whenever we moved to a new site they revelled in telling anyone we met about the day Bela Lugosi had turned up at their factory to put in half a day's graft as a welder.

I had to get up at five in the morning and we worked most Saturdays on the Leicester job, too. Luckily, I got paid overtime for the Saturdays, and didn't have to work for free as part of the punishment of failing my 'A' levels. With a nine hour day, and a further four hours a day in the van travelling, six days a week, I was absolutely bushed most of the time. I rarely made it out on a Saturday night, which left just Sunday lunchtimes down the local with my Dad and his uncles to indulge my taste for real ale. The beer was alright but it wasn't the most ideal location, or even time of day, for meeting girls. Not only was work having an impact on my social life, it was having an impact on fulfilling the rock 'n' roll fantasy; but not as much of an impact as the Gothic Girls had had apparently.

The Angel, The Thrill and I were no longer storming along the heavy rock super highway to hell, we were about to go pixie dancing down a country lane flanked by silent hedges and flat fields[1]. We formed a gothic band: The Imps of the Perverse. The Angel played the bass and sang, The Thrill was on the drums, and I played guitar and also sang a couple. If I remember correctly the band name came from an NME interview with Bauhaus, rather than from the Edgar Allen Poe short story. We were what today would probably be called a tribute band; in that we just did covers of Bauhaus songs, with one by the March Violets and one of our own, the self titled 'The Imps of the Perverse' thrown in. I actually wrote some of the lyrics to this one. Then I'd got a bit stuck after just the one verse and purloined the rest from several Bauhaus songs.

With not a single 'O' level in Art between us, I think we must have decided to form the band with the somewhat misguided idea that, as sixth form had been filled with the Gothic Girls, it would translate out into the wider world, and therefore provide a fresh field of groupies to cultivate. And to an extent it did; there was a club in Birmingham that The Thrill raved about.

The Thrill had fully embraced the culture, and even though I was never fully comfortable with the gothic scene, especially after the Dracula episode, I went along to the gothic club one Saturday night to see what the fuss was all about. It was okay. Some of the music was alright and to be fair, all of the girls looked identical, so there was no need to worry if any sort of 'goggles' incident occurred. However, on going into the gents of said club, I stumbled across three blokes adjusting each other's makeup in front of the mirrors. Not for me. While it wasn't quite a Tuesday Night Disco[2], I wasn't comfortable with it at all now. The writing was on the rose-garden wall.

..... *"Fuck me, Ted. Thuzza bloke in the bogs purin' fuckin' mare-cup on."*
"Wotcha doo, Bazza? Did yow fuckin' twat 'im wun?"
"Nah, arr day. Ar wuz gunna, but ar fuckin' osked 'im if 'e wuzza berra fuckin' welder thun Bela Lugosi.".....

We only ever played the one gig as the Imps, opening a five band bill in the village hall that Sea Witch had been banned from. We should've remained banned. The performance was far from our finest rock 'n' roll moment. An afternoon in the pub, waiting to soundcheck, meant that by the time we finally took to the stage we were a little worse for wear. We proceeded to drunkenly stumble and bumble through our set; in front of what was a predominantly very unappreciative and rock oriented audience. After the gig The Thrill passed out backstage and I nearly had a 'goggles' incident with an ex-girlfriend's sister. That's about all I can really remember of that night; in reality I've probably subconsciously wiped all memories of my very brief gothic period from my mind.

In the flat field, I'd got bored. The Imps of the Perverse faded to grey.

The next weekend, on a rare Saturday off, I went out, got my mullet trimmed, and bought myself a salmon pink Pringle sweater, some Farah slacks, a pair of Adidas Trimm Trabb and started following the Wolves again. Even though they were struggling at the bottom of Division Three, and would end up dropping into Division Four at the end of the season, I quite enjoyed this period, without the hindrance of the rock 'n' roll fantasy; money in my pocket, a few beers with the lads, none of whom wore makeup, an afternoon at the football, followed by a several more beers with the lads, none of whom had applied makeup since leaving the football. Looking back now, I'm not sure which was the most ridiculous look; the 'overtly camp makeup caked men in all black clothes' gothic look, or the 'slightly freaky makeup-less teenage Val Doonican in pastel shaded knitwear' look of the football casual. No, it was the gothic look. Give me knitwear in pastel shades any day of the week.

Football had saved me from my gothic-curious fashion crisis; although by doing so it had plunged me headlong into a new and more expensive one. John the Roadie saved me from my gothic-curious musical crisis. He feared that he was losing a fellow disciple of rock and wanted to save my soul from an arty-farty, jingly-jangly guitar purgatory. As salvation, and to get me back on the righteous path that would lead to the super heavy ~~rock~~ metal highway to hell, he lent me Metallica's 'Ride the Lightning' and Anthrax's 'Spreading the Disease'. The guitar work blew my mind. It was way beyond my level of proficiency, but they rocked. They rocked, hard! If only I'd have heard these in the sixth form; I'd have never gone pixie dancing at all. The problem now was, that with a trimmed down mullet, salmon pink Pringle and Farah slacks I wasn't really going to fit in at a heavy metal club, or a Metallica gig for that matter. That said, I can remember going to a rock club in Brierley Hill once with John the Roadie. I'd come straight from the Wolves still wearing my latest pair of Trimm Trabbs, a pastel green Lyle & Scott jumper and Pepe stone washed baggy jeans.

Nearly a year under the fine tutelage of Teddy and Barry had passed. I felt that I had applied a 'maximum effort, minimum sloth' work ethic and had grafted very hard indeed. I went to see my Dad to discuss the possibility of a pay rise and explained my new found work ethic. I then summarized that, amongst the many skills I'd learned, I was now an extremely proficient fetcher of sandwiches, a very accomplished painter of great, huge, steel girders, and, that as none of the buildings I'd welded girders for had fallen down, I must also be quite good on the arc welder too. I further highlighted that, even though I'd had extensive and exhaustive training in Erection Engineer vernacular, I had not used a single one of Teddy or Barry's swearwords in front of my Mom or either Nan. I glossed over the fact that on two separate occasions Teddy had had to talk me down from thirty feet up a ladder; a fear of heights would not be on any essential or required skills list for the post of Erection Engineer, Trainee or otherwise.

.....*"'E fetches a fuckin' great sarnie, our Matty Boy. Eh, Bazza?"*
"Arr, yam not fuckin' wrung. 'E doh loike goo-in up thum fuckin' lodders, tho', duzzee? But dun yow remember when 'e fuckin' cum t' werk as Bela Lugosi? Med me loff, Ted. Med me fuckin' loff, it did. But 'e fuckin' grafted 'ard that day, day 'e?".....

Having received a good report from my mentors, my Dad relented and relaxed the 'failing 'A' levels' punishment. I got a pay rise. A hundred and fifty percent pay rise! A hundred quid a week. I thought I was minted. I'd be having one of those money trees myself soon. I wasn't lusting after a new guitar and had no girlfriend to waste my new found wealth on; time for a holiday, I thought. Other than Paris, the last time I'd been abroad I still wanted to play in goal for Wolves. Big Trev was in, but we couldn't find any other takers. We booked up a fortnight on the Algarve.

A couple of months later we arrived in the resort, surprisingly already slightly the worse for wear, and hit the bars. The first day all went a bit blurred from this point on. There were a lot of bars, and like kids in a sweet shop, we wanted to try them all. I have vague recollections of chatting up some Welsh girls and crashing and burning badly, and a vaguer memory still of the sun going down. After that, neither of us is so sure. I'm convinced that the following actually happened; Big Trev reckoned that I either dreamt it, or had some sort of continental lager induced hallucination. It's a genuine X

File, although I'm not that certain Mulder and Scully would get to the bottom of it.

.....*I'm lying down. Where am I? I can hear a siren in the distance, getting closer. A funny one, it sounds like a police car in a foreign film. A bloke leans over me and says something that I don't understand. Then a girl leans over me and says that I'll be alright. I can understand her.....*

.....*I'm still lying down. I can hear the funny siren again, very close and constant. A bloke leans over me and says something that I don't understand. He appears to be wearing a uniform. Where am I?.....*

.....*I'm still lying down. The siren is still going. A bloke leans over me and says something that I don't understand. His uniform? It's a paramedic's uniform. Am I in an ambulance? I'm in an ambulance, I'm in a bloody ambulance. Think. Think. Why am I in an ambulance? It wasn't Millwall in the cup today was it? No, I'm in Portugal, I think.....*

.....*Still lying down. There's no siren now. It's very quiet. Where am I now? I feel a bit sick. It's very bright in here. I close my eyes.....*

.....*Still lying down. A man in a white coat comes to see me and says something I don't understand. He takes my temperature. He walks away. Am I in a hospital? I'm in a hospital, I'm in a bloody hospital. I feel really sick now. I lie back down.....*

.....*The man in the white coat, a doctor I presume, comes back again. Again, I don't understand what he says. A nurse, where did she come from? She says something to me I don't understand and hands me a bowl. I sit up. She leaves. I throw up violently, several times. I knew I felt sick. Feel better now. Just lie down for a moment. Rest, need to rest.....*

.....I wake up, the light isn't as harsh. I feel better; woozy, but better. I remember where I am. I panic. Shit! I'm in a foreign country and have just had an ambulance ride and hospital treatment. This is going to cost me a million pounds. A MILLION POUNDS! I haven't got a million pounds. I panic some more. I run. That's good, my legs still work. I find a fire exit and burst through it into a dark street. I wonder what the time is? Where's Big Trev? I run some more, my feet hurt though. I'm lost. Very lost. I find a small square and lie down on a bench. Sleeeep.....

.....I wake up. It's raining. Does it rain in Portugal? Where are my shoes? That's why my feet hurt. It's still dark. Where on earth am I? I wander around some more until I find a larger square. A taxi rank. Excellent! No taxis though, not so excellent. Where am I going, anyway? SHIT! I can't remember the name of the resort. Hotel, errr, hotel? Hotel Sollyma? I think so. A taxi arrives.

"Hotel Sollyma?" I ask.

"Blah, blah blah." No, not a clue. Sorry, mate.

"No? Errr, Sollyma? No?" I try again. This is harder than French.

"Blah, blah, blah bl-blah blah," he says, gets out of his car and goes to a pay phone. He makes a quick call and returns. "Wet you," he says.

"I know, it's been bloody raining, mate."

"No, no. Wet wet."

"Errr, yeah, wet, I know, mate. The rain. Very wet wet, the rain," I make a raining motion with my fingers.

"No, no. Wet wet, blah bl-blah blah," he says and points to the ground before climbing into his cab and driving off. I can see that the ground is wet; he didn't have to point it out for me. I sit down on the kerb. Yes, it is indeed wet. It starts to rain again. Great! I'm not exactly dressed for this weather eventuality; shoeless, in bright green Nike jogging shorts and a luminous yellow Fila muscle vest. I won't get run over though.

I'm starting to get flustered again when a taxi pulls up. It's the same one. The passenger window winds down.

"Is good wet here you," a teenage girl pokes her head out of the window. "My brother he telefon and say Eeenglays boy in square. Many distress. I come help. Where go you?"

"Errr, I dunno. Do you know where the Hotel Sollyma is?"

"Sollyma? Hotel Sol e Mar, maybe? In blah blah?" I don't catch the last bit but it sounds right.

"Yeah, yeah, that's it Hotel Sollyma." I climb in the back of the taxi. We pull away. I drift off to sleep.....

..... "Hey, Eeenglays boy, we here," the girl shakes me awake.

"Errr, what? Errr, yeah," it looks like the right place. "Errr, How much?" She points to the meter, eight thousand escudos. Wallet? Phew, wallet. I pay up. If I've still got my wallet, then I haven't been mugged. Good job I had eight thousand in there. I must've left my shoes in the hospital then. Thirty five quid for a cab ride? I get the key and go up to our room. Big Trev isn't there. I climb into bed. That must've been a fair distance then. Sleeeeeeeep.....

.....I wake up. I can hear someone moving around. I look around. Yes! I'm in our room. It's Big Trev.

"What time is it mate?" I ask him. I'm quite surprised that while I have the most god-awful taste in my mouth, I only have the faintest trace of a hangover.

"Half eleven, I've only just woken up. Heavy night, eh?" He responds.

"Yeah. Where'd you get to then?"

"I dunno, can't remember much. We were walking down the main drag and then you weren't there. I went for a couple more beers on my own, I think. Where'd you go?"

"You won't believe me when I tell you. Half eleven, is it? We are on holiday, mate. Those dusky Portuguese maidens aren't going to chase themselves. Fancy a beer then? I just need to go and buy some shoes first."....

We returned home a couple of weeks later, both with very sun burnt backs (neither of us would apply sun cream to another man)

111

and with a fortnight's worth of crazy beer stories. If they didn't end with a spirited finale about being very drunk and crashing and burning very badly with some tasty Scouse / Cockney / Welsh / Scottish / Irish / German / Dutch girls, then they usually contained the words 'bloody hell, she was a big unit though, wasn't she mate?' followed by a stuttered excuse that continental 'goggles' were way stronger than the ones we had at home. Not a soul believed my hospital tale.

Being a Trainee Erection Engineer was never going to be the same again.

Never mind the rock 'n' roll fantasy, I had a new dream: I wanted to be a Mediterranean[3] Play Boy. I was going to make this one work and vowed never to graduate to full erections. Teddy and Barry were going to be disappointed; they'd have to find someone else to buy The Daily Star soon.

[1] 'Silent Hedges' and 'In the Flat Field' were songs by Bauhaus.
[2] Tuesday Night Disco: Unashamedly borrowed from Al Murray the Pub Landlord.
[3] Portugal, while classed as a Mediterranean country, is not actually on the Med. 'Atlantic Play Boy' just doesn't sound right to me, I'll go for Medlantic from here on in.

8. A Portuguese Misadventure

"Do not dwell in the past, do not dream of the future, concentrate the mind on the present moment."
Buddha

I didn't need to dwell in the past or dream of the future at all. I was totally concentrated on living in the now as a Medlantic Play Boy. A more realistic description was probably a scruffy Medlantic beach bum, but nevertheless, I was living in the sun and most definitely in the present moment.

Birmingham Airport looked like Tan Son Nhut airbase during the fall of Saigon. People were everywhere. Bodies occupied every single piece of available space. Bored kids ran around. They screamed and fought with each other. Parents looked sullenly at the departure boards. Every single flight was delayed. Great! Bloody great! The bloody French! I wanted to jet off and become a Medlantic Play Boy. French Air Traffic Control had other ideas. They had chosen that very weekend to go on strike. Six hours delay. Six bloody hours! It wasn't even long enough to go home. By the time I would have train, bus and bussed back, I'd get an hour at home, before it would have been time to bus, bus and train it back to the airport. Not worth the effort, or expense. Those dusky Portuguese maidens were going to have to wait a little while longer.

What would a real Medlantic Play Boy do faced with a six hour delay? I reckoned that he'd hit the private lounge for a couple of cocktails. Good plan. I didn't have access to the private lounge though. I made my way to the seething mass of disgruntled humanity that was the public bar.

"Yes, sir?" the barman asked when I finally arrived at the bar.

"A Special Brew, please mate, errr," I paused. I remembered, rather vaguely remembered actually, my first ever airport to Portugal all dayer. I didn't want to lose another pair of shoes in a mysterious hospital, eight thousand escudos from wherever I was staying. "Nah, sorry, mate. Scrub that, just a pint of Stella, please." Nice and sensible; getting acclimatised to the continental lager early doors. I

113

found a space to squeeze into and sipped at my Stella. I watched the minutes tick by; very slowly. At least queuing for the next pint would eat some time up, I thought.

After my third pint of Stella, I decided to go for a walk. I checked the departure boards. An extra three hours delay had been added to my flight.

"SHIT!" Three pints of Stella had lowered my ability to politely adhere to social etiquette norms. It looked like it might have lowered someone else's too.

"FACKIN' FRENCH GRUMBLES!" The voice belonged to lad about my age, and a Londoner by the sound of it.

"How long, mate?" I asked him and wondered what a grumble[1] was?

"Nine fackin' hours!"

"Me too, where are you going?"

"The Algarve. Eventually. I hope."

"Me too! Fancy a pint? I'm Matt."

"Yeah, why not. I'm West Ham," he said and held out his hand. I shook it and we made our way towards the seething mass of disgruntled humanity to indulge in a couple of sherbets[2]. I found out that everybody called him West Ham because he was West Ham through and through; born on Green Street and from a very long genetic line of West Ham. He'd come straight from seeing West Ham lose 4-0 at Villa Park; which explained why he was flying out of Birmingham. He showed me his West Ham tattoos and passport by way of further illustration; his middle names were Peters, Moore and Hurst, after the three West Ham players who'd won the World Cup with England in 1966. The tattoos were cool; wrong team but cool. He was good company too. We ended up having several more Nelson's[3] and got seats together for the flight.

By the time we finally boarded the plane the following day, at one in the afternoon, eighteen whole hours late, West Ham and I were well and truly acclimatised to continental lager. Unsurprisingly, continental lager acclimatisation meant that we were more than a little worse for wear. It had been a good job that the bar had closed at two in the morning for four hours. However, it still looked quite possible that I might be losing a pair shoes tonight. I wondered if they would still have my pair from last year.

"What's your plan then, Matt?" West Ham slurred, as we took our seats. Like me, he was also jetting off to become a Medlantic play boy. He'd done it last year too. Unlike me, he wasn't doing it to avoid having to climb up thirty foot ladders; this year he was doing it to avoid a court case, something about a minor misunderstanding with the Old Bill outside the Boleyn Ground.

"Plan?" I slurred back. Other than getting to Portugal and becoming a Medlantic play boy I hadn't really formulated a plan. I had hoped it would just happen. "Errr, yeah. Errr, plan. Errr, I'm going to Portugal. Errr, chat up some dusky Portuguese maidens. Errr, that's about it really." Should I have made a more detailed plan?

"You ain't got one? You're a fackin' rare 'un, my san. I doff me titfer," he laughed. "Ya don't wanna be on your Jack, though. Why dontcha cam wiv me? Meetin' a cappla boys from last year. Four-way split we could getta decent French[(4)]." I didn't fully understand, but to my Stella fuddled brain, it sounded as though I might now have a plan.

"Blindin'. Whereabouts you going?" He told me. "You're joking? The Resort? That's near where I went last year. Errr, I think. Yeah, okay, I'm in. Sounds like a plan. Celebratory beer?" I had a plan. Sorted!

"You're a rare 'un, Matt. Off yer fackin' bacon," he laughed again, as we climbed into the sky and waited for the drinks trolley to come along.

......"*Fuck me, Ted. Arm fuckin' luckin' foah-wad t' this, ay yow? Fuckin' Portugal."*

"Arr car fuckin' wet, Bazza. Gunna be tits 'n fanny all ower the fuckin' shap. Ar woh loike the fuckin' bayer, tho'."

"Yam not fuckin' wrung, Ted. Fuckin' lager. Yow car goo chessin' fanny on fuckin' lager."

"Yow fuckin' car. 'Ay, dun yow remember the toime when Bela Lugosi cum t' werk 'n did sum fuckin' weldin'?"

What are Teddy and Barry doing on the plane? They've got a good point there, though. This Stella is quite strong. I wonder if they've scored the blonde air-hostess out of two yet? She'd get at least.....

"Matt, Matt. Wake up mate. We are fackin' 'ere, my san," West Ham shook me awake. Bloody Stella! My head really hurt, although as a bonus, that flight had passed really quickly. Along with a fear of heights I'm not a very good flier either. I may just have discovered the cure for my flight anxiety; an eighteen hour delay and many-several pints of Nelson.

It looked like I'd started as I meant to go on: please don't let there be an ambulance ride tonight. We wobbled off the plane and made our way unsteadily through to the baggage hall. Even though it was late April, it was certainly warmer than where we'd come from. Combine that with many-several pints of Nelson, a day's intake of high salt content junk food, and nearly four hours locked inside an aircraft cabin, I was dehydrating faster than a beached whale on a Caribbean beach in high summer. To accentuate my rapidly dehydrating bodily discomfort, the wait for our bags to appear on the carousel seemed to last forever, and then just a while longer. We both cheered as they finally made their triumphant entrance through the black rubber flaps. Not quite the last bags off the flight, but almost.

Ultimately reunited with our bags and raring to get on with becoming Medlantic Play Boys, rather than heading for the exit and a speedy onward transit to The Resort, we sensibly sought much needed rehydration in the air-conditioned confines of the airport's bar. I'm not sure of the exact figure, but three or four pints of 5.2% Super Bock later, we were completely rehydrated. I'd lost count because of the metric system; the bar didn't have any pint glasses, just 250ml ones. That's a sip, or two, short of half a pint, which made the pint calculation somewhat difficult; never mind having to remember how many 250ml glasses we had drunk. It's a good job the pub industry in Britain hasn't been fully metricated: *'I'll have 0.568261 of a litre of your finest ale, please landlord, oh yes, and 0.284131 of a litre of shandy for the missus'*, it doesn't quite have the same ring. And, if they rounded it down to 0.5 of a litre to give a metric 'pint', what right minded British bloke is going to go to the bar and order in halves? Bureaucrats in Brussels, take note.

In the bar, although we had not agreed on the actual litre to pint conversion, we had decided (obviously with more than a little help from Super Bock) that we had both had a decent harvest from our respective money trees this year. Instead of taking the ultra cheap bus travel option we decided to get a taxi to The Resort. And once there, rather than staying in the particularly economical local Youth Hostel, we decided to check into a decent hotel for a couple of days while we waited for West Ham's mates from last year, the Two Bobs, to arrive. On exiting the bar we poured ourselves into the nearest taxi and took it in turns to slur our best Portuguese pronunciation of The Resort at our uncomprehending driver. At length, a smile of realisation spread across his face, he knew where we wanted to go: The Resort. Yes, we'd already said that, mate, several times. As we raced out of the airport and westwards on to the N125 I thought that maybe I should've done a bit more Portuguese study before I came out. Then I wished that I'd visited the gents one more time, too. Luckily, Portuguese taxi drivers only have two speeds: Warp Factor Two and Stop. Within forty minutes we were eight thousand escudos lighter, but finally, just over twenty four hours since walking into departures at Birmingham Airport, we were at The Resort. Wow, that must've been at least a twenty-five mile ambulance ride last year.

West Ham paid the driver. I dashed into the nearest bar. For the second time in the last forty minutes or so, I wished I had put in a bit more Portuguese study; I couldn't find the gents. I looked around desperately and then caught the barman's eye. I knew 'please' and that the Portuguese for 'the' was 'o'; which is sort of pronounced like the 'oo' sound in glue. Unfortunately, I didn't know the words for 'where are' or 'toilets'.

"Errr, por favor, errr," I was way out of my depth. I furtively glanced around in the hope that I'd spot them before having to continue. No. *"Errr, oo, oo, errr, oo, errr, oo, oo,"* I repeated, as I held my crotch and hopped from one foot to the next. I probably sounded and looked like a chimpanzee who knew how to say the Portuguese for please in a Wolverhampton accent, but nothing else.

117

Given the near twenty four hour drinking session, in the same clothes and without a bath, shower or even a wash, I probably smelt like one too. The barman looked on bemused, as did several customers. I was getting beyond desperate. I leaned towards the bar and employed the last resort: shouting, in English. "THE TOILET?" Like the taxi driver forty minutes ago, a smile of realisation spread across his face. He slowly raised an arm and pointed towards some stairs at the back of the bar.

Adequately relieved I returned to the bar and had a couple of post relief beers with West Ham (I knew where the toilets were here) to celebrate our final arrival at The Resort. Just like a year ago, it all went a bit blurred from this point on. There must be some sort of first day in Portugal memory loss syndrome that I suffer from. I have a vague recollection of checking into a hotel and then an even vaguer one of being in a bar again and chatting to some girls. I have no recollection of whether I'd had a shower and got changed by this time. Hopefully I had.

The next thing I knew it was the following day. I had woken up in a bright orange, cocoon like structure with a rather large hangover. I didn't remember our hotel room having fluorescent orange decor, or that it was this small, or that it was this bright without the lights on either. I looked around the tiny space. It certainly didn't look like a hospital. I was on my own too. It took my continental lager soaked brain a few moments to realise that I was in a tent. What on earth? I panicked and frantically scrabbled about, then calmed down when I had gathered together all of my clothes. Excellent! I had got changed after all. I still had my wallet too, with plenty of escudos left in it. And most importantly, on remembering last year, I was still in possession of my shoes. I wondered if I'd had an ambulance ride to get here. There were more pressing questions than that, though: what was I doing here? Where was here? And, where the Aylesbury was West Ham?

The sound of the tent's zip being yanked open made me jump. A smiling red head popped through the open flap, quickly followed by the rest of her. Hey, not bad either and not dressed like a nurse, so I definitely wasn't in a hospital. My continental lager soaked cogs whirred and gradually put two and two together. Blinding! Mission achieved first day. I had no idea how, and even though I'd undoubtedly been wearing them last night, I'd achieved it without the need for the 'goggles'! I smiled proudly to myself; I am a Medlantic Play Boy.

"Am yow oright, chick?" Hold the Medlantic Play Boy right there. She sounded like she might be the daughter of Teddy or Barry. Did they have a daughter? I didn't think so, but she really did sound like she could be. She continued, "Ar got yow sum coffay. Ar gorra goo to werk soon, day shift today, ay it. An' the weather's gunna be great an' all, ay it?"

"Errr, yeah. Coffee, great. Yeah, ta. Errr, you haven't got a beer have you?" I did need to rehydrate. I also needed a clue as to how I'd got here and indeed, where on earth here was. "Errr, never mind the beer, where do you work then? And, is your Dad called Teddy or Barry?"

"Wha? Teddy or Barry? Doh yow remember, chick? Arm Shaz, ar werks in the bar, doh I," she laughed. No, not a thing. Seeing the mystification written all over my face she prompted again, "Ar werks in the bar yow wuz in last noight. Yow and that Lundun bloke. 'E rit yoah 'otel nem on yoah bellay, day 'e."

Did he? I looked down at my belly. He had. In big letters, Hotel Dom Carlos and the street name, was scrawled on it in black biro. Very thoughtful too, the addition of the street name. If nothing else, at least I knew which hotel we'd checked into and where it was. While I was happy that I knew where I was supposed to have stayed last night, I was more than a little disappointed at the start of my Medlantic Play Boy dream; I'd travelled two thousand miles to chase dusky Portuguese maidens, not end up in a tent with a ginger barmaid from Wolverhampton. I could have done that at home.

The next couple of days passed pretty much in the same continental lager blurred way, while we waited for the Two Bobs to make their respective ways to The Resort. We did get the occasional free drink out of Shaz, but I didn't return to her tent. At least I don't think so; you can never be one hundred percent sure after a severe continental lager blurring. Once the Two Bobs had both arrived, I was introduced to them by West Ham. After a brief interview, where

119

I introduced myself and outlined my vast experience of the Portuguese ambulance and hospital systems, I was accepted into the group as the fourth musketeer. We needed somewhere to live though. I couldn't afford to stay in the hotel for the whole summer. They were also pretty strict on not allowing you to take girls up to your room. An overzealous night porter had apparently been the reason why I'd ended up in Shaz's tent. I wasn't going to be able to show any of my etchings if I stayed in a hotel.

Scouse Bob was knocking on thirty and had been doing Portugal for the last six years. He could even speak Portuguese. We bowed to his wisdom and experience and let him resume his role as the father figure. He could do the house hunting. I hadn't done any house hunting to this point in my life and it didn't sound very interesting to me either; especially when there was sun to sit in and bars to drink at. Scouse Bob agreed that he was the best man for the job, and we arranged to meet back up in a couple of hours, while he went off to scout around for an apartment. By the time he returned, Villa Bob, West Ham and I had visited several of the local bars. The warm sun and luxuriant glow of continental lager had washed over us; several times.

"I've found an apartment, boys. Big enough for the four of us. Clean, cheap, but it is on the eleventh floor," Scouse Bob said, as he approached our table. That's not a very strong Scouse accent, I thought, through the early stages of a continental lager haze.

"Arggh," the other two groaned in unison. I didn't understand why; Scouse Bob was nearly thirty, he must know what he's doing.

"Eleventh floor? Has is it got a television?" I slurred excitedly.

"What do you want a television for? Are you missing The Wombles?" Scouse Bob asked. The Wombles? How did he know? Ah, of course, the famous Scouse wit. I thought the answer was obvious, wack; to throw it out of the window, while scantily clad dusky maidens danced around the room.

He told us how much the apartment would cost. I was amazed. Splitting the rent four ways was going to cost me less than the board and lodging I'd had to pay my parents back home, and with the change I could afford a couple of second hand TV's: just in case we ever had any wild parties. West Ham and Villa Bob, although still grumbling about the eleventh floor, reluctantly approved. We took out a four month lease on it, paid in full and moved in that evening. It was all working out pretty well for me so far.

"You still the time share king?" West Ham asked Villa Bob forty minutes later as we sat around outside our new local. It would've been ten minutes later except the lift had broken down and we'd had to hike up and down eleven floors worth of steps. I knew what the groans were for now.

"Of course, big marketing push on this year," Villa Bob responded. He was several years older than me and not from Birmingham either, or even an Aston Villa fan, as I'd assumed. The Villa in his name came from his job working for a time share company. He did pretty well at it by all accounts too; it was his third year in The Resort. "You back with John the Builder?"

"Yeah." West Ham had sorted himself out with his job from last year. What's all this talk of jobs? In my infinite wisdom, or lack thereof, I hadn't really thought about having to get a job. I was still in a holiday mind set and didn't really fancy jumping straight into one either; especially as I'd just left the building sites of Britain behind. Fortunately, the British builder West Ham was going to work for again only wanted the one site labourer. Good news indeed and how would a Medlantic Play Boy know the correct mix for mortar anyway?

"How about you Matt? I could get you onboard our sales force. Decent remuneration package if you can make target," Villa Bob immediately tried to recruit me to his team. I certainly didn't fancy jumping straight into one that was commission only.

"Errr, I'll think about it," I replied. Yeah right, I'll think about it for less than one second.

"You need a job Matt, before the season kicks off proper. There'll only be bar work left if you leave it too late, and not much of that then either," Scouse Bob joined in. He sounded every bit the father figure now. "What skills you got, Matt?"

"Errr, painting great, huge, never ending, steel girders, errr, a bit of arc welding, and, errr, I'm a pretty good sandwich fetcher. Errr, that's about it," I said. Not much of CV, I acknowledge. I didn't like the sound of this job talk, I needed to deflect it away from me, "how about you, what do you do?" I asked.

He told me that he played guitar and sang as part of a duo called 'The Bobbles' in one of the bars for just four nights a week, leaving the rest of the week free to do as he pleased. Now, I liked the sound of that; 'minimum effort, maximum sloth', with a guitar in the sun, appealed to me no end. He then, although he didn't realise it, offered me a job.

"Got a bit of a problem this year though, Les isn't coming out. I've got two weeks to find another guitarist." My eyes lit up.

"I can play the guitar," I said. I'd forget to mention that on my CV.

"Really? Do you know the Beatles?"

"Not personally, I'm a bit young, mate," have some Wulfrunian wit. "But I am familiar with their material." I knew their songs, although I didn't know how to play any of them. When I'd been learning I'd given Beatles songs a very wide berth indeed. They were always full of those damned F and B chords.

"Have you got a guitar?"

"'Course I have," oh, hang on. I realised what he meant. "Errr, back in England, like." My job interview wasn't going very well at all.

"C'mon," Scouse Bob laughed. "Let's go back to the apartment and try you out on mine. If you can play, we'll go into Faro tomorrow and sort you a guitar out." It looked like I might have a job after all.

"Errr, yeah. Cool. Can I go to the toilet first?"

.....*The latest Europap boomed from the PA system and echoed around the walls. Finally it ended, the lights went down. A cheer went up from the crowd as they surged forward towards the small, darkened stage. A smell of sun cream and insect repellent filled the cramped and clammy room. Cigarette smoke filled the stage. Lights flashed. Two acoustic-guitar wielding heroes could be glimpsed through the swirling smoke. The crowd cheered. This is the life, the younger one thought, as he swaggered towards the microphone.*

"ALGARVE! ARE YOU READY TO BEATLE?".....

I passed the audition. It didn't take me long to pick up a repertoire of Beatles songs from Scouse Bob's huge song book. The bar we played in always attracted a young crowd, especially being near the hotel that catered for 18-30 holidays. We played four thirty minute sets per night, from Wednesday through to Saturday. The crowd could change several times across the night and we learnt to tailor our set to whoever was in at the time we went on stage. If it was predominantly lads, 'Twist and Shout' and 'Hard Day's Night' always went down well; if it was predominantly girls, we used to give them a bit of 'Norwegian Wood' or 'You've Got to Hide Your Love Away'. While we never really saw the Portuguese in the bar, the Dutch and Germans loved it all, and if there was ever a big Irish crowd in? 'Wild Rover'. I had trawled my memory for my early guitar lessons and we rocked up 'Wild Rover'. Not a Beatles song, but it worked every time. On changeover day, which was a Thursday in The Resort, we usually busked for a couple of hours outside the hotels in the afternoon, as the airport transfer coaches disgorged hundreds of pasty tourists, and handed out flyers to promote 'The Bobbles'. We would've changed the name, except the bar owner who had booked Scouse Bob and Les for the season had already had all of his promotional flyers printed. I doubt Scouse Bob would've gone for 'Matt Black' as the name anyway, and 'The Bobbmat', if we were going to remove Les' name and replace it with mine, sounded like a public laundry that cost five old pence a wash.

Regardless of the band's name, it was brilliant. I was getting paid thirty quid a week by the bar owner, for what was essentially eight hours work. Then on top of that we were splitting the whip rounds we did after each thirty minute set. These could sometimes net us as much as five hundred pounds in a week, particularly when we progressed from mid-July into August, and were rarely less than three hundred, even in May and June. Spending all day on the beach, playing the guitar and meeting girls at night? It wasn't even work! Never mind being a rock star partying in an eleventh floor hotel room, I was actually living a Medlantic Play Boy Rock Star dream in an eleventh floor apartment on the Med.

It was all working out pretty well for me.

Villa Bob and I even went into business together. I had talked about, even though I wasn't that enthused about the name, getting T-shirts printed for 'The Bobbles' and selling them in the bar. Villa Bob, being much more commercially astute than I, picked up the idea and ran it up a flag pole to see if I saluted it.

"Too limiting, Matt. The target market will be a few star struck girlies and as many drunk lads as you can find in the bar daft enough to participate in a commercial transaction. A single bar. We don't want a micro-market, we need a macro one, with a macro-demographic to suit a generic product. Big picture thinking, Matt," Villa Bob said. While slightly unsure as to what he actually meant, it did sound quite impressive to me. Mind you, in less than twenty years time I'd be waving an imaginary bottle of tomato ketchup vigorously in his direction.

"Errr, yeah. Errr, sounds good to me, mate. Errr, any ideas?" I asked hopefully. Other than 'The Bobbles' shirt, I had none.

I let Villa Bob's enthusiasm carry me along and the 'ALGARVE BEACH BUM' t-shirt was born: big black print letters, just like the 'FRANKIE SAYS' t-shirts, on a white shirt. I wasn't convinced, and also felt they were slightly tacky; we were in a Medlantic beach resort not bloody Skegness. But what did I know about European beach fashion and aggressive marketing practices? I bowed to Villa Bob's commercial acumen and hoped that he knew his macro-demographics.

We had two hundred printed and had totally sold out in two days. At a four hundred percent mark up! We re-invested all of our income and had a thousand more printed, half of which were a luminous yellow muscle vest (nothing says Tuesday Night Disco like a luminous yellow muscle vest with the word 'BUM' in huge letters on the front of it). It only took us two weeks to shift, I doubt 'shift' features in Villa Bob's business vernacular, this batch. Our profit and loss account was looking pretty healthy. We took an income and re-re-invested the balance. As well as Medlantic Play Boy Rock Star I could now add T-Shirt Magnate to my curriculum vitae.

It was all working out pretty well for me indeed.

There was one minor problem however; although as a twenty year old who was enjoying myself way too much and actually working fairly hard when not enjoying myself, it was easily pushed to the back of my mind and conveniently forgotten about. A case of out of sight, therefore very easily pushed way out of mind. I was an illegal immigrant.

I hadn't even considered that I was also working without a work permit, street selling without a street vendors permit, not paying any dues to the Portuguese Musicians Union and I certainly wasn't paying any taxes directly into the Portuguese treasury coffers. The Portuguese Daily Mail would have had a field day. In my defence, I was contributing considerably to the local bar and garment printing industries.

I blame my illegal immigrant status on two things. Firstly, Portugal hadn't yet joined the European Union and secondly, I couldn't speak Portuguese. On entry you got a three month tourist visa stamp in your passport. Yet, at the end of your three months all you had to do to renew it was take the train across to Vila Real de Santo António on the Portuguese border and then a short ferry ride over to Ayamonte in Spain. After a leisurely lunch in Ayamonte you crossed back into Portugal and received a fresh stamp in your passport, valid for a further three months. Illegal immigrant status rectified with one pleasant day out. Easy.

Well it should have been, except, as I couldn't speak Portuguese much beyond ordering beer and asking where the toilets were (two very useful phrases in any language), I didn't like leaving the mainly English speaking safety of The Resort on my own. Having missed the first time when the Two Bobs and West Ham went over to Spain, I somehow always managed to miss when anybody else from The Resort's ex-pat tourist visa community was going to catch the train for a passport stamp update too. Probably usually due to some form of late night contributing to the local bar economy, or maybe it was more to do with the fact that they always wanted to go the day after changeover day. Ah, hah! It would definitely be down to a very late night contribution to the local bar economy in the presence of a fresh batch of holidaying girls.

"What the fack?" West Ham was incredulous. "You're well chicken, mate. Chicken fackin' oriental," he continued and waved his half full pint glass at me in disgust. A month or so ago I'd have thought he was calling me a coward. Even though I still couldn't really speak it, I had an almost fluent grasp of Cockney and knew that he was not questioning my bravery at all. Instead, he had stated, quite categorically, that I was mental. With the extra emphasis on the expletive, it actually meant something more along the lines of stark bonkers raving mental. I shrugged my shoulders apologetically and stared at my empty beer glass.

"Go steady on the lad," Villa Bob butted in before West Ham could continue his incredulous rant and then turned to me. "But Matt, you know the house rules, mate. They are there for our own protection." I shrugged my shoulders apologetically again and continued staring at my empty beer glass. I had never thought that they would take the news this badly.

"Rule number five, Matt," Scouse Bob was up to bat. "Never get involved with a local girl. Trust me, too many potential problems."

"C'mon, lads. I understand the one about keeping your passport up to date. Which, yes, I know I need to sort out pretty damn sharpish. But, going out with a local girl? What problems?" I questioned. I genuinely had not thought of any.

"Have you not considered any jealous knife carrying ex-boyfriends?" Scouse Bob asked.

"Errr, no, I hadn't," I replied. Should I have?

"How about over protective and xenophobic big brothers, who don't like seeing their little sister on the arm of a foreigner? No matter how handsome or honourable he may be."

"Errr, that's another no from me," then as an afterthought I added, "thanks for the handsome though." It didn't look like he was finished yet mind.

"Angry fathers with shotguns and connections to the local police and or mafia?"

"Errr, I hadn't thought of that one either." Oh dear, it looked like love wasn't just a case of English boy meets Portuguese girl then. Scouse Bob sounded like a man who may well have experienced all three.

"Errr," my head swam with these new dating considerations, I didn't really know what else to say. "Errr, fancy another beer, lads?" That'll do nicely. I waved the waitress over before they could plant anymore concerns into my mind. Oh, I've thought of one, what if her sister is better looking? The waitress arrived, the moment to share with the group had passed, so I ordered up some more Super Bock and then made a mental note to enquire about all of Fernanda's ex-boyfriends and whether she had any elder brothers the next time I saw her. I'd save the questions about whether her sister was fit and her dad's weaponry for a later date, if indeed, there was going to be a later date after the ex-boyfriend and the brother questions had been answered.

The truth was I missed having a real girlfriend. The lads were brilliant company and somehow, given our disparate back grounds, we'd all bonded and become pretty good friends. And, I couldn't deny that I had been having the time of my life either, but I had started to feel that something was missing. There were a couple of things missing actually; more than a couple, when you add the lack of an up to date passport stamp to the list.

Taking into account rule five (covered above), then rule six (not to get involved with a girl who worked or lived in The Resort, regardless of nationality) and the fact that the available female population was essentially transient (changing every week or two), it all added up to mean that any chance of an embryonic real girlfriend experience developing was extremely limited. Oh, yeah and adding honesty to truth, I was absolutely rubbish at chatting girls up; unless I had the goggles on or the handsome continental lager dribbling buffoon was their type, then I couldn't really fail.

However, a handsome continental lager dribbling buffoon I was. A near continuous failure to generate even a trickle of vacuous and meaningless one night stands (and it should've been so much easier to achieve out there than in a pub or some townie club back home), and the constant effort of having to go on the pull had become a bind, a huge bind; way too much effort for very little result. It certainly wasn't fulfilling the first part of my 'minimum effort, maximum sloth' creed. I reckoned a real girlfriend could address these feelings of emptiness and therefore remove the effort of having to chat them up.

Then there was Portugal. I was missing Portugal. Not missing it in the 'longing for' sense, I was missing it in the 'I'm in Portugal, but not seeing any of it at all' sense. Don't get me wrong, The Resort was brilliant. The sun was brilliant. Playing guitar in 'The Bobbles' was brilliant. Living in an eleventh floor apartment overlooking the Medlantic was brilliant. The cost of living was ridiculously cheap and therefore, by extension, brilliant too. Yet, for all this I wasn't experiencing Portugal or Portuguese culture. I couldn't even speak Portuguese, because I didn't need to; other than a couple of waiters and waitresses who worked in the bars we frequented, everybody I knew in The Resort was either British, Dutch or German. I'd also guess that ninety percent of the people who holidayed there were either British, Dutch or German too. In fact, for all intents and purposes, The Resort could've been any British seaside resort (apart from the sun, the cost of living and an unusually large amount of Dutch and German holiday makers).

Fernanda came along just at the right time. I'm glad she did too; I was starving and wanted to order a beer and some lunch. A couple of weeks before the above conversation I had found myself on my own one day. Villa Bob and West Ham were at work and Scouse Bob wasn't in the apartment. Not sure where he was, though I'd hazard a guess that it was something to do with scoring one of those elusive, vacuous and meaningless one night stands. We were waiting on the next batch of t-shirts from the printers, having sold out of our last lot, so I had no t-shirts to sell. I had no Beatle strumming work of my own to go to later either. Rather than go and hang out on the beach with the other ex-pat workers, like I usually did in these circumstances, I decided to go and explore the far edges of The Resort. Maybe immerse myself in some Portuguese culture.

On leaving the apartment I headed along the main tourist drag and popped into the English Bookshop where I bought an English-Portuguese dictionary. I continued past Angie & Den's Bar, The Queen Vic, The Coach & Horses, De Vliegende Hollander, O'Murphys, Der Bierkeller, The Cheshire Cat, and several other ex-pat owned bars, until, towards the end of the promenade, the names of bars began to change: Bar Pescador, Casa Lisboa, Bar Caranguejo. I was in Little Portugal.

I liked the look of Bar Caranguejo. A few faded plastic tables and chairs with a mix and match of different beers advertised on them were outside, shaded under a reed grass canopy. Euro-pap and Tuesday Night Disco tunes emanated from a radio behind the bar. Never mind being musically confused, I was becoming bloody musically celibate out here. A chalk scrawled blackboard menu hung from a rusty nail by the bar. Using my very limited Portuguese I could decipher that today's special was 'bifanas'. I didn't know how to decipher 'bifanas'. There didn't appear to be anyone around, but I decided that this was where my immersion into Portuguese culture was about to begin.

I sat down on a Super Bock chair at a Heineken table and flicked through my newly acquired dictionary while I waited for someone to appear. Ah, caranguejo translates as crab; I'm in The Crab Bar then. Bifana wasn't even listed though. I tried difana just in case the menu writer's chalk skills were poor. No, no difana either, or anyfana for that matter. I gave up on the translation of bifana, and focussed instead on putting together some useful bar ordering phrases. I waited some more.

The unceasing wait continued. I took in the surroundings and appreciated my first taste of Portuguese culture. The Medlantic waves rolled in soothingly against the golden sands, the menu swung gently on its nail in the warm Medlantic breeze, the Euro-pap / Tuesday Night Disco coming out of the radio was awful. That spoiled the ambience somewhat. But, hardly anyone walked past; your average The Resort tourist doesn't venture too far away from The Queen Vic it appears. I was just about to conclude that it takes forever to get served at a local establishment when a waitress walked towards me. About bloody time! But at least she was a waitress and a dusky Portuguese maiden at that. Marks out of two from the Wolverhampton judge? *Um*. No, actually, the judge from Wolverhampton has amended his score to a definite *dois*[5] (that's *um* twice).

"Olá, blah blah bl-blah drink blah blah?" she asked and smiled at me. My brain raced to try and translate, but no matter how hard I tried the only word I got was 'drink'. Good job I knew the answer to this one.

"Olá, four beers, please," I replied confidently. She raised an eyebrow, a dusky Portuguese maiden's eyebrow. SHIT! I was that used to ordering for The Two Bobs, West Ham and I, it must've become an automatic response. *"Errr, no, is only is the one, please,"* I corrected, my confidence rapidly draining.

"Sim. Blah blah bl-blah eat, bl-bl-blah?" Oh, dear, I'm not following this at all. Hang on, yes! I got the word 'eat'. Right, let's unleash my new found linguistic skills.

"I am like to eat the bifana of you," I replied. The look of concentration on her face said I might have been slightly adventurous with that sentence, or, bifana also doubles as a colloquialism for a lady's nether regions.

"Sim," now that's 'yes', *"blah blah bl-blah?"* followed by a question. Nope. As West Ham would say, I ain't got a fackin' Scooby dahlin'.

"Errr, bifana?" I tried answering the question with a question and a slightly different pronunciation of bifana.

"OK. Yes. But is like the how many you?" Ah, cool. She could speak English. I still didn't know the answer to this question though, and this was in English! The chalk scrawl on the menu said one hundred escudos. By employing deductive reasoning, a burger and chips on the main tourist drag being around the six hundred escudo mark, I deduced that four sounded like a reasonable number to order.

"Errr, four?" I said, answering her with yet another question.

"Four? Is like the four you?" Apparently, not a reasonable number to order, or has she just questioned my fondness for the number four.

"Errr, two?" I tried again, and then, just in case, added in Portuguese: *"dois?"*

"Ah, sim. Blah blah bl-blah." Sorted. Two seemed to be the correct number. She smiled again and disappeared towards the bar. I hoped that my heavily flushed cheeks would dissipate before she returned with my beer. Delving into my dictionary I tried to

formulate some basic opening gambits. I'd obviously forgotten that I was a continental lager dribbling buffoon, a handsome one mind, and that I couldn't form opening gambits in English, let alone in a foreign language that I'd only started to learn ten minutes ago. Why did I buy a dictionary? A phrase book, now that would've been a much better purchase. I could've tried to raise a smile with a badly pronounced 'do you have a single room' and followed up with 'how much is it for the night?'

Just as I was about to keel over with hunger and severe dehydration, the dusky Portuguese maiden returned with my beer and a plate containing two bread rolls with some sort of filling in them. Bifana is possibly the Portuguese for sandwich. She placed the plate on the table, took the knife from my cutlery and cut each roll into two.

"Is now, I is gives the four you," she winked at me. Is she flirting with me? Damn! I hadn't thought to formulate any sort of Portuguese response to this eventuality so I just grinned back inanely. With hindsight, it might have been a good idea to look up the word for 'thank you' before I'd even considered expanding my 'wooing the ladies' vocabulary. If only I had that phrase book; 'is there a chemist near here?' would've developed the conversation way better than any inane grin.

I tucked into my bifanas, very pleased to taste succulent fillets of tender pork loin that had been soaked in a garlic, piri-piri, paprika, herb and red wine marinade, and then served in a soft bread roll, rather than finding some sort of questionable foodstuff from an unknown genus. It beat a burger and chips in The Cheshire Cat by a margin of one point six kilometres. Four would definitely have been too many, although a side order of *batatas fritas* wouldn't have gone amiss. Half way down my beer, and now so deeply immersed in Portuguese culture that I knew it would take at least a demi-epoch for a second to appear, I waved the dusky Portuguese maiden over to order another.

Four or five beers later I was borderline continental lager dribbling buffoon, but for some unknown reason, I was holding back from jumping over the line. The waitress and I had developed a flirty pidgin Portuguese / pidgin English relationship. To be fair, it was mostly one word answers or just inane grins from me (I am fluent in inane grinning), and very difficult to follow English from her. BUT! There was a connection; well, I thought there was. I hoped she did. Ah, there's the reason for not jumping over the dribbling buffoon threshold. Regardless of that, I thought it was probably better to disappear before I turned into the full blown buffoon and tried my luck with a continental lager dribbling attempt at asking her out. Something about discretion being the best part of continental lager dribbling. Surprisingly, or luckily, she wasn't around. Cool, no self induced embarrassment to be had. I left some escudos on the table and got up to leave. As I walked away, I heard a scuffling sound come from behind the bar.

"Hey, Eeenglays boy. Comings for the morning more time you?" she shouted after me. I gave her my umpteenth inane grin of the day while I tried to decode her English.

"Errr, morning?" I replied and fired off another inane grin.

"Yes. Is for the morning. Bar to here is yes you?" More unintelligible English begets more inane grinning, my girl.

"Errr, bar?" I stuck with my one word grinning strategy.

"Yes, crazy Eeenglays boy. Is not for you me understandings is for the morning more time you?" Not really, no. Sorry. That just sounded like you wanted to randomly shout a load of vaguely English sounding words at me. Hang on. Through the haze of a mild continental lagering, it slowly dawned on me, I was understandings that. At least, I thought I was understandings that of her. Oh well, in for a penny, in for an escudo or *dois*.

"OK," yes, that was all that I said, it really wasn't meant to be a one word answer. Honest. I had been trying to figure out how to add 'see you tomorrow' in Portuguese but it wouldn't come to me. Stupid dictionaries! Scrambling desperately through my brain for a follow up, I'd briefly toyed with the idea of using sign language, but although I'd sussed how to do 'see' and 'you' in a nano-second, I couldn't figure out how to do 'tomorrow'. Instead? I grinned inanely and gave her a thumbs up. I know how to woo the ladies. I'd only pulled a bird in the Crab Bar! Hopefully an even deeper immersion into Portuguese culture is not too far away. I walked back to the resort with a spring in my step.

..... "Hello, is that the British Consulate, the one in Portugal?"

"Yes, we are indeed a British Consulate, sir. And for one's information, we are located in Faro, the administrative capital of the Algarve, which, for one's further geographic benefit and confirmation, sir, is indeed in the fair Iberian country of Portugal. Now, how may I help?" Alright mate. I'm sorry that I don't speak like I've been rogered senseless by the First Fifteen. Several times.

"Excellent, you speak English, mate," have some sarcasm back, pal. Hopefully I sounded like I'd rogered senseless several dusky Portuguese maidens. Several times. "Right, with a bit of luck maybe you can help me. If I somehow lost my passport, can you issue me a new one?"

"In those circumstances obviously, yes sir, of course we can issue you with a new one." Oooh, sounds promising. Better tone my sarcasm down mind.

"Excellent, again. In fact, very excellent, you are indeed looking after our British interests, excellently," and the toning down of the sarcasm came where? Errr, right, yeah. "Errr, sorry. Errr, would you be able to add in a fresh three month stamp for me? Starting today, maybe?"

"Of course, sir. That will be no problem at all." B-B-B-BINGO! Very helpful indeed! Three cheers for the British Consulate, hoo-rah. I don't know why the lads keep banging on about the three month stamp thing. All you need to do is ring the British Consulate and tell them you've lost it. No need to get that early Friday morning train to Spain at all. Sorted.

"Oooh, while we're at it then, can we change my occupation status from 'Trainee Erection Engineer' to 'Medlantic Play Boy Rock Star T-Shirt Magnate and Wooer of Dusky Portuguese Maidens'?"

"I didn't realise that was a real job, sir."

"Well, it is what I'm doing now."

"Then I'm not so sure that would quite fit on our forms, sir. Perhaps there is a shorter version one would like to use?"

"Errr, I don't know, I never progressed to Full Erection Engineer. I bet that would fit on your form though?"

133

"Indeed it would, sir. However, on the subject of employment, I do have to inform you that Her Majesty's Government was of the opinion that after you'd given up on dinosaur hunting and space travel you wanted to play the electric guitar in a rock band, sir."

"You can't sort my passport out at all, can you? This is a dream isn't it?"

"I'm afraid it is indeed a dream, sir. And if one is still listening, sir, and if one would allow me to plant a suggestion in that tiny conscience, one really ought to think about obtaining the requisite passport stamp, applying for a valid work permit, as well as a valid street vendor permit, not to mention registering with the Portuguese tax authoritzzzzzzzzzzzzz"

"Sorry, you totally lost me at tax authzzzzzzzzzzzzzz".....

I went back to the Crab Bar the next day and the day after that. The day after the day after that, I didn't see the dusky Portuguese maiden at all. I played beach football for England against a Scottish, Welsh, Irish, Dutch and German coalition. Even though West Ham had managed to get himself sent off for an X-rated and very, very late tackle on a German when we were 4-2 up, the ten men of England went on to triumph 14-11. The day after that, I really should've gone to Spain and got my passport stamped. But no, (who listens to advice given in dreams?) the day after the day after that, I discovered that the dusky Portuguese maiden was called Fernanda. It had taken me a few days to realise that inane grinning and sign language was never going to illicit her name and I'd finally resorted to the dictionary to learn how to ask it, and added a few other key words to my vocabulary. I put these into action once I'd discovered her name.

"Fernanda, tonight disco go you me?" I couldn't figure out from the dictionary any of the important gluey bits that would bind them into a more complete, flowing and coherent sentence. Luckily she was somewhat used to my unique, grammarless and often mono-syllabic or even signed version of her native tongue; she answered in the affirmative. I had my very own dusky Portuguese maiden girlfriend. Score! With the aim of improving our communication I went and invested in a phrase book; Fernanda knew way more

English words than I did Portuguese ones, and at least she knew some of the English gluey bits too, but when she glued them together I ~~always, nearly always,~~ no let's make that always struggled to fully comprehend her intended meaning.

August drew to a close and with it the end of the lease on the apartment was also in sight. The Bobbles were only booked to play until the end of the second week of September; though Scouse Bob had negotiated the same deal for us again next year. It was time to start thinking about what to do until meeting up next April. West Ham decided to go back England in time for the football season, hoping that the police had forgotten all about him. Scouse Bob was going to back pack across Europe and onwards to Liverpool once his 'Bobbles' commitments were fully discharged. Villa Bob worked for the time share company full time and wasn't due to leave for their UK office until the end of October. As it was the end of the main season he could get himself subsidised accommodation in one of the time share apartments, and said that I was welcome to share if I was going to stay on, although it would be more expensive than our current place. I didn't really want to return to England; I loved Portugal, I guessed it was just like being at university without the inconvenience of having to attend lectures or write essays (it was!).

With September approaching we'd not bothered having a further batch of t-shirts printed when we hit our re-stocking levels, so there wouldn't be that to keep me occupied once 'The Bobbles' were finished. The t-shirt business had provided a decent income, added to my guitar wage and whip rounds, and then the discovery that the food and drink prices on the far edges of The Resort were about half compared to the main tourist drag, I'd amassed a tidy pile of escudos. I did some sums and realised that I could stay until Christmas without really needing an income. All I had to do was budget, live sensibly and buy my flight home now. I bought a flight to return home in December; as least I'd got one of the criteria covered.

I turned Villa Bob's offer down after a visit to The Village with Fernanda. It was a quaint little place where Fernanda lived, a twenty minute or so bus ride from the Resort and what my Dad would call Proper Portuguese. A very small ex-pat community lived there, so, if

I ever felt the need for a break from grammarless and frequently mono-syllabic grunting with hand gestures, there'd be someone around with whom to converse freely in my mother tongue. There were six bars too, located around a small, tree shaded square; all but one were Portuguese owned. In the first one I ventured into I discovered that, not only did they do bifanas and Super Bock, but that it was even more economical than in Little Portugal; food and drink being almost seventy-five percent cheaper than back in The Resort. Further investigation was required. With the resultant knowledge that I could rent a room in an authentic Portuguese guest house just off the square for the insanely small sum of fifteen hundred escudos a week (roundabout seven pounds), I'd even have money to spare. As Villa Bob would say, 'it was a very deliverable paradigm shift' or down a level for my benefit, 'it was a no brainer'. I was sold.

Back to 'minimum effort, maximum sloth' for me, I just had to remove Rock Star and T-Shirt Magnate from my job title and concentrate on being a Medlantic Play Boy and Wooer of a Dusky Portuguese Maiden until the end of the year. I'd got it all planned out. When Fernanda wasn't working we could go and explore the Algarve, or even further afield; I quite fancied seeing Lisbon and we could also pop over to Spain to get my passport sorted out. When she was working I could sit in the square and concentrate on some fiscal restraint combined with sensible living; drinking very cheap beer, eating very cheap bifanas and studying my phrase book.

My Portuguese idyll was progressing nicely.

While I probably wasn't exactly living that sensibly (cheap booze and bifanas), the cost of living in The Village (cheap booze and bifanas) meant that I was almost certainly applying some fiscal restraint without having to try. I even landed a part time job driving a van, after a chance encounter with an ex-pat businessman in the one bar in The Village that wasn't Portuguese owned.

My new boss, Mr Daley (not his real surname) appeared to run his business from a bar stool in The St George (not the actual name of the bar). From about midday until whenever, you could always find Arthur (not his real first name either) sat on a stool, sipping an espresso, feeding a constant stream of small coins into the bar's payphone and yabbering away in either English, Portuguese or Dutch; sometimes, a mixture of all three. Undoubtedly in a couple of year's time he would be one of the first people to own a mobile phone on the Algarve.

Like the majority of ex-pat businesses I'd come across, Arthur's was also a purely cash up front, no questions asked and very little, if any, paperwork involved at all (I'm not saying that every ex-pat business on the Algarve was involved in the grey economy, just the majority of the ones I came across). This was pretty good for me as I still hadn't renewed my passport, let alone made enquiries about a work permit. He didn't pay that much, but he did let my work coincide with when Fernanda was working down in The Resort, so it suited me fine.

Some folks would no doubt have referred to him as a shady character. I liked Arthur though, and thought of him more as a likeable rogue than shady. And at least he practiced his own particular brand of commercial enterprise without the use of any of Villa Bob's ridiculous business-speak. To me he came over as urbane and rather intelligent, although I suppose that after four months, where the only topics of conversation had been about girls' breasts and extreme alcohol consumption, almost anybody was going to appear sophisticated. His mantra was, that if there was an escudo to be made, then Arthur Daley knew just where and how to make it. If he had had a business card it would probably have read something along the lines of:

Arthur Daley Esq.:
Import-Export Fixer for the Ex-Pat Community on the Algarve
(Also: Discount Booze, Snacks & Fags; General Wheeler-
Dealering; Speaker of the Local Lingo; and Airport Transfers.
No cheques accepted.)

And, a company motto to accompany his business card: 'A Digitum in Omnis Pastillus' (a finger in every pie). I collected and delivered parcels; once I even collected a very docile looking Alsatian from the airport. I delivered discount booze, snacks and fags to ex-pat bars up and down the coast - although I only ever seemed to collect this from another van, or lorry, on the side of a quiet road, very early in the morning (no questions asked, no paperwork, I assumed the cash had already been up-fronted). I even helped with odd jobs around ex-pats' villas after Arthur learned of my building trade back ground, luckily I didn't have to climb any ladders.

My Portuguese idyll was progressing very nicely, indeed.

And then one day in the flash of a Guarda Nacional Republicana (GNR) motorcycle patrol's blue light, it all changed: forever.

I'd just left The Other Resort, only had a couple of booze, fags and snacks deliveries left to do, and was looking forward to an afternoon on the beach before having to pick up Fernanda from The Crab Bar. As I headed along a quiet stretch of road that led up to the main coastal route a GNR motorcycle, with its blue light flashing, appeared alongside me. The rider motioned for me to pull over. I checked my mirrors only to see a second motorcycle behind, also with its blue light flashing. I bumped onto the side of the road, bought the van to halt and began to wonder about what I'd done wrong. I didn't think that I'd been speeding. It couldn't be about running away from a huge hospital treatment bill last year, could it? I began to panic. Panic? I hadn't even considered my immigration status yet.

The front cop kicked his bike on to its stand, took off his gloves, climbed off the bike and walked towards me. The rear cop kicked his bike on to its stand, took off his gloves, climbed off the bike and lit a fag up, without walking towards me. I went to wind down the window, then began to panic because it wasn't working, before I realised that it was already down. Calm down, Matt.

"Blah blah blah bl-blah blah?" the GNR said as he put his hands on the window opening and leaned in towards me.

"Errr, Portugal no speak me," I hadn't really been studying that hard with my phrase book.

"Eeenglays?" he growled menacingly at me.

"Errr, English me yes." After several weeks with Fernanda my English had deteriorated somewhat.

"Papers?" he asked, holding his hand out. This didn't compute. All I could think was that I like The Times but Teddy and Barry had made me buy The Daily Star, but they haven't got either out here.

"Errr, I didn't buy one today," I said and tried an inane grin with an apologetic shrug.

"Papers?" he tried again, it sounded slightly impatient.

"Papers?" I tried my 'answer a question with a question and an inane grin' strategy that had worked so well for me when wooing Fernanda.

"Papers? No?" he said, and shook his head just like a teacher would when you've told them you don't have any homework to hand in. OH SHIT! Papers! Now I was panicking big time as it dawned on me, 'papers' as in: driving licence, vehicle registration, vehicle insurance, work permit and passport. I'd got my driving licence and passport to hand (I still hadn't been to Spain though) but I worked for Arthur; no questions asked, no paperwork. I'd never asked about the vehicle ones and he'd never asked about my non-existent work permit. I tried to figure out how to broach this but all that went through my head was; *'Why haven't I been to Spain? Why Haven't I been to Spain?'*

"No papers," I lied and shook my head like I was telling a teacher I didn't have any homework to hand in. I'd watched The Bill loads of times: lie, act demure, buy some time, let them shout at you, come up with some more lies, act demure, ask for a brief, get released. Sorted! Not the greatest plan I'd ever come up with, but a plan it was. A malevolent smile spread across his face and he nodded a couple of times thoughtfully.

"Wait," he said, and then slowly walked back to his colleague. After a brief discussion, the other GNR finished his fag, mounted his bike and rode off; the blue light no longer flashing. The one word GNR returned to my van. He still wore that malevolent smile. "Problem," he said and nodded at me.

"Problem?" I questioned. *'Why haven't I been to Spain?'* was replaced with *'I'm too pretty for prison. I'm way too pretty for prison.'*

"Papers? No?" Come on, my mono-syllabic enforcer of law and order, we're going to be here all day.

"No papers," I shook my head again. *'Why haven't I been to Spain? I'm too pretty for prison. Why haven't I been to Spain? I'm too pretty for prison.'*

"Out," he signalled for me to get out of the van. *'He's going to take me into the woods and shoot me. He's going to take me into the woods and shoot me. Oooh, that would be preferable to going to prison. I'm too pretty for prison. Oh dear, I'm way too pretty for prison. Yes, please shoot me. Hang on, can I go to the toilet first?'* As I climbed out of the van, with very shaky legs and an urgent need to use the toilet, my passport and licence fell out of the pocket of my shorts and landed at the GNR's jack-booted feet. He looked at me, down at the passport and then back to me. "Papers, no?"

"Errr, papers, yes," I was busted, fortunately my bladder held. I picked them up and slowly handed them to him. He spent what felt like an age looking at my driving licence before handing it back to me.

"Is good," he said. *'I'm in the clear, I'm in the clear.'* Then he opened my passport and began perusing it with a Holmesian attention to detail. I wasn't quite in the clear, just yet. "Problem," he nodded. The malevolent smile turned up a few notches and morphed into a distinctly dastardly grin.

"Problem?" That's all that came in to my head. That and a rather vivid picture of what Portuguese prison showers would look like.

"Well," here we go again with the single words I thought. But no, he had paused for effect, "big problem, or maybe small problem. Is for decide you," he nodded again and stroked his chin. Given the limited choice available, the small problem sounded like my best option.

"Small problem, no?" I asked hopefully. *'Let small problem mean no prison. Let small problem mean no prison.'*

"Is good. Is good small problem," he looked at me and waved my passport at me. "I keep passport of you," not so good at all, "when fifty thousand escudos you make me, I make passport back you. I happy, you happy, every peoples happy." Every peoples happy? He wants to pimp me out? Can I have the big problem instead? Hang on, 'make passport back you', has he used 'make' for 'give'?

"Errr, make you fifty thousand? Make you?" I wasn't sure I wanted to know the answer if he hadn't used 'make' for 'give', but I did need to verify, even if it meant questioning his linguistic capabilities. "You mean 'give you'? Because, how would I 'make you' fifty thousand?" I asked nervously, but very pleased that my English had returned.

"Make me, give me, I no care. Fifty thousand, five days, yes?" Phew! He didn't want to pimp me out; it was a shakedown for approximately two hundred and twenty quid. *'I'm not going to prison. I'm not going to prison.'* "If no fifty thousand? Problem. Big, big problem." I bet it's prison. "Eeenglays boy, no papers. Is prison maybe. Is big problem for Eeenglays boy. Big problem, yes?" Yes, I'd say so, sir. I'll take the shakedown I thought and skipped a happy little 'not going to prison' jig. The jig was skipped in my mind, not in front of the corrupt copper.

It took a while longer (make that a long while longer) to sort out the finer intricacies of how to pay off a corrupt government official. I had the money to spare, but feared a further shakedown, so I hadn't let on that the money wasn't a problem. Once he'd finally ridden off, I ran into the woods to find that I no longer needed the toilet. I returned to the van and sat shaking while I smoked quite a few fags before I set off to finish my deliveries. By the time I had made the last one I'd realised that maybe Medlantic Play Boy wasn't for me after all, not in a country where you couldn't trust the forces of law and order, no matter how sunny and cheap. Mind you, I did quite like van driving.

Within seventy-two hours I'd given Arthur two days notice and my December flight ticket (he'd sell it), booked my passage out of Portugal (no flights available so had to take the fifty-eight hour bus journey to London option), handed a wad of cash in a brown envelope to an off duty police officer, got my passport back, and was sat on said bus about to encounter another 'small problem' at a northern Portuguese-Spanish border crossing.

It would be another nineteen years before I set foot on Portuguese soil again, and that time I made sure all of my papers were very much up to date and in completely in order.

.....It's a relief to be in the shower at last. I really hate long bus journeys. I let the warm jets of water sooth my aching and cramped muscles. Damn, I've dropped the soap. I bent down to pick it up. This wasn't the shower in my mom and dad's house. I had a vague recollection of having seen it before though. I felt a hand on my shoulder. I turned in surprise, and then screamed in shock as a double Portuguese murderer emerged through the steam brandishing his.....

".....Matt, Matt. Is okay you?" Fernanda shook me awake as the very uncomfortable bus bounced on through the night in the northern Spanish countryside. "Is sleeps you and is shouts."

"Errr, sorry," I said and began to drift back off to sleep. "I no go prison ever....."

[1] Cockney rhyming slang. Grumble and Grunt: a swear word. As in 'that estate agent, he's a right grumble'. You can figure out what it rhymes with yourself. Over the next eight months I would learn many more.

[2] Sherbet Dip: a sip, usually pertaining to beer. As in 'Coming down the rub-a-dub for a few sherbets?'

[3] Nelson Mandela: Stella (Artois), strong Belgian beer. As in 'A few sherberts of Nelson, and he ain't got a fackin' scooby'

[4] French Plait: Flat, or in Portugal, an apartment. West Ham didn't offer any slang for apartment.

[5] Dois: The Portuguese for two. Um is the Portuguese for one.

9. Trucks of Drugs and Sausage Rolls

"You have to give people something to dream on."
Jimi Hendrix

Jimi was no doubt referring to mind altering hallucinogens. I liked his statement more for the sentiment; I wanted something to dream on again, but I needed someone to give it to me. After a month or so I realised that van driving was a bit shit. During those long and lonely hours in the cab, I had also realised that all of my dreams were in tatters (goalkeeping for Wolves; opening Wolverhampton Civic Hall for Judas Priest; living a Medlantic Play Boy lifestyle; driving a van). I was leaning more towards Jimi's original meaning after that particular revelation. Where on earth do you get some hallucinogens from?
The Thrill saved me; he didn't know where to get hallucinogens, but he did give me something to dream on.

After almost eight months in Portugal returning to England came as somewhat of a culture shock. You couldn't bribe government officials here for starters. On reaching Dover, we missed the bus onwards to London because of an immigration official who was convinced that Fernanda was going to disappear off into the wilds of Great Britain and then hoover up all available part-time bar work away from British people. Struggling to understand Fernanda's English he'd had to call me over to help translate. Then, thinking that we were speaking code with our Portuglish means of communication, he had called a colleague over to ~~hassle, deal,~~ no, definitely hassle me. That I had already entered the country didn't appear to matter to them at all. The contents of my bag were unceremoniously dumped on a table in the arrivals hall, then very, very slowly rifled through. I suggested that maybe there was something else I could do that would speed our entry. There was a distinct bristling at this, so I declined to expand that my suggestion would be fifty thousand escudos, perhaps? If they had taken me into a back room and pulled on latex gloves I would've made very vocal my suggestion and upped it to one hundred thousand escudos. Once they were sure we had definitely missed our bus, they relented, gave

Fernanda a four week visitor's visa and let both of us enter the country.

Travellers tip: *If you ever want to buy train tickets at Dover station at seven thirty in the morning, make sure, if using cash of course, that you have British pounds and not Portuguese escudos. In my defence, if it had not have been for the* ~~over-zealous,~~ ~~bureaucratic,~~ *no, definitely over-zealous immigration officer, we'd have arrived, on our bus, in London, during bank opening hours.*

My parents had a mild culture shock too, being more than a little surprised when I turned up on their doorstep with Fernanda. I understood 'surprised' because she wasn't expected. Nor was I, for another five weeks for that matter. But I didn't understand 'surprised' that she was foreign. If only Teddy and Barry had made me buy The Daily Mail, I might have had an understanding or at least the tiniest of insights to this 'surprised'. She was a girl, that's all, surely? And it wasn't as though I'd fallen for the female of a rare breed of Portuguese sheep, was it? Even though we didn't have any Welsh genes in our family, if we had have had, and it was a Portuguese sheep that I'd bought home, should it have been a problem? The result to this particular question in a survey of two anonymous Daily Mail readers was inconclusive. One said 'yes, it would've been a problem', the other said 'no, there is no bloody Welsh blood in our family'. The Daily Mail didn't have the Portugue in their sights in 1987; given the survey results, it looked like it needed to.

I had lived under Lads House Rules for almost eight months, and they had only ever been a rough guideline. The transition to Strict Parental Law was an extreme culture shock to me; a bit like going from a 1960's Haight-Ashbury hippy commune and being parachuted straight into Kabul under the Taliban: without the beheading, stoning or AK47-ing that being parachuted straight into Kabul under the Taliban would've entailed.

Poor Fernanda, she experienced the biggest culture shock of all. Add to her shock, a severe bout of homesickness, then her reluctance to try and understand crazy Eeenglays culture, then further add a tendency to fly off the handle at the slightest thing (or had we just arrived in England as the communists had seized control?) and the writing was on the wall. In the space of a week or so, my dusky Portuguese maiden lost her lustre; she'd turned into a dour Portuguese moaner. It was too cold, which she moaned about incessantly. The food wasn't Portuguese, which she moaned about incessantly. It was very expensive compared to Portugal, which she moaned about incessantly. She didn't like me getting drunk with my crazy Eeenglays friends, which she...; you get the picture, total broken record. Next time I speak to Scouse Bob I'll tell him he can add this concern to his knife wielding ex-boyfriends, xenophobic brothers and shotgun carrying fathers theory.

At Dover I'd thought the immigration officer was a right fascist bastard. With hindsight, I'd have given him fifty thousand escudos not to let her in now and I was certainly thanking him for just the four week visa. Before it expired I sorted a flight back to Faro for her and counted down the days before she'd be on the big silver freedom bird.

"But how marry you me? If Portugal no come you?" she said to me in the airport, as she waited to go through to the departure lounge. What? She knew that I had no intention of going back to Portugal until there had been a thorough crackdown on police corruption. Hang on. Did she just say 'marry'?

"Sorry?" I said after computing what she'd just said.

"One time say you me. In disco one time say marry you me," she explained. I paused to compute. Right, errr. No, it was still news to me. I racked my brains.

"Errr," I continued to fight for some recollection of this marriage proposal. It doesn't sound like something I'd have said aged twenty.

"But how marry you me? If Portugal no come you?" she moaned. Ah, got it. But it does sound like something a twenty year old continental lager dribbling buffoon may have said.

"Errr," now I had my explanation, I needed an appropriate answer. "Errr," I couldn't think of one.

"If Portugal no come you? No see you me more times. Is many important is marry you me," she continued. Is many important? It was many important that I came up with an appropriate answer. Ah, got it. I would have to lie.

"Errr, Spain go you, Spain go me," it was quicker to speak Fernanglish than speaking either English or Mattuguese and then having to say it again in Fernanglish anyway. "Spain more time come you me."

"Is when more time come you me?" she whined. I glanced at my watch, five very long minutes until the departure gate was due to open.

"Errr," four minutes fifty-eight seconds. "Errr," four minutes fifty-six seconds. "Errr, more soon Spain you me," I lied shamelessly. I glanced at my watch again; it wasn't a very long lie. Four minutes fifty-one seconds. This is going to be the longest four minutes fifty-one seconds of my life.

Genius! A spark of sober genius too! I pointed at my watch and said, "train go more quick no miss me. Flight good have you. Bye." I turned and ran for it.

As well as having a unique way of wooing the ladies, I also have a unique way of un-wooing of them. Although this was possibly not as unique as having a pint of lager poured over your head in a packed pub surrounded by friends. In my defence, I thought that by having her friends there it would provide for a rapid and accessible support network. Thoughtfulness, ladies like that.

With Fernanda gone and my reluctance to return to Portugal (doubly so now, after the continental lager dribbled marriage proposal revelation) the Medlantic Play Boy dream was well and truly finished. That the dream was completely over was further bought home by the fact that, as soon as Fernanda was somewhere over the Bay of Biscay, Strict Parental Law doctrine was ramped up, fundamentally. Five times a day I was pointed towards the Job Centre and had to listen to them wail 'what are you going to do with your life, we can't afford for you to sit around here all day strumming a guitar'. To which I was then forced to answer with the correct intonation of 'Musthaffajob, willgetajob. Musthaffajob, willgetajob.'

Before you could say the word 'brainwashed' I'd had my hair cut, shaved off my facial hair, put on clean clothes and charged head first into the Job Centre. KABOOM! The first interview they sent me for, I was given the job. Goodbye Medlantic Play Boy, hello Vehicular Delivery Operative. It was the Job Centre's will. Luckily I had developed a taste for van driving in Portugal. While pleased that I wouldn't be sitting around all day strumming a guitar, Strict Parental Law doctrine still deemed that I now had to listen to a new wail. Fortunately, I was going to be out at work all day, so least I would only have to listen to 'but you could do so much better than driving a van' once a day. And that would only be if I hadn't managed to sneak off to sit around and strum my guitar all evening. [1]

The weekend before I was due to start work I thought it would be very rude not to celebrate my new found freedom (I probably should have put 'employment' there). Pub crawl was called. I can't remember who exactly, but there were ten or twelve of us: Big Trev, The Thrill, The Angel, John the Roadie, Sport Billy and Jezza were all definitely there. Not wanting to end up proposing to any of my mates, I steered well clear of any sort of continental lager and stuck to half the strength British beer. However, after several pints, I realised that, due to my high continental lager tolerance level, I was way behind everyone else in the slurring stakes. I got in a sneaky couple of large G&Ts as a means of performance enhancement. By the time we had landed in the curry house we all seemed to be equally well lubricated.

I was just about to tell my mates (for the fourth or fifth time) that I had missed them and that it was good to be back and see them all, when a hush descended on our table. That just does not happen on a table of ten or twelve very drunk twenty year olds, at midnight, in an Indian restaurant. Ever!

"We haven't got enough to pay the bill," Big Trev whispered. Around the table there were several looks of concern, a couple of unconcerned bleary eyed grins and one very slurred whisper.

"Whys dush weesh wantsh to kill anyonesh?" slurred the whisperer. It was followed by some not very muffled giggles.

"Seriously, we haven't got enough to pay. Empty your pockets, lads," Big Trev whispered in earnest. Hands fumbled in pockets, loose change was dumped on the table, Big Trev counted furiously, and waiters, having that mystical power of being able to hear one hundred decibel 'whispers', hovered by the table nervously.

"No, still not enough, lads, come on," Big Trev pleaded. The waiters collected un-touched drinks and un-eaten desserts from our table.

"RUNNER!" A nano-second of hush descended on the whole restaurant. Disdainful heads turned towards our table. Our eyes darted left then right. BANG! As one, nine or eleven of us responded to the call and exploded from the table. Chairs flew in all directions. A single mass of giggling inhumanity charged through an eruption of small change, flying pint glasses and clouds of airborne lager. The waiters retreated as the mass crashed (staggered, lurched, swayed, stumbled - all would work here) towards the door and ultimate financial freedom.

To this day, no one has ever admitted to being the originator of the shout. The only person we can definitely rule out is Big Trev. He had remained inside trying to marshal the additional small change, in the hope that we may have had enough for the bill, and that if anyone was going to get banned it would not be him.

We bomb burst out of the restaurant door and somebody, unsure of which way to run, immediately stopped dead and caused a huge human pile up. A tangle of uncoordinated, yet still giggling, limbs and bodies crashed to the pavement outside. I must've been pretty quick off the mark, I thought, as I found myself at the bottom of the pile. As one, we looked up. A lager soaked Big Trev (internally and now externally) was still inside. He was stood at the window holding up five fingers, he mouthed something at us (later discovered to be 'we only need a fiver, you fuckin' twats') and beckoned for us to come back in. Untangled from the giggle heap, a couple of lads obviously didn't want to face the music for short-payment of an exotic food bill and decided to continue the runner. They charged off into the night, laughing maniacally. As the giggle fest abated the remaining seven or nine of us untangled ourselves and trudged, rather sheepishly, back inside to several rather judgemental looks from the other diners. On a much closer inspection of our pockets we miraculously found a fiver, and two more for that matter. Big Trev insisted we leave those two as a tip. He really didn't want to get banned.

I stayed at Big Trev's that night. It was a good mile-long, uphill all the way, walk from the curry house. Except that when you drunkenly stagger three steps forward, then two backwards, it is more like five miles of distance covered before you reach your intended mile away destination (spreadsheeted it, story checks out). The next morning I awoke and rose to go to the bathroom. I immediately crumpled to the floor. That's strange I thought. I had known how to stand up yesterday. Overnight I'd lost the ability to stand? I refused to believe that and tried again. Same result. I tried yet again. Same result again, except this time, emerging through my alcoholic cloak of analgesia and flawed understanding, when I did crumple to the floor, I experienced what I could only describe as a slight twinge of excruciating pain. I looked down at my legs. Phew, they were still there. Big Trev hadn't cut them off in the night as a punishment for being first runner out of the door. It warranted a closer inspection. Both knees fine, good. Left ankle fine, good. Right ankle fine, errr, no. In the words of a corrupt Portuguese copper I had problem, big problem. It was the size of a bloody football.

Five hours later, and nursing a huge hangover that was admittedly being numbed nicely by some very strong pain killers, I emerged from A&E on a pair of crutches sporting a huge plaster cast on my right ankle. The extreme pain had indeed confirmed my suspicions that this time, unlike last time, there was no conspiracy (refer to Chapter Five: The Broken Ankle Conspiracy). I'd properly, not probably, but properly broken my ankle: no doubt exacerbated by unknowingly walking five miles back to Big Trev's house on it. I still marvel at the remarkable analgesic powers of a gallon or so of British beer. To be fair, even if there had been a conspiracy this time, I'd have played along. Signed on the sick for ten weeks? Who wouldn't? I hadn't even started my new job yet. I rang them on the Monday, with the ~~good~~ unfortunate news of my immediate ten week absence. They took it quite well, 'see you in ten weeks then' they said. I still had a job, without even starting it! Happy little jigs of joy were called for. I jigged, happily. Obviously, only in my mind, how else could you do a happy little jig in a plaster cast and still justify a ten week sick note?

This called for a celebratory pub crawl. I hobbled back over to the phone.

"Alright (Big Trev, The Thrill, The Angel, John the Roadie, Sport Billy, Jezza – use whoever you would like me to be calling)," I said when the phone was answered.

"Alright, Matt," whoever said in return.

"Pub crawl?" I said.

"Sound. I'm in. When?"

"Ten weeks from today, mate."

Ten weeks of convalescence ensued: under the ever watchful and judgemental gaze of Strict Parental Law. It could gaze and judge all it wanted; I had a ten week sick note. So, in full view of that watchful gaze and at the risk of being judged, I sat around the house all day and strummed my guitar. Another important part of my convalescence was trying to avoid being told 'but you could do so much better than driving a van'. And, if I couldn't avoid being told, I tried to avoid responding with 'I know, but there weren't any Rolls Royce driving jobs going that day'.

A couple of weeks after my plaster cast was removed I received a call from The Thrill.

"Still got the lot, mate. I've been playing quite a lot of guitar lately too," I said to his enquiry about whether I'd sold all of my gear before heading out to Portugal.

"Cool. I'm in a band again. We're looking for a new guitarist, interested?" The Thrill asked. Excellent! It's about time I got back to the serious business of rock.

"Of course," hold on. "It's not some gothic shit is it? I ain't poncing around on stage in make-up." A five minute debate ensued on the merits of the gothic music genre. The Thrill argued for the defence; I argued for the prosecution that it was indeed shit, with a secondary argument that it wasn't natural for men to wear any sort of make-up. The Thrill countered this by questioning why it should be a problem for men to wear make-up. To which I closed my case with the question of whether he still liked to watch football, any sport?

"What? Of course I do. Anyway it's not gothic, okay?"

"What sort of stuff is it then?" I asked.

"Well, sort of like a fusion, a sonic melting pot where retro post-punk meets grebo," said The Thrill, sounding very much like he'd been updating his CV to apply for a job on the NME. Unbeknownst to him, there was an imaginary tomato ketchup bottle being vigorously shaken at my end of the line. Grebo?[2] Not a scooby. And what is 'retro post-punk', or a 'sonic melting pot', for that matter?

"Errr, right. No keyboards? No make-up?" I sought for extra clarification, but deemed it pointless to ask about the exponents of, or even, who they sounded like. At least I was fairly confident that they wouldn't sound like any of the Euro-pap that had been assaulting my ears on the Algarve recently.

"Definitely not,"

"Errr, grebo, eh?" I didn't want to let on that I hadn't a clue. "Errr, go on then, I'm in." Let's get back to the serious business of rock. Did 'retro post-punk meets grebo' rock? I hoped it did, because as yet, I was totally in the dark. I hoped that the groupies were fit too.

..... *"Wolverhampton! Are you ready to non-descript rock?" The singer shouted.*

The crowd shouted back in the affirmative.

The new guitarist was pleased to note that none of his fellow band mates or male members of the audience were wearing make-up.

"I CAN'T FUCKING HEAR YOU. ARE YOU REDEEEEE TOOOO NON-DESCRIPT RAHHHCKK?".....

I'd spent the last couple years in a musical wilderness; musically confused teenager followed by total musical celibacy in Portugal (other than playing Beatles songs and 'Wild Rover', that is). Although for some reason, probably because I'd heard it at least one thousand plus times, I had been quite taken with Mel & Kim's 'Respectable'. I needed a crash course in what was happening out in the proper music world. I limped up to the paper shop to buy a music paper. Back when I'd been a regular on the music paper buying scene, I'd always bought Sounds. Sounds had covered tattoo swathed bands that made your ears bleed. Those tattooed gods of rock played

151

growling and exotically shaped guitars through mountains of huge speakers; whereas, The NME covered flowery shirt attired bands that played jingly-jangly guitars through tiny little amplifier-speaker combinations. They made my ears bleed for a different reason. A 'no brainer' really; I bought Sounds.

That week's edition seemed to be one long REM and U2 love in, as well as coverage of several other bands that appeared to be attired in flowery shirts. I checked the cover. It was definitely Sounds. I was still partial to some pre-'The Unforgettable Fire' U2, not a clue about REM though. On closer inspection I did find an interview with Metallica on page thirty-two. Now, I was very partial to a bit of Metallica indeed, even if their guitar work was way beyond my level of competency. Although, not wanting to be reminded of my lack of ability, I'd never progressed any further than 'Ride the Lightning' with them in my record collection.

I delved deeper into Sounds, the only mention of 'grebo' I could find was in the Musicians Wanted section. Ah-hah! So at least it was a genre recognised by more than just The Thrill. Damn! Why had I deemed it pointless to ask him about who the exponents of grebo were? I could've cheated and invested / wasted (delete according to individual taste) some money on a couple of records. According to Sounds though, it looked very much like I did need to invest in a couple of flowery shirts. With Sounds read cover to cover, twice, I remained clueless, yet I did wonder whether it was the NME that now covered those tattoo swathed gods of rock. I hedged my bets and bought one flowery shirt and, just in case, REM's 'Document' too. They weren't grebo, but it is still an album that I occasionally listen to today; other than AC/DC from 'Powerage' up to and including 'For Those About to Rock' there are not many pre-1990 albums in my collection that I can say that about. I gave up on AC/DC after 'For Those About to Rock'; though to still listen to five albums by one band is pretty impressive, even by my limited musical attention span.

Eventually signed fit for work I climbed into the cab of an ancient (and very unreliable) Transit van and set to the task of delivering hardware and building supplies around the Midlands. The van had no radio / cassette player installed, which made for some very long and very boring days at the wheel, in what was essentially a very boring job. If only there really had been a Rolls Royce driving job available that day. The only thing of note from these early days on the highways and byways of the greater West Midlands conurbation was that I developed a keen taste, which bordered on addiction, for Yorkie bars and Ginsters sausage rolls.

Being signed fit for work now meant that at long last I could get on with the serious business of rock. I arranged with The Thrill to meet up with the band: Incee Wincee Spider. None the wiser as to what a 'sonic melting pot where retro post-punk meets grebo' sounded like, or indeed what the band members of said genre would look like, I made my way to a small back street rehearsal room in The Lye. I was pretty nervous when I finally walked in to the room to meet the other two members of the band. Plum Fingers, the singer, looked every inch the rock star; flowing long hair, fag in hand and slurping on a can of Special Brew. There was a sort of Jim Morrison vibe and more than a bit of the throwing televisions out of eleventh floor windows about him. That's a good start; Special Brew, fags and he's not wearing make-up. Stevie Boy played the bass guitar; he looked every inch like he'd just stepped out of a Bros video. To be fair to Stevie Boy, while I wasn't wearing my luminous yellow muscle vest with 'ALGARVE BEACH BUM' emblazoned on it, I did look like someone who had been left on a sun-bed for eight months, with the setting on eleven, as well as someone who hadn't had their mullet attended to for a not dissimilar amount of time.

Outgoing Guitarist was also there to give me an intensive induction to their songs. Like Plum Fingers he too looked like a rock star, albeit in a sort of leather jacketed gothic way (though without the make-up). Not one of them, apart from me, wore a flowery shirt. I set my amp up in a corner of the room and strapped on my gleaming fire red and freshly strung Ibanez Destroyer. I was ready to non-descript rock.

"What the fuck is that silly shaped banjo?" Plum Fingers asked, on seeing the Destroyer. "We ain't Metallica or bloody Iron Maiden." Oh. Instant disappointment combined with instant relief. Disappointed, because it didn't look like growling and exotically

153

shaped guitars were used in a sonic melting pot. Relieved, because I didn't have the technical ability to play like either Metallica or bloody Iron Maiden.

"I think it looks cool," Stevie Boy said. Ah, then again, maybe it could still be used in a sonic melting pot after all. It didn't change my technical ability mind.

I plugged it in and banged out a couple of dirty power chords. Outgoing Guitarist walked straight over to my amp and turned the overdrive knob down. What? I was gob smacked. Totally gob smacked. You just don't twiddle with another man's knob, especially without asking. Ever! I banged out a couple of jingly-jangly 'very much lacking in power' chords. What on earth? At the resultant sound I looked at everyone in disgust, then turned back to my amp and twiddled with MY overdrive knob. To make sure I had definitely re-twiddled it back to the appropriate 'rock' setting, I fired off a couple of dirtier, meatier power chords. Ah, that was better. To my relief, Plum Fingers, Stevie Boy and The Thrill all nodded their heads in acknowledgement of this newer, dirtier, meatier sound.

"What sort of stuff do you like then Matt?" Plum Fingers asked.

"Errr," I wanted to say anything that rocks, but, still unsure of what musical ground I was standing on, I didn't. I shrugged and uttered the all encompassing "Errr, all sorts really," I couldn't bring myself to admit to Mel & Kim being in the all sorts.

We spent the next couple of hours going through their (now, our) songs. I quite liked most of them, especially when played with the newer, dirtier, meatier sound. At the end of the session I was welcomed into the band with a can of Special Brew and a bag of chips from the chippy around the corner. Later, The Thrill lent me a couple of records; he'd noticed my discomfort when we'd been talking about what bands everyone was going to see or currently listening to. There hadn't been a grebo scene in Portugal, I was clueless. He lent me 'Unbearable', a single by The Wonder Stuff, and a Pop Will Eat Itself album: 'Box Frenzy'. What? Pop Will Eat Itself used a sample of Mel & Kim's 'Respectable' on track eleven 'Hit the Hi-Tech Groove'! I could've said I liked Mel & Kim after all. I quite liked The Wonder Stuff, with their catchy guitar based rock, and guitar parts that were a lot easier to figure out than anything by Metallica. I could get into these, no problem. Pop Will Eat Itself, on the other hand, with their sampling and rapped lyrics, was a change of taste too far for me at this point, given my recently starved musical palate. Even with The Thrill's records I still couldn't get my head around 'retro post-punk meets grebo', and anything I wrote sounded like 'Love' era The Cult turned up to eleven. I'm not sure any of the others knew how to get their heads around the 'retro post-punk meets grebo' conundrum either, as most of my songs, once Plum Fingers had put his lyrics to them, were happily accepted by the band.

Once we had got what we thought was a decent set together, we began the process of getting gigs lined up. Luckily Plum Fingers was a bit of a face on the local music scene, so, rather than having to play tiny pub backrooms to a few coerced friends and a couple of mild-drinking regulars who were just waiting for their racing pigeons to return home, we jumped straight into some of the more established Midland's music venues: The Barrel Organ in Birmingham; Moseley Town Hall; Tamworth Arts Centre; and the legendary JB's Club in Dudley, where Plum Fingers managed to get us a monthly slot. We also made the occasional foray, and often more than rewarding, trip down to London: The Sir George Robey in Finsbury Park and The Tunnel Club in Greenwich were two of the most enjoyable places that we played down south.

Now, I grew to love Dudley's finest rock venue, but, before I get all misty eyed about it, I did have a love-hate thing going on with JB's which stemmed from an early experience there. It was great for music, there were live bands on every night of the week across a pretty wide spectrum of genre and also, unfortunately for music purists, at times very average and sometimes very below average. If truth be told, the crowd was pretty, let's make that very, difficult to please too. However, the hate part of my relationship stemmed not from the difficult audience or sometimes below average quality of band, but from an incident when I was seventeen or eighteen. The Angel and I, both desperately trying to deny, or hide totally from our ill-fated gothic period, had gone to see The Hellfire Club there, a local heavy rock band that we both liked. The Hellfire Club rocked! On leaving the club and heading to the car park (I was the designated driver this evening; strange but true) I heard a shouted 'Oi' and heavy running footsteps. I turned around to see what the commotion was all about. My eyes focussed on a huge fist that was about to land on the side of my face. It did. It hurt.

"What the? What was that for?" I asked, rubbing the side of my face.

"Yow spilt me pint," replied my assailant. Ah, I see, how remiss of me. My new friend had just used one of the two great 1980's meathead excuses for battering you: if you hadn't spilt their pint, then you'd obviously looked at their girlfriend. I must've spilt his pint though as I doubt I'd have given a second glance to this particular gentleman's lady friend, goggles or no. He was a great, hairy, tattooed, fat bastard and it was quite easy to tell that he wasn't one of life's intellectuals either. He also had two equally great, hairy, tattooed and grinning fat bastards standing behind him. From the look of this pair, I wouldn't have looked at either of their girlfriends. Not even with the full goggles on.

"Errr, sorry mate, errr, I didn't mean to," I didn't think I had, in fact I doubt I had been anywhere near his pint, let alone looked at his girlfriend. I didn't really know what else to say. I couldn't see The Angel anywhere. Where was my backup?

"Wharram-the fuck-am yow gonna do about it?" he said menacingly and moved (more like staggered) towards me with raised fists. I knew what I wanted to do about it. However, while he was obviously drunk, he was rather on the big side, and did have an equally large two man support team and my backup had deserted me. But he had just punched me. Got it! Weapon. I needed a weapon. I glanced around and noticed a loose brick in the car park wall. Now I had a plan. This was going teach him for falsely accusing me of spilling his pint. I looked back at the fat bastard and was about to make a grab for the brick, when I noticed a twelve inch Bowie knife hanging from his belt.

"So, wharramyow gonna do about it?" he repeated impatiently. With a decent lump of Ibstock I reckoned I could take two of them down easily, that would just leave one left to deal with, but I really didn't fancy being stabbed in the process. Metaphorically, I bent over, dropped my trousers and presented my backside: I chose cowardice as the better part of valour!

"Errr, tell you what, Fat Boy, I'm going to run away, and very fast too." I charged off down the road, laughing maniacally, "try and catch me, ya fat bastard!" He didn't, and he didn't try for that long either. It was quite a few months before I returned to JB's though. The sight of a twelve inch Bowie knife to a seventeen, possibly eighteen, year old boy is quite an effective door policy.

After my school band days, a brief flirtation with 'goth' and strumming Beatles songs in Portugal, Incee Wincee Spider should have been a halcyon period in my rock career. We regularly played in front of one to two hundred people at decent venues across the country. It should have been groupie heaven and I should've been at the top of the groupie league. The other three were all birded up and The Three Yokos followed us everywhere to keep strict watching briefs over them. Groupies couldn't get within ten feet of us before being met with a Gorgon stare from one, two, or at times, all three Yokos. Then, no matter where we played we always seemed to end up on a bill with a 'goth' band, I couldn't escape it: Every New Dead Ghost, Scream Dream and the Sex Gang Children to name but a few. Even the music press labelled us an 'up and coming Midlands goth outfit'. This further limited the groupie scoring opportunities somewhat, they weren't really into 'retro post-punk meets grebo' especially when they thought they were going to see an 'up and coming Midlands goth outfit' and did I really want to hook up with a girl who looked like a month old corpse? Even after I'd have confirmed that she was indeed a girl and not an effeminate looking male month old corpse, the answer was still no.

To further compound the lack of any groupie action, although we didn't really recognise it at the time (or did we recognise it and refuse to believe it?) we were, in all honesty, a bit a shit. We would never have inspired Aristotle - our whole was not greater than the sum of our parts, our whole didn't even appear to be in the vicinity of the sum of half our parts. We'd launch enthusiastically into our set, yet within a couple of minutes there was a steady migration of punters towards the bar area. Forty minutes later, as the last vestiges

157

of our signature ethereal power chord finish reverberated around an almost empty venue, there had been a very healthy upsurge in bar takings, and tumbleweed blew past The Three Yokos, alone near the front of the stage. The world, it appeared, was not ready to non-descript rock to the eclectic musical stylings of Incee Wincee Spider, although, the only place this didn't seem to happen was in London. Plum Fingers was once forcibly reinstated on the stage by a gang of Highbury skin heads demanding an encore. They must've grasped the whole 'retro post-punk meets grebo' thing.

The rock 'n' roll fantasy was dying again. As the gigs started to dry up I considered getting a new identity (I got the new identity idea from watching Edward Fox in The Day of The Jackal, it seemed quite easy to do) and heading back to Portugal to team up with Scouse Bob for another season of drunkenly banging out Beatles songs in The Bobbles. Ultimately though, after some considered heart searching and several nights enduring a recurring nightmare where I kept dropping the soap in a Portuguese prison shower block, I decided against going back to the sixties; I still wanted to rock.

During the heart searching process I also realised that fame, fortune and after show parties filled with nubile young ladies of particularly low moral values was not going to happen overnight in Incee Wincee Spider (if ever) and consequently I still needed the not very rock 'n' roll burden of the day job. Having got rather bored of driving around the Midlands I found a new job as an Extra Large Vehicular Delivery Operative (the 'Extra Large' pertaining to the size of the vehicle and not my burgeoning sausage roll and Yorkie Bar fed waistline) delivering urgent medical supplies into hospitals across the country. Quite pleased with my career advancement, I told the purveyors of Strict Parental Law that they had indeed been right, I could do so much better than being a mere Vehicular Delivery Operative. Surprisingly they accepted that I had made a positive move forward and without too much mention of it not being a very big step forward; although they did flinch when I told my Nan that I was now essentially employed as a drugs mule.

The Three Yokos became Four. I figured if you couldn't beat 'em, you had to join 'em. I located myself a Yoko too. By extension, Incee Wincee Spider became an even more impenetrable unit guarded by not three, but four formidable Gorgon sentries. At a rare rehearsal without a single Yoko present, we, with the aid of several cans of Special Brew each and without the encumbrance of said Four Yokos, decided to book into a recording studio. It was time to immortalise Incee Wincee Spider on tape. The rest of the rehearsal was spent arguing over what songs to record, rather than actually rehearsing them. Still, without reaching any sort of agreement on what tracks to lay down, we adjourned to the pub next door to continue the debate. With further mediation, and extra help from some more Special Brew, Banks's Bitter and several bags of pork scratchings, we not only arrived at three songs to record, but also came up with the brilliant idea of committing them to vinyl on a self financed seven inch single. I say brilliant because I'd been thinking of quitting the band and going back to Portugal again, and from gossip picked up from My Yoko (I hadn't mentioned Portugal to My Yoko, but I had become rather taken with the new identity idea), the other Yokos had been talking about one, two or possibly all three of the others leaving the band. It was news to me and I guess it might've been news to the other three too, depending on what weight you gave the provenance of Gorgon gossip. However, with all things considered, it did look like we were in a failing marriage and, rather than talking about it and trying to resolve the problems, we were burying our heads in the sand and about to conceive a child.

Within a few weeks we walked into a recording studio on an industrial estate in Cradley Heath. Not exactly AIR in Montserrat or The Record Plant in New York or even Abbey Road for that matter, but it was cheap, and, through a subsidiary company, they did record pressing too. In five hours we recorded 'Don't Know Anythin'', which became the A-side, 'See My Love Shine' and 'Dream Baby'. In true Spinal Tap fashion we spent at least two of the five hours trying to get an alarm clock to go off in the right place at the end of 'Dream Baby', eventually giving up and letting Sound Engineer splice the tape instead. We then spent a further five hours mixing it. Continuing in the Tap vein, four of these five hours were spent arguing, and then sulking if we'd lost our own individual argument, about how high up in the mix the voice / guitar / bass / drums should be.

"The only way you are going to get eight minutes of music on the B-side, lads, is by doing it on twelve inch," said Sound Engineer, with more than a little hint of the pound sign in his eye. Twelve inch vinyl was more than double the cost of seven inch at this particular purveyor of vinyl pressings.

"No, that's not right. You can," I jumped in. I knew you could.

"No, you can't," he didn't believe me.

"Yes, you can. Gillan did a nine minute thirty three second version of 'Smoke on the Water' on a seven inch B-side. Pressed it at 33RPM." Gotcha! I even had the proof at home.

"I've never heard of that." He still sounded as though he didn't believe me.

"Gillan? The Ian Gillan Band? Deep Purple's singer? Has a guitar shaped swimming pool at his mansion in Oxfordshire? Or, a B-side being done at 33RPM?" The Thrill knew of my heavy rock heritage, so I was only bemusing half of the band with my encyclo-geekic knowledge of seventies rock legend Ian Gillan. And probably Sound Engineer by the looks of it.

"Well we can't do that at our pressing plant." That was that then. As much as we'd have loved to release a twelve inch slice of non-descript rock, we couldn't afford to. An additional three hours of arguing about whether it should be 'See My Love Shine' or 'Dream Baby' as the B-side ensued. Ultimately 'See My Love Shine' and the recording studio / pressing plant won the day. Thirteen hours to record eleven minutes of music, five of which didn't even make it on to the bloody single. It had been a very expensive recording session indeed.

I'd finally ticked a rock 'n' roll fantasy box though; still hadn't got the wild after show party ticked, but I had released a record. It even got a half decent review in Sounds although we were once again referred to as a 'Midlands goth outfit'. I might be pushing the 'half decent' there, unfortunately I've lost the scrap book from the Incee Wincee years, but I do remember that it was better than the review in The Melody Maker. They weren't that keen. The NME, having already given us a below average review for a gig in London, didn't even bother reviewing it. The local music rag Brum Beat did. They didn't like it at all. We'd been counting on this one; they had reviewed a couple of gigs and had us marked down as a 'shambolic yet entertaining live outfit'. Of the five hundred pressed, we used about fifty as promotional material, sold another fifty odd to whoever we could persuade to buy one, and the rest either got made into plant pots or started to gather dust and grow mould in darkened cupboards.[3] For the fifty odd we actually sold, it worked out at a cost of somewhere in the region of sixteen quid a single.

The gossiping Gorgon Nostradami had not been far wrong. Within six months of the single being released, without ever having had a single wild after show party, we put the child up for adoption and went our separate ways. Monetary differences were cited initially rather than the traditional musical ones as the reason for the split.[4] Call me a conspiracy theorist, but I've always wondered whether The Four Yokos played some part in the band's ultimate disintegration.

.....Brrrr, brrr. Brrrr, brrr. The phone rang on and on. I was starting to think that I'd dialled the wrong number. Surely Ian Gillan would have an answer phone; he's got a guitar shaped swimming pool. Now I bet that's seen some action. Brrrr, brrr. Brrrr, br-click.

"Hello," a croaky voice finally answered.

"Ian, is that Ian? Ian Gillan?"

"Yes, who is this?"

"Cool, Ian Gillan, it's really you. Errr, just a quick question, mate. You can press a seven inch single with one side at 45 and the other at 33 and a third, can't you?"

"Yes, I remember doing a nine minute thirty three second version of 'Smoke on the Water' on a B-side once. Who is this? How did you get this number?"

"Knew it. I knew you could. I thought I had a copy of that, but must've swapped it for, errr, some Bauhaus. Or made a plant pot, I'm not quite sure and I've made quite a few of those lately. Errr, one more question, what guitar shape is your swimming pool? Is it a Flying V?"

"Who is this?"

"Errr, and while you are on, you're not after a new guitarist by any chance?"

161

"What the?" Click. Brrrrrrrrrrr. The line went dead.....

[1] I hope the 'Googling' I did for this section hasn't put me on an FBI watch list.

[2] I could've done with Google back then! I'd have been able to discover that 'grebo' was a late 1980's and early 1990's musical subculture based largely in the English Midlands; and that in addition, it was a Kru language used almost predominantly in the extreme south-west of Liberia.

[3] I discovered several boxes in my loft about five years ago. Through ebay and my (now defunct) web site I've sold another fifty or so: mostly to Germany, Japan or the East Midlands. None of these were mouldy and there are still a few left!

[4] Plum Fingers went on to form Belch Pop Frenzy who have only recently changed their name to The Disco Tramps and still occasionally play around the Black Country. The Thrill joined a band called Pyschedelia Smith, before deciding to become an optician. More of Stevie Boy in Part Three.

DISC THREE
The Flaming Drambuie Years
1989 – 1992

Selected Soundtrack
Pixies – 'River Euphrates'
Throwing Muses – 'Counting Backwards'
Stone Roses – 'I Wanna be Adored'
The Wonder Stuff – 'Ten Trenches Deep'
Inspiral Carpets – 'Dragging Me Down'
Blur – 'Bang'
Fret Blanket – 'I'm Going to Buy a Hang Glider'
Mega City Four – 'Awkward Kid'
Nirvana – 'Smells Like Teen Spirit'
Buffalo Tom – 'Bird Brain'

Also getting burned on to poor quality CD's
REM, Smashing Pumpkins, Jesus Jones, Carter USM,
Senseless Things, The Family Cat, Midway Still

10. Subterranean Pub Band Blues

"Dreams are true while they last, and do we not live in dreams?"
Lord Tennyson

Yes, possibly. But by the same token, sometimes we also live in nightmares and they seem beyond true for the duration. Time was about to stand still; whereas playing Beatles covers in Portugal it hadn't, playing cover versions in tiny pub back rooms in the Midlands was a clock stopper of Faustian nightmare proportions. And I'm not talking about Paco Hernández's guitar work here either.

With the demise of Incee Wincee I once again had no band to occupy me. I focussed on work instead, volunteering to take the longer routes and monotonously slogging up and down the M5 / M6 / M1 / M42 / M62 (if the road had an M in front of it I'd been on it) making sure the country's hospitals were well stocked with drugs. The only highlight was when there was a hospital to deliver to that I hadn't been to before (rarely), or, a road to drive down that I hadn't driven down before (very rarely). I didn't even get to ogle any nurses. Sadly back then they didn't tend to employ nurses to drive a forklift truck in the stores. To make matters worse, following a couple of minor reversing incidents and a slightly more troublesome low bridge one, I'd been taken off the big truck and demoted to van driver. The final straw came when I drove into the back of some stationary traffic waiting at traffic lights in Leeds city centre. I had been trying to determine whether I had the A to Z the right way up, while trying to make my way from Leeds General to St James'. When the highlight of your day, outside of a truck stop bacon, egg, sausage and tomato sandwich with a sausage roll starter and Yorkie Bar dessert, is the equivalent of writing down the number of a train in a little note book, I knew I had to do something about it. Change jobs? No. Go to college and get some qualifications? No. It was time for a holiday. The easy quick fix: 'minimum effort, maximum sloth'.

I hadn't got around to changing my identity so Portugal was off the cards. For some reason I didn't fancy Spain (strange but true), probably because it was so close to Portugal. France? No, I'd been to Paris a couple of times; way too expensive and my French was rubbish. The travel agent wanted the sale and continued working her way across Europe. Italy? Don't really like pizza; Yugoslavia? I'm reading the broadsheets again these days, so I know there's an anti-communist insurgency brewing up; Bulgaria? Where? I finally settled on Corfu, made sense, I knew no Greek whatsoever.

A fortnight in Corfu with My Yoko was just what I needed to recharge the batteries. I returned with a rejuvenated energy for work and a very unhealthy red glow. The red glow came from a heady mixture of too much sun, too much taramosalata and way too many Flaming Drambuies. Ah, the Flaming Drambuie. I'd never found Drambuie to be much of a drink, but take a lowball glass with a double shot and add the visual theatre of swishing it around the glass, setting fire to it, slapping your hand on top of the glass palm down, waving hand with now attached glass above your head, shouting something in Greek and then downing in it one. Never mind Special Brew, I choose Drambuie with a bit of fire. I also came back with a renewed desire to join or form a new band. I had scouted out the possibilities of getting a live music gig in Corfu similar to my Portuguese one, but there only seemed to be openings for TV installers who knew how to leave MTV on at full blast in the bars out there.

Yes, it was time to get back to the serious business of rock. But what type of rock? The long hours in the cab had sort of helped broaden (actually, more accurately would be the word define) my musical horizons. Having spent quite a few quid on 'recommendations' from the music press I found I didn't really like much of what was out there. Why wasn't I listening to John Peel? I was either in the pub or in bed if I had a three in the morning start. I persevered with the gamble method and finally found that after several listenings, I was particularly taken with Pixies (they didn't use a 'The', the singer screamed incomprehensibly a lot and he was called Frank Black!), Throwing Muses (Kristin Hersh and Tanya Donnelly; two girls with guitars, step sisters in fact. That's almost twins! This opened up a totally new rock 'n' roll fantasy. I did check their lyrics; they did not appear to be of a lesbian leaning), and, errr, REM (not a clue what their lyrics were on about but I could work out most of the guitar parts). I was going to be wearing that flowery shirt after all. I would be looking to join an American indie rock band.

Could I find one? I scoured the Musicians Wanted section of the local papers and notice boards in the local music shops. There seemed to be an abundance of heavy metal bands looking for original, versatile and superfast guitarists; that was me out on all four counts. There was also an excess of bands 'into The Smiths'; my shirt was nowhere near flowery enough for that. 'U2 influenced' featured in quite a few ads too. The rest looking for a guitarist were from a smorgasbord of musical genres, none of which I had a clue about; hardcore, grindcore, melodic crossover thrash, shoegazing, space rock, noise pop, grebo (there's that grebo again), neo-psychedelic goth (who names these genres?). I only wanted to rock. Found it!

ROCK BAND REQUIRE 2ND GUITARIST
Own gear and transport essential
AC/DC, Diamond Head, Judas Priest
Call: ███████ on XXXX XXXXXX

It couldn't be? There was a ███████ in AC/DC. Not exactly American indie rock, I grant, and while I hoped against hope, I somehow doubted it was a supergroup being formed by the fore mentioned bands either. The needing your own transport sort of gave that away. But, it did say 'rock'; I may not have known how to grindcore or shoegaze, I certainly knew how to rock. Furthermore, I knew how to play a lot of their songs (if it was indeed the supergroup that was being formed), and if not, 'second guitarist' usually meant you could hide any shortcomings in ability behind the principal anyway. It had possibilities. I gave ███████ a call.

Sadly, it wasn't a supergroup being formed and they just did cover versions. They were a decent bunch of lads though, looked the part, had all the gear and my Destroyer wouldn't look out of place here (I'd been meaning to replace The Destroyer for a less exotically shaped guitar for ages but never managed to get around to it). Weighing the odds, I decided to put the flowery shirt back in the wardrobe and join them.

.....Dry ice swirled around the foot of the stage, the guitarists stood in unison, legs apart, head's to the sky, ringlet perms blowing in the breeze of the wind machine, they segued seamlessly from a dual harmonic solo and windmilled their arms to punch out the final crashing power chord. The crowd roared. The new guitarist, resplendent in skin tight, royal blue, shiny spandex leggings, adjusted his open to the navel sleeveless white silk shirt and gave a nonchalant flick of his ringlet perm. The singer swaggered towards the microphone.

"Wolverhampton! Are you ready to look ever so slightly camp?".....

We played together for a couple of months and had done a few gigs, just small pub back room affairs to about thirty people. Five of those were usually the girlfriends. It was not anywhere near the realms of my rock 'n' roll fantasy at all. My heart wasn't really in it. And then, ███████ wanted to introduce Boston's 'More than a Feeling' and Foreigner's 'I Want to Know What Love is' to the set list. What next? Toto's 'Hold the Line? Hey, while we're on, why not do some Meatloaf and Bryan Adams too. The thought of strumming along to chick rock's (I claim the credit for naming this genre - see Chapter 5) greatest hits of the last three decades held as much appeal as driving up the M5 / M6 / M1 / M42 / M62 every day. I left the band. Totally my decision; there was no Yoko conspiracy here. The sleeveless white silk shirt went into a charity bag.[1]

It was back to the ads then. The same story ensued, in fact it seemed as though I was looking at the same ads I'd looked at last time. And, I was still asking myself the same questions, foremost amongst them: what on earth is 'grindcore'? A change of tack was needed. After revisiting my groupie theory calculation, even though when My Yoko was applied it always came back to zero, I thought that given recent results, I'd better have a go at singing again. Having sung backing vocals in The Bobbles and Incee Wincee I had gained in confidence somewhat since my last foray as a front man. And, as long as the song was in the key of E, I had almost an octave range! Not one to be deterred by any limitations in my ability, I thought yes, I could be a singer again.

Armed with the decision to use the singer approach to joining a new band, while it didn't make the ads any more understandable, it did open up several avenues that looked worthy of an enquiry. After an enquiry and a subsequent audition, I'd found a band. I had finally got to wear my flowery shirt. Yet the band was ill fated almost from the off and extremely short lived. We played to just eight people in a small pub back room at what was only our second ever gig. They weren't exactly grooving on our REM pub rock cover versions. We split up half way through the set. Total apathy rather than musical differences here. The landlord wasn't too happy about it but the crowd of eight never even noticed; I reckon they were waiting for their racing pigeons to return home.

It had taken a while, but I was finally getting a clearer picture of what I really wanted to do and it certainly didn't include half heartedly strumming cover versions in pub rock bands. Incee Wincee had given me the taste, and the last two bands had fully confirmed it for me. Then add to that my groupie theory calculation, although I still hadn't figured how to make it greater than zero with My Yoko in the equation, I had my answer: I wanted to be playing my own material as the singer and guitarist. And, while I'm compiling a list of desirables, I would like to play at decent venues too. It was no good looking for a band to join; I was going to have to form a band of my own.

Stevie Boy and I had become good mates during Incee Wincee and I'd even recruited him into the last band just in time for the break up. I knew he was free at the moment, so that was the bass player sorted. I knew a few drummers, and as I definitely knew that G7 (from the last band) was also free at the moment, I gave him a call first. He was in. That saved a few phone calls. We nearly had a new band. However, if I was going to be singing and playing the guitar, there was a slight problem; I'd always had trouble singing and doing fiddly guitar bits at the same time. We would need another guitarist. We formed a new band anyway. We didn't have a name. We didn't have any songs. We didn't have a full line up. We didn't even have anywhere to rehearse. Rather than doing anything about it we met up in the pub instead and talked about it over a couple of Flaming Drambuies. It was time for some action.

"Tell you what, lads," I said, "I'll lock myself away for a couple of weeks and sort some songs out. You go away and sort the rest out, sorted?" They agreed. We were taking action.

"Lemon Tree Creek," said G7 as we sat around our new rehearsal room behind Donovan's Music in Stourbridge.

"Lemon Tree Freaks?" asked Stevie Boy. It looked like they might have further delegated the tasks between themselves. It was better than the first one I thought, but only just.

"Mighty Lemon Drops, The Lemonheads, Red Lemon Electric Blues Band, that's a lot of lemons," said Fardy, our new guitarist. Ah, the joy and pleasure of trying to name a band by committee.

"Matt Black?" I offered.

"Isn't that a bit too much like Frank Black?" Stevie Boy knew of my penchant for Pixies. "How about a single word name?" I liked where this was going, there were loads of single word band names currently out there: Cud, Ride, Curve, Blur, Suede, Lush, James, etc, etc.

"Like what though?" said Fardy. We randomly shouted out words for a few minutes, none of which came up with a majority vote.

"Let's do it Bowie style." I threw Stevie Boy a copy of Hamlet. Why I had a copy of Hamlet in my guitar case? I've no idea. "Open it to any page and randomly place your finger. The word it falls on, that's the name." The other two looked at each other, turned back and nodded. We had a majority consensus on using this method. Stevie Boy opened Hamlet, gave a theatrical flourish of his hand and stabbed at a page.

"Prithee?" he said. G7 and Fardy groaned.

"No wonder Bowie's lyrics were so shit," said Fardy.

"Try again," I encouraged.

"Fie?" More groans.

"Errr, again?" I encouraged some more.

"Mercenary," Stevie Boy looked up then said it again. "Mercenary?" That would do for me.

"I still like Lemon Tree Creek," said G7.

"Lemon Tree Freaks?" Had he still not heard G7 correctly or was this Stevie Boy's suggestion?

"Nah, too many lemons," said Fardy.

"I like Mercenary," I said. "Or Matt Black."

"Nah, too many blacks. Sabbath, Crowes, Flag and then, what about Matt Bianco?" Fardy jumped in and quashed Matt Black once and for all.

And that is, after throwing it around several more times (it seemed like forever), the story of how we ended up with Mercenary Tree Freaks as the name. I never really liked it and always referred to us as MTF. It was still a couple of years before we could have used the internet and Google. If it had existed back then I wouldn't have referred to us as MTF at all. Type 'MTF' it into a search engine and you'll get a plethora of links pertaining to 'Male to Female' transgender procedures, 'Male to Female' transgender support forums and plenty of dubious looking 'Very Hot Triple X MTF' links, no doubt pertaining to the results of 'Male to Female' transgender procedures, originating in Thailand and full of pictures of fragrant lady-boys in varying states of comportment. Not wanting to end up on a register, I've never clicked through.

In the two weeks prior to this point I'd managed to knock five songs out, including the lyrics. Well, nearly all the lyrics. Leading up to writing them I had been listening to a lot of Pixies, Throwing

Muses, REM, Tin Machine and, still not fully able to leave my rock past behind, AC/DC. If we were to pigeon hole them in a specific genre it would have to be a new one: 'throwing pixies in an electric tincore', or as one reviewer in an obscure fanzine called it 'confused indie'. In retrospect he or she wasn't that far wrong, but at the time we thought they were pretty good. Stevie Boy had found a gem in Fardy, he's the best guitarist I've ever played with by a long shot, and once he had added his guitar playing to the rough bones they began to morph into mighty 'throwing pixies in an electric tincore' anthems. Overall we were very pleased with how things were shaping up. This was more like it; the rock 'n' roll fantasy was on again. Almost.

The line up was in place, the band name was sorted (still didn't like it), I'd finally traded the Destroyer in for a huge whale bodied semi-acoustic Antoria Jazzster guitar, we had seven songs (I'd written two more) and a place to rehearse them but, other than at JB's, without Plum Fingers' contacts we didn't have anywhere to play them live. Stevie Boy had arranged our debut at JB's, but that was it. We needed some more gigs. We could've just hired tiny pub back rooms. No. That was not part of the MTF road map. The better venues wanted to hear what you were like before booking you, unless you had Plum Fingers' contacts of course. We needed to record a demo tape. We chose a studio in the Northamptonshire countryside. When there was a multitude of studios in the Midlands, I can't remember why we chose Northamptonshire, but would hazard a guess that it had something to do with the price. Never mind that whatever we were saving would be eaten up by the fuel cost of taking two cars down there.

In the rehearsal room the week before we hit the studio, rather than rehearsing, we wasted the whole time arguing about which songs we should record. Three songs were settled upon in the rehearsal room, so in the pub afterwards we only had to argue about which order they would appear on the tape. Luckily no one had the genius, yet money sapping, idea of committing them to self-financed vinyl. Been there, done it, can't really afford the t-shirt. Off to Northamptonshire we went.

G7 and Fardy, not having been to a recording studio before, were impressed when we arrived. Stevie Boy and I looked around disappointedly. It wasn't exactly AIR, The Record Plant, Abbey Road or even Cradley Heath for that matter. Though we'd only ever been to the Cradley Heath studio (me twice with different bands), this was more like a converted large living room than the custom built one we'd used before. There was one benefit though, American Girl, the sound engineer for our session, gave it a rather pleasing aesthetic. She managed to ease our obvious concern by reeling off a great list of bands who had recorded there. Between us we'd even heard of a couple of them. Furthermore, she sounded like she knew what she was on about and was very enthusiastic about laying our tracks down. There were a lot of 'Hey, guys, that's cool' and 'Geee, yeah guys, go'. Not really speaking American we took these as positive noises. I later learnt that she was the girlfriend of ex-Bauhaus guitarist Daniel Ash. I just couldn't escape, there was a gothic connection everywhere I touched a bloody guitar! If I remember rightly, The Thrill's next band went and recorded there after he had heard this little gem of gothic trivia.

It took four hours to record three songs, about half of this time spent on the singing. I kept losing key or forgetting the words (in my defence they were fairly new songs). Then a further three to mix them, at least two hours of this was spent arguing, and then sulking if we'd lost our own individual argument, about how high up in the mix the voice / guitars / bass / drums should be. Eventually we had our first demo tape. It sounded nothing like 'throwing pixies in an electric tincore' anthems should sound at all. In fact it sounded nothing like we even sounded in rehearsal. Carried along on a wave of Californian [2] 'Hey, guys, that's cool' enthusiasm we had let American Girl dress us up in flowery shirts and turn us into a jingly-jangly indie band right in front of our very eyes.

'Disintegrating' was an attempt at a Pixies song, lots of loud bits with lots of quiet bits in between and at a fair old tempo. Somewhere along the line we managed to lose the pace and she managed to lose the definition between the loud and the quiet. 'Mascara', not about my days in a 'goth' band, was Throwing Muses inspired, so much so that I just used their lyrics from the song 'Dragonhead' rather than write any of my own (I was still having trouble writing lyrics). The title came from the lyrics too. We had wanted a 'raw' feel here, yet she made it sound 'nice', let's make that 'too nice', or even 'way too nice'. As for the final song, 'Dying Without You' (there's me having trouble writing song titles, never mind the lyrics), it should have had a 'Document' era REM vibe and yet American Girl turned it into something that made us never, ever want to play it again. Ever! Or listen to it for that matter. We didn't do either.

This was a problem. The next rehearsal, rather than rehearsing or writing a new song to replace the one that we were never ever going to play again, was spent debating (slightly more civilised than arguing) about whether to use the three we had recorded as the demo tape or not. Our choices boiled down to either, bite the bullet and use them, or, re-record them at another studio. If we re-recorded them we wouldn't have had any money left to have the demo tapes run off. Eventually we reached the compromise of just re-recording 'Disintegrating'.

We booked three hours at yet another studio, this time in The Lye, and hoped that three hours would be more than enough to record one song and get it mixed. Sensibly, we scouted it out first. This studio wasn't in someone's converted living room, this was the real deal, and dare I say, even better than the one in Cradley Heath. Stevie Boy and I looked at each other and nodded approvingly. G7 and Fardy were even more impressed than they had been in Northamptonshire; they joined in with the approving nods.

On recording day we announced our arrival on the security intercom and the sound engineer came to get us from the reception area. Oh my god! OH MY GOD! OH MY GARD!

"Alright, lads, I'm Brian," he said. Let us rock. It was Brian Tatler, the guitarist from Diamond Head. One of my rock god school boy heroes was going to be sound engineering our session. Even

Metallica thought he was a rock god; they covered Diamond Head songs too. And, he used to play a Flying V just like Wellington Womble's. He seemed smaller than I remembered him on stage though.

"Fuck me, I know who you are," I said. Talk about meeting someone famous, that you also admire and not having a clue of what to say. Fortunately, in my star struck daze, I didn't flash him a devil horn salute. Let's just hope I never get an OBE.

Taken aback he regained his composure and indicated for us to follow him, "c'mon, down to where the magic happens." After Northamptonshire we could do with some rock god magic on this session.

"Who is he?" Fardy whispered, as we humped our gear down the corridor towards where the magic happened.

"Brian Tatler," I whispered back.

"Who?"

"It's Brian Tatler, the Brian Tatler,"

"Who the fuck is Brian Tatler?"

"Diamond Head,"

"Who?"

"Never mind." I may as well have been talking to my Dad. Fardy, quality guitarist though he was, did not have an early eighties rock heritage.

Four hours later we had finally finished getting the song on tape. We were yet to mix it though. Brian turned out to be somewhat of a perfectionist and had designs on being a producer rather than just the sound engineer. He kept on wanting to know whether something or other was in fifths or eighths. Fifths or eighths? We wanted to rock not do bloody fractions. One particular guitar part he made me do over and over and over again. I thought I'd got it, the band thought I'd got it, he reckoned the timing was out. Again. He made me do it again. I doubt he'll be calling me up next time he wants a second guitarist. And then he made me harmonise the vocals. This didn't really work on two counts; firstly, it wasn't what we wanted, and secondly, you try harmonising when you have less than an octave range. I doubt he'll be calling me up next time he's after a singer either.

Mixing it also took an hour longer than we'd anticipated. A school boy error here on Stevie Boy's and my part; we'd forgotten to factor in the time it takes to argue and sulk about how high up in the mix the voice / harmonised voice / guitars / bass / drums should be.

"What do you reckon then, Bri?" I asked, once we finally had the finished article down on tape.

"Not really my thing, lads," was all he said. The tone suggested a certain level of strained diplomacy. A rock god had crumbled before my eyes.

"Oh," I was a tad disappointed. "Your 'Canterbury'[4] album wasn't really my thing either, mate." That was the last time I ever spoke to Brian Tatler. And yet, for all his fifths, eighths and obsessive perfectionism he had delivered a new improved version of 'Disintegrating' (apart from the vocal harmonies) and had at the very least, made it sound a lot closer to how a 'throwing pixies in an electric tincore' anthem should sound. Our problem now was that the other two songs, when put side by side with new improved 'Disintegrating'[3], sounded like they were by a totally different band altogether, from a different genre even. We could not afford to re-record these two though and had to settle for what we had on tape. A hundred copies were all we could afford to run off. It would've been two hundred copies if we hadn't overspent somewhat on our budget. At this rate a two-up two-down in Wolverhampton was going to be way out of my reach, never mind a Home Counties mansion with guitar shaped swimming pool.

.....Empty Drambuie bottles were strewn around the room. Discarded clothes lay in random heaps across the marbled floor. The two lovers lay in bed and stared awkwardly into each other's eyes. A thought momentarily crossed Tanya's mind: 'I bet he's only with me to steal my lyrics'. He stared back at her with a satisfied grin on his face. He rubbed his bruised cheek and contemplated: 'I wonder if Kristin would be here too if I hadn't asked whether they were

lesbians?' He got up to go and fetch another bottle of Drambuie from the kitchen. Making his way there he paused briefly in the bedroom doorway, an even bigger grin spread slowly across his face. He glanced around furtively as a new thought entered his Drambuie fuelled mind: 'Now I wonder where she keeps her lyrics book'.....

(1) ███████ and the boys went on to become one of the Midlands' many eighties rock, or as I prefer to call it 'chick rock' tribute acts.

(2) American Girl, while definitely American, may not have been from California. She might have been Canadian come to think of it.

(3) A friend of an older friend's brother-in-law's sister's daughter reckoned she heard it played on John Peel's show. We've never been able to confirm this although several others also believe that they've heard this and other MTF songs played by the great man.

(4) 'Canterbury' was Diamond Head's difficult third album. It was an almost complete shift in direction from their previous two, that ultimately saw them dropped (understandably if you ask me) by their record label.

11. Cheggers and The Man With a Singing Dog

"When defeat comes, accept it as a signal that your plans are not sound, rebuild those plans, and set sail once more toward your coveted goal."
Napoleon Hill

I didn't think we needed a signal as to how sound our plans were. Our JB's debut went really well (apart from what we wore, but I've never been one to shy away from a rock fashion faux pas), plaudits included members of that difficult Dudley crowd and none other than Jonn, the singer from Ned's Atomic Dustbin!
Then I went to see The Wonder Stuff at The Hummingbird in Birmingham. This wasn't a mere signal that our plans were far from sound, it was a Damascene moment. I had drunk the Kool-Aid, and then come back for a second glass. You were either on the bus or not. G7 got sacrificed on the high altar of indie power pop and we set sail once more; this time at 152BPM or faster.

Given that our debut reception at JB's had been far greater than we'd ever dreamt of, it was clear to me that my brief foray into the realms of 'throwing pixies in an electric tincore' was over. Not entirely, as I still listen to Pixies and Throwing Muses today, but as for the band's direction it was time for a radical change. The rest of the country had gone baggy and was raving away in ridiculous flared jeans to the Madchester scene[1]. In my day job I had moved even further up the Vehicular Delivery career ladder by now and was a fully fledged owner-driver who regularly delivered into Chester. It didn't seem that mad to me at all (I had hours of fun telling this to floppy fringed Mancunians on holiday). I liked The Stone Roses mind, yet their guitar work was way too intricate for me to think about banging this particular drum. I also liked Inspiral Carpets, and they used keyboards! So I wouldn't be hitching myself to this individual caravan either. I knew exactly where I was headed: catchy guitar based rock, or as the music press had dubbed it 'indie power pop'. Pop? That didn't sound very rock 'n' roll at all. 'Indie powercore', now that would've been way, way better.

With the plan rebuilt all I had to do was write some 'indie powercore' songs: easier said than done. I needed some pointers. The Thrill had taken his Wonder Stuff records back ages ago; while they had stirred something, they hadn't set the same spark alight as seeing them live had. I rushed out and bought everything by them I could get my hands on (that being up to and including 'Circlesquare'). I spent a week listening to them solidly in the cab and then a further week analysing the new purchases in my bedroom. It was deconstruction for the modern man crush. At the end of this process I was very pleased with myself and yet, in spite of this self pleasure, I was also very concerned. Pleased: because I could figure out how to play all the guitar parts and how the songs were put together. Concerned: for exactly the same reasons. Was it really that simple? Did you really not have to be a virtuoso guitarist? Had I been trying to over complicate everything for the last fifteen odd years? And, at the forefront, why hadn't I been to see The Wonder Stuff earlier? Fighting through the murky fog of these concerns was the conviction that through my deconstruction I had discovered a formula for 'indie powercore' superstardom.

We'll put aside the fact that my lyrical ability still worried me, not to mention a slight lack of confidence in my voice. When applying my formula to the music side all you needed was: a bouncy opening riff (doesn't have to be too tricky), a continued bouncy theme for a four line verse, catchy three (maximum four) chord chorus, repeat first three steps, then do a changey interludey bit (lyrics optional) for four (sometimes eight) measures, bouncy build up to a double (occasionally quadruple) chorus end. I never did learn to read music. Once I had done all that several times over (I had titles and the odd snippet of a verse or chorus but still needed to produce a full set of lyrics), I took the new songs to the lads for the final fitting. Stevie Boy added in his bass lines and Fardy worked his fiddly fingered magic. Et voilà! We had several less than three minute slices of 'indie powercore' magic (there were also a couple of slices of not so magic 'indie powercore', these never made it past a second rehearsal). This blueprint served me well for the rest of MTF's natural life. In fact, whenever I deviated from my formula, the resulting song never had the same feel, never quite had the requisite power and never, ever turned out like I'd heard it in my mind's ear.

.....*The lights went down. A cheer went up from the crowd, etc, etc. Yeah, OK, I get the picture. The elevated drum riser was bare. Three guitar wielding heroes emerged through the whirling dry ice. The singer-guitarist swaggered towards the microphone.*

"Wolverhampton! Are you ready to 'indie powercore'?"

The crowd roared in the affirmative.

"Hang on, before we do this thing. Does anyone know a drummer?".....

"A drum machine? Are you serious?" Stevie Boy was incredulous. I'd just told him how I thought we should fill our vacant drummer's seat.

"Yes," I replied.

"A machine though? Not a real drummer?" Although Fardy hadn't yet chipped in, this idea wasn't going down that well with Stevie Boy at all.

"Errr, yeah, why not? We've gone through a few and not found anyone who fits the bill yet."

"You're not trying to turn us in to fucking Depeche Mode or some robotic Kraftwerk shit?" That was quite a good 'why not'. I wasn't sure I had a decent enough counter to this.

"No, of course not." That wasn't a very good counter at all. I also had the problem that even if I did manage to convince him, I didn't have the first clue about drum machines or even where to get hold of one, never mind how much one might cost. Hang on! I might just have something to convince him after all, "errr, Pop Will Eat Itself use one." I knew Stevie Boy liked PWEI.

"My mate has got a drum machine. I'll ask him if we can borrow it for a while. Let's see how it goes." Fardy settled the argument, brokered a compromise and contributed the solution all with his one and only chip in.

This set us up for a couple of weeks of hard work as Fardy and I beavered away trying to get to grips with the finer intricacies of drum machine programming. It was pretty time consuming and not the most interesting part of music making I've ever been involved with at all. In reality, it was even more boring than turning up four hours early at a venue and waiting around to sound check with only a bag of chips and twenty fags as company (since missing the passport stamp train in Portugal I've never liked being late). Beats per minute (BPM) became our creed, we could now ramp up the speed of songs, and then maintain that speed for the full two minutes fifty seconds.

I could understand Stevie Boy's robotic worry though. We really needed to come up with something other than a metronomic four click intro for each song, and running it alone without any accompanying music didn't have the same feel of a live drummer either. Nevertheless, once we'd got used to playing along to it, MTF morphed from its early very loose and at times rather shambolic form, into a very compact and extremely tight unit indeed. I loved it. Bar some initial arguing and sulking, the MTF sound was finally taking shape. We were almost ready to unleash MTF 3.0. We threw our flowery shirts away, donned stripy tops, fancy waistcoats, combat trousers and chunky trainers (Stevie Boy, not being able to get his enormous feet into chunky trainers, went for monkey boots). All I had to do now was to write some decent lyrics.

.....The lights went down. A cheer went up, etc, etc. Yeah, OK, I got the picture last time. The elevated drum riser was bare save for a tiny little white plastic box. A shiny back lead plugged into its side trailed away to stage left. Three guitar wielding heroes emerged through the whirling dry ice. The singer-guitarist swaggered towards the microphone.

"Wolverhampton! Are you ready to 'indie powercore'?"
The crowd roared in the affirmative.

"Hang on, before we do this thing. Does anyone know Tanya Donnelly's phone number? I need some new lyrics.".....

The transition period of going from having a drummer (G7), to not having one, to having a drummer once more (JSus), to not having one, to having the phone number of a possible drummer, to finding out it was the phone number of a Chinese take-away, to finally employing a drum machine, represented a several month hiatus from playing live. We'd only managed two gigs since MTF's inception as it was, and had had to cancel a return to JB's. We needed to get out there and start gigging. Luckily the reaction to our first demo tape, just like the debut JB's reaction, came as something of a surprise, and possibly justified paying the extra to re-record 'Disintegrating'. We had several venues, mostly across the Midlands and a handful in London, wanting to book us for a gig. We accepted them all; including one opening for a heavy metal band in a staff social club at a mental hospital (I assumed the crowd would be mad for it). I probably wouldn't have accepted this one had I known about the heavy metal band. As it turned out, even though we had a rather nervous start (stage fright of a very different kind), we ended up playing an encore. We were told which song to play, mind. And when a rather large group of gentlemen in some serious biker attire tell you to play 'the reggae one', you don't really want to say no. As a matter of fact, saying no was probably not an option open to us. Once we'd nervously determined that 'the reggae one' was one of ours and not one of Bob Marley's, we played it. This is what we call in the trade a 'character builder'.

The most intriguing response to our demo tape mail out came from Sky Television, then a fledgling satellite broadcaster. A letter dropped through the door of MTF HQ inviting us to audition for a 'music programme' that was in the pipeline. Although I didn't know anyone who actually had satellite television I could see a 'Sold' sign going up on the Home Counties mansion with guitar shaped swimming pool. That the audition was in a tiny pub back room in the wilds of Islington should've been a dark portent of what was about to unfold. The 'Sold' sign clouded all rational thought processes. We accepted.

With our new line up and sound ready to be unleashed on to a wider gig going public (by this time I'd written all the lyrics to all of our new songs) we decided it might be best to get these down on tape before we changed direction again. We booked some more studio time to record our second demo tape 'Schooosh'. Cost was again the predominant choice factor, even more so as we were currently questioning the fiscal wisdom of dropping to a three piece now that it would be a three way split on cost rather than between four. With that in mind going back to Brian Tatler and The Lye was out of the question; we'd hardly been able to afford Mr Tatler's perfectionism and our arguing and sulking on one song, never mind four.

A studio in the Shropshire countryside just about fitted into our budgetary constraints. As before we went on a recce mission to make sure it wasn't set up in someone's living room. On arrival at a huge farmhouse we were met by an awfully well spoken lady, carrying a baby, and an extremely threatening and rather large dog. The awfully well spoken lady, still carrying the baby, had shown us around an impressive looking studio in a converted barn set aside from the farmhouse. She told us that her client base was predominantly film and television production companies, yah! All three of us looked at each other nervously. Was this place going to rock? She must've sensed our apprehension and assured us that she had a fine boy (her exact words) who looked after the pop groups for her. Pop groups? Nervous beggars cannot be serene choosers. We sucked down a valium and booked it.

Tech Boy was the fine boy who looked after the pop bands. Even though he was more into dance music than our brand of pop group he set to work with an enthusiasm that became infectious as the session wore on. The drum machine was an absolute blessing in the studio. Live drums take ages to set up, then ages to mike up, then ages to get the sound levels sorted before you are even ready to record. This can really eat into your session time. To compound things even further, if the drummer fluffs his beats, you have to start the whole song again.

Tech Boy just plugged the drum machine into his thingy jigger, tapped a few keys on a computer whatssit and announced that he was ready for the guitars. We set to the serious business of 'indie powercore'.

Sleeve Notes: 'Schooosh'

It should've been 'Schwooosh', the sound a Teenage Mutant Ninja Turtle's shinobigatana (sword) makes as it scythes through the air. Don't ask. Veiny, a graphic designer who did our artwork for guest list inclusions rather than actual monetary payment, had probably been away with the reggae fairies when he put this sleeve together.

Track 1. 'Marshmellow Brain' (sic) 148BPM

Stevie Boy wanted the BPM's added to the sleeve just like PWEI did. I stole the title from the lyrics to 'Mania', a Throwing Muses song, but changed the 'mallow' to 'mellow'. The rest of the lyrics were my own, as were all on 'Schooosh' and every MTF song thereafter. It told a cautionary tale of the dangers of being seduced by mass marketing and the blatant consumerism bought on by the Thatcher years: XR3i's, wine bars, gold signet rings, all that stuff. It was possibly semi-autobiographical. We played this live right to the end of MTF's days.

Track 2. 'Silly Stupid Eyes' 134BPM

MTF's slowest ever song! And as we discovered at the mental hospital, apparently it was our reggae song. This was definitely autobiographical. My Yoko and I had been going through a bad patch – what do you mean 'rock is your life'? My man crush had gotten worse; I stole this line from The Wonder Stuff's video 'Welcome to the Cheap Seats' (stolen way back then and resurrected for this book). What did she think I meant? Evidently, that had been the wrong thing to say and I found myself single again. It took a while to get the lyrics down for this one. The awfully well spoken lady kept walking in and out of the studio carrying the baby when I was trying to sing 'You make me so fucking angry' in the chorus. I wanted to be a rock star, yet I still had a modicum of social etiquette; I was only a foul mouthed fool (man crush) in front of the ladies when I was on stage.

Track 3. 'Mr. Twilight' 160BPM

This was MTF's fastest song at the time and my last ever attempt at writing a Pixies type tune. It didn't really work. I hadn't followed my formula either, so it failed on two counts. It begs the question: why did we put it on 'Schooosh'? Tech Boy grooved on it though, which may have been the reason we kept it on the tape. While recording it, it looked like he wanted to down a handful of disco biscuits and start throwing some very fast shapes indeed. Fardy never liked this one; possibly the reason it didn't stay on our live set list for that much longer.

Track 4. 'Alfie Can't Stop' 152BPM

It was back to the 'indie powercore' formula here and was definitely my favourite from the 'Schooosh' session. It was about a bloke who had a rather unhealthy and ever growing fondness for Flaming Drambuies. I suppose you could say this was autobiographical too. I can't for the life of me remember why, particularly as the kids (there's that man crush again) were still shouting for it months after we'd stopped doing it, but 'Alfie' also got dropped from our live set not long after.

Feeling pretty pleased with what we'd put down and especially pleased with how quickly we'd put them down (cheapest recording session ever!), we left the studio with a slot booked to return in a week for the mixing session. Unsure of who would argue and sulk on the drum machine's behalf we still hoped that it wouldn't take too long to get mixed with just the three of us throwing toys out of the pram. Even so, to help pay towards the inevitable arguing and sulking, we cancelled that week's rehearsal. Money saving aside, the cancelled rehearsal room doubly made sense, as even though we had the television audition to attend, we had no gigs the week prior to it. We'd be able to keep in shape practising alone, playing along to 'Marshmellow Brain' from a tape of the version we had just recorded.

"Tut, tut, guys," Clipboard TV Girl appeared slightly stressed as we walked into the pub in Islington where the audition was being held. "Guys, guys, guys. You are SO late." We were only ten minutes late, we'd have been thirty minutes early if there had been any parking spaces anywhere near the pub.

"Sorry, nowhere to park the van," I offered. "Where do you want us?"

"Follow me, guys," she sighed and then spoke urgently into her headset. I was impressed by the headset. "Quickly," she added. Luckily we'd had the forethought to carry all our gear down with us. We clattered and cursed behind her down a narrow corridor that led to a room full of people. Although not taking much notice of them I did think that there were a lot of people who were going to be assessing our performance.

"Ok, guys. There's the stage and Marcus. Say hello to Marcus, guys." We mumbled 'hellos', it was like your first day at infant school. "Five minutes to get ready, away you go." She disappeared out of the room, as fast as she'd entered it. Marcus, another television type wearing a headset (no clipboard), was waiting on the stage for us.

"No drummer, guys?" Marcus asked. Was 'guys' a southern thing or a TV thing?

"He's in here," Stevie Boy said holding up our little white plastic box.

"Ah." This sent Marcus into a frenzy of activity as he dashed about trying to decide how a drummer who fitted into a little white plastic box would look in front of the cameras.

"Matt, Matt," Fardy whispered to me furtively.

"What?" I asked impatiently, as I rushed to set my gear up and get my guitar in tune.

"There's a fucking clown over there," he whispered. Did I just hear that correctly, a clown? I looked up.

"There is a clown over there," I said, more to myself than anyone else. I surveyed the room slowly. It didn't compute. They certainly didn't look like the type of people who should be assessing a rock band's chances of appearing on a music programme. Among the many people sat there staring at the stage, not only was there a clown, there was also a twelve year old girl in a diamante leotard clutching an equally sparkly hoola-hoop, a bloke shuffling a pack of cards in full morning attire, six bouncy teenage girls straight from the set of 'Fame' and two, errr, (....searching for the politically correct word), errr, people (that'll do) who could only be described as a heavy duty drag act. I stopped my surveillance. This looked like an audition for some sort of crappy talent show. Ah, I've got it.

"Errr, Marcus, mate, I don't think we're at the right audition like," I said.

"Yep, you are," he said, a smile began to spread across his face.

"Errr, what programme is this for?" I asked. Marcus' smile widened.

"Keith Chegwin's Star Search." Phew! We were at the wrong audition.

"No, we are at the wrong audition, mate. We're here for the music programme." Marcus' smile widened some more. I was developing an intense dislike for this Marcus guy.

"We haven't been able to get many bands to respond to the 'Star Search' letter, so for bands we changed it to 'music programme'. We get a lot more bands these days." At least he didn't say pop groups.

"There's a fucking clown over there," Fardy said again. Stevie Boy and Fardy looked at me. I shrugged my shoulders; part in apology, part in confused submission.

"We're here. We may as well do it. Might get to meet Keith," said Stevie Boy. I slowly nodded in the affirmative; Fardy kept shaking his head and muttering something about clowns.

We did it. It was a disaster. Tech Boy had done something to our drum machine in the studio that meant it wouldn't work through a

188

sound system.[2] Five minutes of random button pressing and head scratching ensued. We gave up. Marcus appeared to be enjoying our discomfort immensely and suggested we just play without the man in the little white box as we were really holding up the proceedings. Everyone else looked on, bemused and bored in equal measures. We reluctantly agreed and raggedly sped through the most shambolic version of 'Marshmellow Brain' we've ever played.[3]

We got the gig. I remember Fardy not being that keen about doing it. The lure of a television appearance, regardless of how cheesy it might be, was too much for Stevie Boy and me to turn down. Those Home Counties mansions with guitar shaped swimming pools weren't going to buy themselves! We wished we had stayed to see the clown's audition, though. Taking our audition as the benchmark (and it was bad, very bad), he must've been totally shit; the sort of shit that is so awfully shit it is totally brilliant. We kept looking, but there wasn't a single clown (save for us three) anywhere to be seen in London Weekend Television's studios (LWT! The ones on the south bank of the Thames, where The South Bank Show comes from!). After waiting around for hours trying to spot the clown, any clown, we were summoned to makeup. Hang on, I've got a site delivery to Teddy and Barry tomorrow, I thought. I am not wearing makeup. No way!

..... *"Fuck me, Ted. Did yow see Matty Boy on the fuckin' tele?"*
"Arr fuckin' did, Bazza. 'E wuz wearin' fuckin mare-cup an' all. Doh 'arf explain why 'e day loike goo-in up thum fuckin' lodders, doh it?"
"Arr, yam not fuckin' wrung, Ted. Bay no wunder thum cor gerra fuckin' drummer, ay?"
"Arr, but dun yow remember when 'e fuckin' cum t' werk as Bela Lugosi? Med yow fuckin' loff, day it, Bazza.".....

I tried to tell the lady that my goth period had been extremely short and completely ill advised. Furthermore, I had a delivery to a building site in the morning. To people I knew. She was having none of it; apparently everybody has to have makeup applied to appear on television. It looked like I had no choice.

We played and sang live in front of a studio audience, Keith Chegwin and the two judges: Derek Nimmo and Lynsey de Paul. I nearly went flying over a stage riser as we launched into the intro. I managed to recover my balance before I became Jeremy Beadle's video out take of the week. It was live, recorded as live, so there were no second chances. I don't think anyone saw me mouth 'shit' or noticed the rasping fart noise my guitar made as I fumbled with the neck during the stumble. Song completed without any further mishaps, I then had to sit on a stool, with Stevie Boy and Fardy standing behind me, while the judges appraised our performance. Derek was very concerned about the lack of a drummer. He could not get his head around it. Lynsey could only come up with 'we were good looking boys', to which I replied (I saw this as my opportunity to get a funny in; John Lennon style) 'errr, I know'. Keith liked that one, nobody else did. Not even the audience! I kept my mouth shut after that. Pffft, it was way better than the cringe inducing knock knock jokes the comic turn had just served up before us. Unlike the clown (that we'd never seen perform) he didn't fit into the 'so shit that it was totally brilliant' bracket, he was just utter shit.

At the end, all the acts had to stand on a stage and wave goodbye to the viewers back home. Being recorded live we were lined up for this rather swiftly. As the camera zoomed in on us all for the closing credits and cheesy wave fest, a TV type (in full clipboard and headset ensemble) could just be seen impatiently pushing Fardy into place on the stage before disappearing from view. You then heard a very loud crack as Fardy put a foot through a sunken stage light. Fardy immediately turned to us and said 'which fucking clown put that there' (unlike the loud crack this wasn't audible to the cameras). Instantaneously Stevie Boy and I exploded into fits of giggles as everyone else around us waved inanely at the camera. A self-importance of TV types glared at us with disdain from behind the camera line (a 'self-importance' can also be used as the collective noun for anyone who carries a clipboard and wears a headset for a living). The giggles lasted long after the cameras had stopped rolling.

We never got to have a chat with Keith and neither Lynsey nor Derek were 'indie powercore' aficionados. Not that we had expected them to be. We finished second last out of six performers. Other than the awful comedian I can't remember anything of the other acts, save for the overall winner: a one man band with a singing dog. A singing dog? It didn't sing, it just yowled occasionally and never in time or tune. In conclusion, Star Search was what we in the trade call both 'character building' and 'an experience'.

.....I woke with a start. Confused. My vision gradually unblurred itself to reveal familiar surroundings. Phew! It had been a dream, an awful dream. Clowns and Keith Chegwin? What on earth could that mean? I rolled over to try and go back to sleep. Oh, hello cat. The cat was curled up next to me. She raised her head slightly and lazily opened one eye.

"Dream? It wasn't a dream you fool." The cat had just spoken to me. In English too!

"Did you just speak to me?" I thought I'd better affirm that I had heard correctly.

"How you could demean yourself?" she said and looked at me with disdain. "On the same bill as a singing dog? I hope you'll be able to sleep better after your duet with Cilla Black tonight.".....

.....I woke with a start. Bolt upright. Confused. Sweating. My vision gradually unblurred itself to reveal familiar surroundings. The cat was fast asleep next to me. Phew! It couldn't talk; of course it couldn't, cats can't talk. It had been a dream, another dream within an awful dream. The cat raised her head, lazily opened both eyes and yawned.

"Again?" she asked. She has just spoken to me! Again! "I hope you are going to wear that nice knitted pullover from granny when you appear on Val Doonican's Christmas Special. Now, either go and get me some food or go back to sleep.".....

.....I woke with a start. Bolt upright. Confused. Sweating. Heart racing. My vision gradually unblurred itself to reveal familiar surroundings. The cat was still on the bed, but sat upright and looking at me with her head tilted to one side. If she's going to talk I thought I'd get the words in first.

"Look, Polly, cats cannot talk. So if you do, I'll know that this is just another dream, okay?"

"Pffft, dreams," she said. Phew! It was another dream. "You appeared on television with a singing dog and you think that we cats can't talk?" Or was it?.....

---

[1] Madchester was the name of a Happy Mondays EP. It somehow got attributed (by the music press?) to the whole Manchester music scene. The Charlatans were often labelled as Madchester, they actually originated in the Wolverhampton area. I know this as Incee Wincee Spider used to rehearse in Wednesbury at the same studios that the early Charlatans did.

[2] If we had read the instruction book, as Tech Boy pointed out later that week, all we had to do was to change it from studio mode to live mode. A three button press procedure.

[3] Not entirely true. We once arrived at a gig in London where we were supposed to open a four band bill to find out that we were the only band who had shown up. The promoter wouldn't let us go on stage until midnight, by which time a couple of us were so drunk that I can't actually remember doing our set. Now, that is another rock 'n' roll fantasy box ticked.

12. The Ego Has Landed

"We are the music makers and we are the dreamers of dreams."
Arthur O'Shaughnessy

*Although 'Schooosh' hadn't captured the power of a live MTF performance
(a bit like a Tony Visconti produced Thin Lizzy album) it received some
pretty decent reviews in the minor music press; even Brum Beat gave it a
good review! We were beginning to believe our own hype and now that I'd
had five minutes of fame I wanted the other ten. When fifteen year old kids,
wearing MTF t-shirts, start asking you to autograph their copies of
'Schooosh' in the middle of Dudley High Street, who wouldn't? Surely we
were only ten minutes away from hoards of rampant groupies besieging the
stage door.*

MTF had grown into quite the cottage industry. Our tapes were
selling well at gigs and through fanzines. We even had some t-shirts
printed. I can't remember, but I guess that it could've been my idea,
given my experience in the European printed t-shirt industry. I knew
a thing or two about t-shirts, I thought. The design phase did lead to
another wasted rehearsal spent arguing and sulking over the design
though. Ah, the joys of design by committee. Once the committee
had a majority vote, we went on to sell out of every batch of the
original 'Gas Mask – Made in Dudley' design we ever had printed.
We then came up with a new design that turned the MTV (Music
Television) logo into MTF. These were doubly popular and hadn't
generated any arguments or sulking in the design process either.

The fanzine was a phenomenon that had carried on from the punk
era. An A5, usually photocopied, booklet (of varying quality of
writing and quantity of readership) that gave voice to and
championed bands that weren't part of the mainstream. They were
the minor music press of their day, and rather like a primitive
internet, helped generate a wider exposure for your band (only if the
editor liked you, if not, they could be as scathing as the major music
papers). We had limited fanzine success with 'Demo-One'; however,
none of us had really believed in that recording and we hadn't really

193

sent that many out. With 'Schooosh' we felt we had something to shout about and carpet bombed them with copies of it. We exploded (more like a cheap firework rather than a drone launched Hellfire missile, but exploded all the same) onto the fanzine scene. Through this exposure we were pretty soon selling tapes across the UK, Europe and the world. We even began to get fan mail:

Liked the tape. Are you playing anywhere near Falkirk? - Scott
Awrite Scott, glad you liked the tape but probably not for a while, sorry - Matt

Brilliant tape. When are you playing in Belfast? - Rohan
Top of the morning Rohan, brilliant might be pushing it a bit, but thanks all the same. Not sure any of our moms would let us go to Belfast, sorry - Matt

We love MTF. You is make play in Stockholm? - Birgit and Tekla xxx
Hej (I looked up where Stockholm was and then, armed with that knowledge, the Swedish for 'hi') Birgit and Tekla, I think the answer to that could be very soon - Matt xxx

Prior to the release of 'Schooosh' we were lucky if we played four gigs a month, now we were doing three or four a week and getting enquiries for many more, as well as for interviews. It was having an impact on my day job. Not because I was regularly getting home in the early hours of the morning, but because I had to keep pulling over to answer my cab phone. It would ring constantly throughout the day with band related enquiries rather than work related queries. I once blocked Nottingham city centre's pedestrian area for thirty minutes while I took a call about playing a gig in London, and then had to try and get hold of Stevie Boy and Fardy at their places of work to make sure they could do it before I rang the venue back. We needed a manager. We put ads in the music press. We didn't get a single response.

194

"A mate of mine is interested in managing us," said Fardy.

"Is he any good?" Stevie Boy asked. We'd soon find out the answer to that particular question.

"How should I know?" Fardy retorted. We'd soon find out that it was a shame he didn't know.

"Let's get him down here, see what we reckon," I said.

Potential Manager came down to our next rehearsal. He said all the right things, or at least we thought he said all the right things: 'regular gigs', 'build a following', etc, etc. A quick committee meeting, (no arguing or sulking) resulted in a unanimous decision and the unconditional offer of a Flaming Drambuie and the post of The Manager. We handed over all our current commitments, about twelve confirmed gigs, along with all the other venue contact details we had, as well as a list of places we'd like to start playing.

"No problem," said The Manager. "Leave it with me." We left it with him. We shouldn't have.

In a term shorter than Brian Clough's time in charge at Leeds United, The Manager cancelled most of the gigs we already had in place (he left just the local ones) and didn't add any at all. I only found this out after one of the venues rang me to confirm our cancellation. When we finally got hold of him (he was very difficult to get hold of by phone) we asked why, to be told that he thought we should be concentrating on local venues and not to worry about elsewhere, particularly London. When I asked if he had added any more local gigs then, he replied that we already played at the local venues and had gigs booked at them before he came on board. I probably then used some choice words straight from Teddy and Barry's school of English; something along the lines of 'fuck me, am yow 'avin' a fuckin' loff?'. Exasperated, we held a brief committee meeting and came to the unanimous decision to sack The Manager. Essentially this led to a deep suspicion of anyone who came along and promised the earth for their ten percent and, although we had a couple of offers, MTF remained self-managed for the duration.

I got back on the phone and managed to salvage half of the gigs The Manager had cancelled. I understood the not playing in London argument to an extent, starting out we'd done the trek down the M1 to play in front of three or four people and the bored bar staff without getting paid enough to cover the fuel to get there, let alone back home. We'd moved on from those types of venues. We were now getting paid enough to cover the fuel both ways, kebabs and chips all round and beers for the non-drivers. We were also starting to generate a minor but growing fan base as well as a minor but growing press interest. A couple of staffers from the music papers were regularly enquiring about when MTF had any dates in town. Town?

"Errr, which town?" I enquired.

"London, of course," Journo replied.

"Errr, is it still called Old London Town then?" I asked, totally exposing my country boy heritage.

There was another reason we enjoyed playing London. Me Brother was at university there. His house, in the wilds of Isleworth, gave us an after show party base (sometimes there were even girls there). To save having to drive up and down the M1 for every gig we tried to arrange blocks of gigs down there across four or five days, sometimes playing twice a day. It was almost like being on tour! To our minds, with all things considered, after show parties probably being at the top of considerations, to stop playing in London at this point in time made no sense at all.

"Which way, lads?" Stevie Boy asked from the wheel of the van. We were trying to make our way from a gig in north London towards the inevitable after show party in Isleworth. We were lost. Me Brother and Veiny, one of his impoverished student house mates and also our cassette sleeve designer, made for very useful and unpaid roadies.

"How should we know?" Fardy and I slurred in unison.

"I was asking the other two," Stevie Boy said, with more than a hint of irritation. "C'mon quick, which way?" Useful roadies they may have been. Future black cabbies they were not. Their grasp of the Knowledge[1] was limited to a two mile radius of their house in Isleworth that took in the Students Union, nine pubs, five pool halls and just shy of a million fast food outlets. It did not extend to underground live music venues in north London.

"Just follow the pretty lights, man," replied an equally slurry Veiny. Somehow Stevie Boy eventually piloted us back to Isleworth.

What was quite a shock to me; given the blatant man crush sycophancy of 'Schooosh', was that no one who reviewed it in the press or fanzines referenced the more than obvious The Wonder Stuff influence. One reviewer, who did give it a decent write up, even likened it to The Fall or early Gang of Four. We couldn't see that ourselves at all, especially as none of us knew what either of those bands sounded like. What the reviews did more than anything though, regardless of misinterpreted influences, was give us a sense of self belief in our songs; a confidence boost if you like (that should probably read 'ego boost'). However inflated our egos were from this sudden recognition it didn't help deter the apathy that had begun to set in from playing the same ten songs over and over again, week in week out. We needed to expand our set list. As I was about to sit down and write some new songs, The Wonder Stuff released 'Never Loved Elvis'[2]. Excellent, perfect timing I thought. I rushed out and bought it. I listened to it, and then listened again. For me it was as disappointing as rushing down the offie for a four pack of Special Brew only to find that all they had on the shelves were small tins of non-alcoholic lager: less 'indie powercore', more 'stadiumbore'. My man crush was over. As it turned out 'Never Loved Elvis' can actually be cited as having the greatest influence on MTF's future career and direction. At the time though, I began to panic: where on earth was I going to get my song ideas from now?

Salvation was not very far away at all; in fact, it was brought to my attention by our Swedish fan club. In a lull in our gigging schedule, Stevie Boy and I went to see Mega City Four (Birgit's favourite band) and Senseless Things (Tekla's favourite band) in Birmingham. As one door had closed, another two were swung wide open. My muse was well and truly thrown. I rushed out and bought everything by Mega City Four and Senseless Things I could get my hands on (neither had reached their tricky third albums yet). I spent a week listening to them solidly in the cab and then a further week analysing my new purchases in my bedroom. It was deconstruction without the modern man crush. At the end of this process I was very pleased with myself and yet, in spite of this self pleasure, I was once again very concerned. Pleased for exactly the same reasons as before: I could figure out how to play all the guitar parts, etc, etc. And just like before, concerned for exactly the same reasons. At the forefront was: why hadn't I been to see Mega City Four or Senseless Things earlier? Fighting through the murky fog of these concerns was the conviction that through this latest deconstruction I could still use my formula for 'indie powercore' superstardom. I set to work.

Mega City Four and Senseless Things would also have another pivotal impact on MTF. After seeing them, Stevie Boy was convinced that we needed to revert to a real drummer. I had never played in a band as tight as we were with the drum machine, so I was dead against it. Then we had a local band, Fretblanket[3], support us somewhere (The Market Tavern in Kidderminster, possibly?). They were pretty impressive, had a real drummer, were powerful, very tight and didn't do slow songs either. This hardened Stevie Boys resolution even further, weakened mine and also convinced Fardy of the merits of a real drummer approach. I was out voted. Damn that decision by committee. I didn't bother arguing. I just sulked while they placed a 'Drummer Wanted' ad in the local music press and got on with writing some new songs.

Combining my newly broadened musical horizons with my 'indie powercore' formula, the new songs I wrote certainly moved MTF away from sounding purely like starry eyed The Wonder Stuff wannabes and transitioned us into the realms of sounding like 'indie powercore' wannanbes, with a slightly wider range of influences: a dash of The Wonder Stuff, a pinch of Mega City Four and a soupçon of Senseless Things thrown in for good measure. Everything appeared to be slotting into place once more; we were developing our own sound, we were gigging regularly, our tapes were selling well (yes, even the first one), kids were walking around in MTF t-shirts (sold at a profit but nowhere near the profit Villa Bob and I had made in Portugal) and the mail bag at MTF HQ was growing steadily.

From this increased mail bag came another letter from Birgit and Tekla that told me they were coming over to London soon to see, among others, Mega City Four, and asked whether I'd be going. I had no intention of schlepping down to London to see a band I would be able to see in the Midlands again soon, regardless of how enticing meeting a couple of Swedish groupies may have sounded. For one, they'd never even sent me a picture of themselves, let alone a pair of either's pants (I don't have a ladies underwear fetish, it was another rock 'n' roll box that hadn't yet been ticked: Tom Jones had them thrown at him, Ian Gillan used to get them sent to him). I wrote back anyway saying that we were busy gigging and also rehearsing new material ready to go back into the studio (all true), so I probably wouldn't be able to make the gigs they were going to. I popped it into the post and thought nothing of it.

"Matt, c'mon mate, a bloke who says he's from Sounds wants to talk to us and Fardy wants to get going back to your brother's pretty soon too," Stevie Boy shouted into my ear, as he tried to make himself heard above the main band who'd just taken to the stage. We'd just played a half drunken set (apart from Fardy who was driving, yet we had played drunker) at The Robey in Finsbury Park. Like JB's it always had live bands on, although it did have a smaller crowd, or it did when we played there anyway; dark and dingy, beer sticky floors, blokes whose girlfriends it would be wise not to look at, never mind avoid spilling their pint. The night before Splodgenessabounds, of 'Two pints of lager and a packet of crisps' fame (the song not the TV show), played there and a couple nights after us 999 ('one of the longest lived groups of the punk era' according to AllRovi.com) were appearing there. How we fitted into this mainly punk venue I'm not sure, but I had played it several times (it was where Plum Fingers had been thrown back on stage by skinheads for an encore in our Incee Wincee days) and we always seemed to go down well there. Tonight had been no exception. I liked The Robey.

"C'mon, Matt," Stevie Boy urged again. "There's the Sounds bloke and Fardy'll go without you." I was sat at the back of the pub, with a couple of pints on the table in front of me, and a Swedish girl on each arm. Birgit and Tekla had shown up to see us play. Groupies, real groupies! Somehow through my post gig euphoria and a rather expensive beer fuelled haze (London prices, I didn't want to go anywhere near the Drambuie this far south of Dudley) we'd hit it off. No doubt I was wearing the 'goggles', yet they were nowhere near on the strongest lens setting, and they didn't need to be either: I'd only got my arms around eighteen year old indie versions of Agnetha and Anni-Frid.

Stevie Boy's urgings had posed me with a rock 'n' roll dilemma though: interview with the music press and chauffeured through the pretty lights back to the after show party in Isleworth, or, Swedish groupies and, errr, what? To be honest, my mind had been well London priced by now, it was beyond thinking any further than the tune to 'Lay All Your Love On Me'[4]. There was only one thing for it, I had to ask myself the question I always ask myself when faced with any sort of rock 'n' roll dilemma: what would Keith Richards do? Errr, actually, never mind consulting Keith Richards, I could've also asked myself: what would Teddy and Barry do?

..... *"Fuck me Bazza, am yow lissnin' t' saft lod 'ere?"*

"Arr fuckin' am Ted. 'E doh loike gooin' up thum fuckin' lodders, wearin' mare-cup on the tele an' now 'e doh even know the fuckin' doings with sum bostin' Swedish fanny? Tay fuckin' roight ya know, Ted."

"Arr, yam not fuckin' wrung, Bazza. 'Ay, but dun yow remember the toime...." .....

Regardless of who I used as my rock 'n' roll dilemma consultancy service, I believe the answer would've been the same.

"Do the Sounds cat without me, man," I slurred loudly back in my best Keith. Slurring back in my best Teddy and Barry would've just sounded like me doing a broader than usual Black Country accent.

"What about your brother's then?" Stevie Boy asked. I knew exactly what Keith, Teddy and Barry would've done here too.

"I'm gonna hang with the Swedish cats, man." I gave Stevie Boy a Keith Richards shrug, which was probably accompanied by a Bill Wyman grin. Stevie Boy disappeared. Fifteen minutes later Fardy appeared, saw that I was busy and let me know they were off. About thirty seconds after that Veiny, who'd been on roadie duties again, bounced over to me with a hopeful look spread right across his face.

"Is there a spare one? C'mon, man, rock 'n' roll," he shouted eagerly as he gave me a high five. If Birgit and Tekla had heard him they didn't let on, although they might have wondered what the high five was all about. Now, I didn't want to seem greedy, and not that Birgit and Tekla had given me any impression that they wanted me to pimp either one of them out, yet through my London priced beer haze I hadn't considered sharing at all, my mind had now jumped to changing the lyrics of 'Knowing Me, Knowing You' to 'Knowing Me, Knowing Two' and was way too busy trying to work out the batting order. Veiny's question threw me another rock 'n' roll dilemma. Essentially this one boiled down to share and share alike, or sort out the batting order and tick a rock 'n' roll fantasy box? What would Keith do?

"Sorry, dude. I'm ticking the boxes." Exactly what Keith would've done!

"Rock 'n' roll, man. It was worth a try." Veiny didn't seem too perturbed, he grinned, gave me a double thumbs up and shot off to find the others before they left him to follow the pretty lights on his own. From there on in everything melted into what I can only best describe as an ethereal experience. I vaguely remember having several more drinks (I must've been holding our appearance money) and at some point beyond that jumping into a cab with Birgit and Tekla (no idea where we were headed, I was way more preoccupied with the batting order conundrum than where we were going). Between jumping into the cab and waking up the next morning, I just have fleeting and very obscure memories that could've happened or were either (more probable) figments of my beer blurred imagination.

I awoke the next morning in the small state of confusion that borders the major state of hung over. Bright light streamed through a crack in the curtains. As my senses battled to make their way through the London priced day after fuzziness, I surveyed my surroundings. I wasn't at Me Brother's house that was for sure. This bedroom was way too modern and clean to be in an Isleworth student abode. Yes, it was a bedroom. Promising. Discarded clothes were strewn around the place, some of them definitely ladies wear. Very promising. There were also a couple of empty bottles of Thunderbird on the floor (I've always known how to woo the ladies). I glanced to my right. Wow! There was a blond girl in bed with me. Score! Ah, just the one though. It was vaguely coming back to me. There were two last night? I swung my legs out of the bed and heard a grunt as I hit something lumpy and blanket covered by my feet. It was a dark haired girl. Another girl. Two girls! Ah, of course, Birgit and Tekla. TOTAL SCORE! Rock 'n' roll fantasy box well and truly ticked. Twice! I wondered if we were on the eleventh floor. I looked down at the discarded clothes to try and locate my jeans. Where were they? I couldn't see them. Oh, found them. Not quite the score I'd thought. I was completely and totally fully clothed, right down to still wearing my chunky Fila trainers (I did like those trainers). Surely after a passionate night of entertaining Swedish lady friends I wouldn't have got dressed before getting into bed? Yet, I had no recollection of much from last night at all, the only explanation I could come up with, and given the taste in my mouth and searing pain when I moved my head it was a very feasible explanation, was that I'd passed out and snored my way through to the morning before any entertaining had begun. If that was the case, I suppose there was the minor consolation that it was way less embarrassing than passing out and snoring mid-entertainment. Forlorn, I tried to cheer myself up with the thought that this must've happened to Keith at some time or other, surely?

The girls made me some coffee and rustled up some breakfast. It was eaten through an awkward and, on my part, embarrassed silence. They were probably mulling over the lyrics to 'Gimme, Gimme, Gimme, A Man After Midnight' whereas I had moved away from pondering Abba song lyrics and was focussed on getting the hell out of Dodge as soon as I could. I finally made my excuses and exited what turned out to be a modern flat complex. After having to climb over the locked security gate, I dropped in to a very quiet and unfamiliar street indeed. During the focus on my immediate extraction plan I should've thought to ask them where on earth we were. It took me fifteen minutes of blindly wandering around wherever I was before I came across any semblance of a busy road to follow. I immediately set off, unbeknownst to me, in totally the wrong direction, before I eventually came across a newsagent.

"I'll have twenty Marlboro please, mate. And, errr, where am I?" I asked the newsagent.

"You're in Camberwell, my son," replied Jolly Cockney the newsagent. Camberwell? Isn't that where Windy Miller comes from? "Errr, Camberwell, eh?" I had no idea where Trumptonshire was in relation to London. "Errr, is it anywhere near Isleworth?" Jolly Cockney laughed at this. Apparently no, and I'd also pronounced it wrong. Once we'd established the correct pronunciation of Isleworth ('eye-zull-wurff'), we then ascertained that he and several of his transient customers had never studied The Knowledge; not one of them could give me any sort of directions towards Isleworth. I was totally lost now then, especially as it was daytime and there were no pretty lights to follow. At length I managed to determine where Trumptonshire was in relation to London, and I asked him to point me towards Old London Town instead. I set off on foot, hoping to come across somewhere or something I recognised. An hour later I reached the Elephant and Castle tube station. Finally a place I knew. They ought to name all the tube stations after pubs; I'd be able to find my way around then. My day job didn't take me into London that often (and never into Trumptonshire) so my knowledge of The Knowledge extended little beyond knowing that Covent Garden was on the Piccadilly line and from there I could get to Osterley, the closest tube station to Me Brother's house. I jumped on the tube to Covent Garden. I had another problem now though. I'd just blown my last fiver on fags and a tube ticket to Covent Garden. I was totally skint. I'd either spent last night's appearance money on beer, taxi's, Thunderbird and this morning's fags or the girls had robbed me after I'd passed out and snored. I remembered a taxi ride and had seen empty bottles of Thunderbird this morning, so while I couldn't be one hundred percent sure, the size of my hangover and London prices probably meant that being robbed by the girls was not the reason for my poor financial predicament.

I could only see two options here: make a reverse charge call to my folks to get Me Brother's phone number (I really didn't fancy doing this one) or, apply to become a Big Issue seller and earn enough money to get the tube to Osterley.

"Big Issue. Big Issue, dahlin'?" I practiced out loud for the interview as I wandered around Covent Garden wondering where you actually applied. "Big Issue, guv?" I was getting a few strange looks, but not bad, I thought. However, no matter how good I was at shouting 'Big Issue' at random passersby I wasn't going to make tonight's gig if I went down this route. Damn! That realisation brought me reluctantly back to option number one. I bit the bullet and made the reverse charge call. Three reverse charge calls (I misdialled Me Brother's number the first time) and two hours later Fardy picked me up from Covent Garden and we set off in search of that night's venue (somewhere in Harlesden, no idea where that was in relation to Isleworth either). Rock 'n' roll! The legend of the Camberwell Foreign Exchange was born. While I've never exactly told the true events of the Camberwell Foreign Exchange (until now I'd always employed 'don't ask, don't tell'), I had never lied about it either; the rest of the band and Me Brother's house mates just assumed whatever they wanted to assume. There is nothing wrong with letting others build your own rock 'n' roll legend.

.....The singer-guitarist and the rest of the band stood nervously at the side of the stage waiting for the announcer to introduce them to the expectant crowd. Stage lights flashed as dry ice swirled around the stage floor. The crowd roared as the introducer shouted the band's name. Three guitar wielding heroes emerged through the whirling dry ice. The singer-guitarist swaggered towards the microphone.

"WOLVERHAMPTON! ARE YOU READY TO ROCK?"
The crowd roared back in the affirmative.....

This wasn't a dream.

This was very real.

We weren't opening for Judas Priest mind. MTF were just about to step out on to the stage of Wolverhampton's Wulfrun Hall in front of nearly seven hundred people. It was the final of The Express & Star's battle of the bands competition, where ninety odd bands had been whittled down to just five hopeful contenders. The Wulfrun is not quite the Civic Hall, but it is part of the Civic Hall complex, and if you were to graph this on a rock 'n' roll credibility scale of one to ten, where appearing on Keith Chegwin's Star Search would've scored zero, it merited at least a six and a half. Earlier we'd drawn straws to determine the running order and had managed to luck the second to last spot out of the five finalists. Brilliant! Everybody should've had a few by then, hopefully that would include the judges too. Last on would've been better, but we happily took second best on the running order. I felt for Jain Faith, one of the other bands who we had played with locally several times. They drew the shortest straw and had to open the evening. If they had gone on later they should've had a pretty good chance of winning it outright.

This was very, very real.

Ticking yet another rock 'n' roll fantasy box real.

We'd done photo shoots and interviews leading up to it and now we had 'Access All Areas' laminates and our own dressing room. The rider was a bit shit mind. Four cans of Harp? I wanted a bowl of blue M&M's, a bottle of Drambuie and Tanya Donnelly's phone number.

I didn't actually shout 'Wolverhampton! Are you ready to rock?' either. Instead, overwhelmed by the occasion, our own dressing room, my shiny 'Access' laminate and performing in the presence of a multitude of the Midlands' rock luminaries, that included the judges Noddy Holder and Dave Hill (seventies rock legends Slade), I blew it. I swaggered towards the microphone, struck the requisite clutching guitar with legs apart rock pose and shouted, "HELLO!"; I didn't even shout 'Hello, Wolverhampton'. The crowd didn't roar back either, it was more like a tailed off response of 'What the...?'. A brief look of self admonishment flashed across my face before I regained composure and launched into 'Marshmellow Brain'. From there on in we rocked our thirty minute set. We loved the thirty minute set length. My 'indie powercore' song writing formula meant that every song we had came in somewhere between two minutes thirty and three minutes dead, depending on how many BPM's we'd ramped it up to on the drum machine. While we had to play at least nine songs, it did mean that we were value for money, as you'd get at least three extra slices of 'indie powercore' compared to most other bands on the thirty minute set circuit.

We stormed it! After thirty minutes of top quality 'indie powercore' we thrashed out the final power chord finish and bounced off the stage to what sounded like, if I'm not very much mistaken, an adoring public. I'd just played Wolverhampton Wulfrun Hall. I'd just played The Wulfrun Hall! That was close enough to the Civic Hall to tick another rock 'n' roll fantasy box. Free Harp lager had never tasted so sweet.

We came last!

What did Noddy Holder and Dave Hill know? Quite a bit actually. Cue assorted quotes from the judging panel:

'The panel was most impressed with MTF's performance' - And why wouldn't they be?

'MTF had fine musical abilities and an impressive stage show' - We had my song writing formula and we did like to bounce.

'The panel was also impressed with Matt Rothwell's performance, a front man with star quality' - The ego had most definitely landed! I'll be booked in for an appointment with Cynthia Plaster Caster[5] before the year is out.

'However, the winners had outstanding commercial appeal, youth and talent' – Never mind that, did you see the last one? Just in case you didn't, it said 'Matt Rothwell is a front man with star quality'.

"Matt, this is G-Man, he's the drummer I told you about," said Stevie Boy, as we stood around The Wulfrun more than a little disappointed at the final outcome. First prize had been three grand's worth of recording; we'd never spent more than five hundred quid, we could have argued and sulked until our hearts were very content indeed during the mixing process.

"Alright, mate," I nodded to G-Man noncommittally. He did look the part though, yet I still wasn't that keen on reverting back to a live drummer.

"Alright," G-Man nodded back with a similar level of reserve.

"What do you reckon then? Fancy joining us?" Stevie Boy asked him.

"Yeah, OK, I'll give it a go," he replied coolly. Fardy was nearby talking to his mate DMO (drum machine owner). DMO's ears pricked up and he leaned into our little group.

"Oh, if you're having a real drummer, then I'm having my drum machine back," he said sulkily.

"Well, I've got my own drum machine, mate. So you can fuck right off." I decided that I was going to like G-Man after all. Forget my earlier reticence, he had just passed the audition without banging a single drum. Hmm, his own drum machine, eh? Now that gave me the idea for a cunning plan.

.....*"Here is a box, a musical box, wound up and ready to play. But this box can hide a secret inside. Can you guess what is in it today?" Didn't the narrator used to be Brian Cant? This narrator fellow sounds rather like Ozzy Osbourne trying to do a Brian Cant impression. A long haired figure clutching a guitar emerges from the box, the musical box.*

"It's Matt the singer-guitarist," Ozzy Brian says. "Hello, Matt the singer-guitarist."

Matt waves at the camera.

"What adventures are we going to have today then Matt? It's a nice guitar, are you going to play us a song?"

Matt shakes his head.

"Are you going to try and pull the Swedish flower seller girls from the town square again?"

Matt nods his head.

"And are you going to entertain them in your hotel room this time?"

Matt looks side to side furtively, then back at the camera and then nods his head eagerly.

"Really?" Ozzy Brian asks doubtfully. "Are you sure? Won't you get so drunk that you pass out without knowing whether you're in Camberwell, Chigley or Trumpton?"

Matt shakes his head vigorously.

"Are you sure?"

Matt pauses then bows his head shamefully and begins to shake it slowly.

"Not to worry Matt. We've all been there, I know I have and you should ask Keith Richards the number of times it's happened to him."

Matt raises his head, looks back at the camera and slowly smiles; 'I knew it' written all over his face.....

[1] The Knowledge: the in-depth study of a number of pre-set London street routes and places of interest that cab drivers in the city must complete to obtain a licence to operate a black cab.

[2] The Wonder Stuff's difficult third album. It sounds like the record company wanted them to shift some units in America. Gone was the three minute power pop, replaced by FM radio friendly stadium rock. Violins and pianos?

[3] In my humble opinion Fretblanket were the best live band we ever played with and should've gone much further than they actually did. They released two albums before their premature demise, citing the lack of support in the British music press. Check their debut album 'Junkfuel'.

[4] 'Lay All Your Love On Me': From the Abba album 'Supertrooper' which also appears in the film 'Mamma Mia'. Proper Wife made me watch it.

[5] Cynthia Plaster Caster: You may want to Google this for yourself. I can tell you that her clients have included Jimi Hendrix, Eric Burdon (The Animals), Noel Redding (The Jimi Hendrix Experience), Clint Mansell (PWEI) and Pete Shelley (The Buzzcocks).

13. Beautifully Absurd

"A single dream is more powerful than a thousand realities. "
J. R. R. Tolkien

*Once my cunning plan to use a live drummer with a stripped down drum kit **and** a drum machine had been accepted (minimal arguing and sulking), G-Man became the vital final piece of the MTF jigsaw. Rock 'n' roll fantasy boxes were at last being ticked with abandon, left, right and centre. The guitar shaped swimming pool may have been a long way off and I still hadn't got Tanya Donnelly's phone number, yet it was becoming increasingly difficult to distinguish between however many realities and the single dream.*

Though 1991 hadn't started that well for me personally, the Wulfrun Hall gig and G-Man's arrival was to set the foundation stones of MTF's annus mirabilis[1]. Just before New Year's Eve I had suffered a recurrence of an old trainee erection engineer back injury. Originally sustained, I guess, from carrying Teddy and Barry's oversized breakfast and then lunch butties half way across a never ending landscape of windswept building sites; although it may have been more to do with all the heavy lifting I did on the ground because I didn't like going up the ladders.

.....*"'E day loike goo-in up thum fuckin' lodders did 'e, Bazza?"*
"Arr, yam not fuckin' wrung, Ted.".....

This particularly bad recurrence had me laid up in hospital for a week and resulted in me not being able to work for a year or so. More disappointing than not being able to do the happy little jig of joy that not being able to work for a year or so entails, I couldn't attend to the serious business of live 'indie powercore' for a while. On the positive side, though we did have to cancel several gigs and I had to employ someone to drive my van (not the most ideal long term business model for a single vehicle fleet, granted), this actually fitted in very well with my attending to the serious business of

211

writing some new 'indie powercore' songs. Under the judgemental gaze of Strict Parental Law I once again sat around the house and strummed my guitar all day. Further adding to the positive side, my long term recovery plan also got me out of: any driving to gig or rehearsal room duties (when I was fit enough to play, obviously), and having to do any of the heavy lifting when we arrived at gig or rehearsal venues. It also provided me with a veritable cocktail of drugs that would've made The Rolling Stones' (1960-70's line up) eyes light up. They were on prescription and for pain relief, mind; although I think there was a warning about not taking the pink and blue ones with alcohol, and come to think about it the yellow ones didn't sit too well on several cans of Special Brew either.

With a whole load of new songs ready and MTF riding a wave of post Wulfrun Hall hype[2], G-Man joined at just the right time. Although G-Man was Yoko'd and was only let out to play once or twice a week, we did have the shared interests of alcohol consumption and making music; we hit it off straight away. He hadn't seen us play before the Wulfrun Hall but had been aware of the band before he'd even seen the 'drummer wanted' ad. Stevie Boy and I used to reverse-shoplift copies of 'Schooosh' into Our Price in Dudley (and possibly into the Stourbridge and Halesowen branches too). We'd furtively sneak up to the cassette singles stand and place a couple of copies of 'Schooosh' straight in at number five and then hang around to see if anyone picked them up. We really didn't have a great deal to occupy our time on Saturday mornings while we waited for the pubs to open. With the reverse–shoplifting idea in mind we'd briefed Veiny to put a barcode on the cover artwork to make it look like a real cassette. He'd told us that it would cost about twenty quid to have a real barcode generated. We checked the MTF bank balance. The cupboard was bare. The last few quid had just been ploughed into another batch of t-shirts.

"We're skint, mate. Errr," I said to Veiny, on learning of the barcode issue.

"You don't pay me as it is, so I ain't fronting it," Veiny replied. Doh! It was a fair point though.

"Errr," I said and racked my brains for inspiration. Now Villa Bob would have said something like 'there are no such things as problems, only solutions'. All I said was, "errr," as I continued to struggle to come up with an alternative barcode idea. "Errr, hang on," there are no problems, just solutions. "You're a graphic designer. Can't you just make one up?" I asked.

"Hmmm," you could tell he was considering the cheaper design challenge. "Yeah, alright then," he finally replied. Problem solved.

Unbeknownst to us at that critical design point in time, Our Price was where G-Man worked. It was from one of these reverse-shoplifted tapes that he first became aware of MTF. Not so much from the music, but from when anyone had attempted to buy it. On scanning the barcode his till had shown 'Durex Exciter – Extra Large'. After several more surprised attempts G-Man gave up, rang it up manually and thought nothing more about it. Veiny obviously conformed to the 'minimum effort, maximum sloth' ethos too; he just copied one from a packet of condoms and added it to the artwork without telling us about the barcode's provenance. Once G-Man had rung Stevie Boy to respond to the 'drummer wanted' ad and found out that it was for MTF, he had rushed over to the cassette singles stand to see if there were anymore of the mysterious condom cassettes on the shelves. There were. That week we were riding high at number two; we just couldn't knock Bryan Adams' 'Everything I do' off the number one spot.

Before we could do anything though, we had to programme G-Man's drum machine. He had Wednesdays off, so on Tuesday nights we met up in the pub, which soon progressed to all night in the pub followed by a curry / Chinese / kebab / chips (depending on whose house we were staying at) before finally setting to work with the drum machine the following day.

Drum machine programming is a dull monotonous task at the best of times; it now became a murderous chore. For four consecutive Wednesdays we sat in a room replete with gallon plus hangovers and the faint, yet fetid and all pervading, fug of the previous evening's culinary delight. For four consecutive Wednesdays the machine

213

pulsed through a Marshall four by twelve speaker cabinet like a platoon of trigger happy insurgents squeezing off very well coordinated bursts of AK47 rifle fire indeed. After an arduous month of Wednesdays had passed, and the last fetid take-away fumes had thankfully dissipated, we had a drum machine full of less than three minute slices of pounding 'indie powercore' rhythms. It was time to hit the live circuit once more. And, maybe it was the right time to hit the studio again.

G-Man made his live MTF debut at JB's in Dudley (where else?) a couple of weeks after we'd finished programming the drum machine. The bite of a live snare drum and attack of the cymbals must have really added to the live MTF experience; we were even called back for an encore! We always did encores, but used to wait for about thirty seconds and then come straight back on and do one regardless of crowd reaction, but this time it was actually merited. Stevie Boy did get slightly carried away during the encore and decided to join in with the stage divers. He forgot that there is a lead, of limited length, that connects your bass guitar to your amplifier. His lead wasn't long enough. As he jumped from the stage, it pulled to critical length, then went past the point of no return. A look of realisation spread across his face in mid jump and a loud pop emanated from his amp as the lead unplugged itself and shot through the air with a ferocious velocity. It missed decapitating a spiky haired girl who was dancing down the front by a matter of millimetres. Not wanting to lose face Stevie Boy danced about in the crowd for a few seconds still playing his now silent bass, then climbed back on stage to looks from Fardy and me that said 'you didn't fully think that one through, did you?'. Oxford, Kidderminster, Leicester and London soon beckoned, as did the studio. Yes, it was the right time to hit the studio again.

You'd have thought that we would have learnt our lesson by now. But no, cost once again dictated our choice of recording studio. We rocked up to an industrial unit on the outskirts of Stourbridge ready to lay down some new MTF less than three minute 'indie powercore'. As before, we had given it a cursory visit prior to giving them a definitive booking. It had all the right looking thingy-jigs with the right looking twiddly bits; the blokes who worked there talked a good game and we knew of several local bands that had used it. What we should've done was asked the bands who had used it what they thought of it.

"You know what you boys need?" No, but I'm sure you are about to tell us, you've told us every other opinion you've had in the last three hours. He hadn't been around during our pre-booking recce but it looked like we'd drawn the short straw with Sound Engineer Guy. I thought I'd better respond to this quickly before Fardy piped up with 'a decent bloody sound engineer for a start, mate'. The session wasn't going that well.

"Errr, no." Not much of an answer but at least it stopped Fardy chipping in.

"Well, what you boys need," he said, before lighting up his tenth pipe of the session. "What you boys really need, and I reckon you do, is an accordion player and some trumpets." If it hadn't been for the thick fog of Hogarth ready rubbed swirling about our heads I might've questioned whether it was crack cocaine in his pipe. "No? I reckon you do, boys." Too gob smacked to even respond, we all stared at him as though it was indeed crack in his pipe. Sound Engineer Guy shrugged and turned back to the mixing desk.

"An accordion? Trumpets?" Fardy whispered under his breath and then in leant towards me. "Who is this fucking clown? Does he think we're trying to shag Eileen?"[3] I shook my head in bemused resignation, popped a yellow one and took a long swig of beer.

Sleeve Notes: '152 or Faster'

I seem to remember that we had a lot of arguing and sulking over what to call this one, but can only remember that '152 or Faster' was the eventual compromise. It should've heralded the arrival of the new MTF 'mega-wonder-things' sound, yet we were totally disappointed with the end product. It was our tricky third album and not because of the songs or any change of musical direction either. It was decided, very quickly too (no arguing or sulking whatsoever), that this would be the last time we'd use a budget studio. There wasn't even any arguing or sulking during the mixing process, we just wanted out of the Hogarth and opinionated miasma as quickly as we could.

Track 1. 'Shot Down, Big Sky' 156BPM

A little bit of politics and Fardy's favourite MTF song (I think; it wasn't one hundred percent clear from his email). I was never overtly, or even covertly, political; although for sport I used to take the polar opposite stance whenever The Thrill (make that anyone) started droning on about politics in the pub. We were twenty something, all I needed to know was where my next pint or female experience was coming from, not how criminal it was that some toffee-nosed, failed Oxbridge barrister was adjusting the payment deficit to suit his own bourgeios needs. Surely that's a given, no matter which side of the fence you represent? Then along came the poll tax. I found a political stance and refused to pay. Then, along came the bailiffs who threatened to take my guitar and gear away as payment. I quickly reneged on my lofty ideals, paid up and wrote this song instead. Right on, brother!

Track 2. 'Bitter End' 152BPM

I didn't really do love songs. I must've been sixteen the last time I wrote one. If there was ever an imaginary tomato ketchup bottle that needed to be waved, it was at the sixteen year old me who wrote love songs. Now, obviously more mature, I did break up songs instead, and not the 'oh, you've left me, I'm so sad' type. They were more along the lines of 'look darlin', you've started to get on my nerves, can you go and find yourself another bloke or should I just dump you now'. The first line of the first verse was *'Another boring night on the sofa with you'*; another line was *'I no longer love the way you comb your hair'*. The twenty-three year old me probably (probably?) merited an imaginary tomato ketchup bottle wave too. Sound Engineer Guy ruined this; in fact it might even have benefited from an accordion and some trumpet work. It certainly couldn't have made it sound any worse, that's for sure. We closed the door and switched the lights out.

Track 3. 'Overdose' 156BPM

'What's the use of telling lies, c'mon baby, let's break those ties'; another break up song that wasn't planned to appear on '152 or Faster'. The session was going so badly that we swapped out the new MTF song we had planned to record and replaced it with 'Overdose'. It wasn't even an MTF song. I had written this back in my Incee Wincee days as an attempt at a 'retro post punk meets grebo' song; I had even slotted in the riff from Pop Will Eat Itself's 'There Is No Love Between Us Anymore'. MTF still played it live occasionally, which meant we already had the drums programmed and ready to go. Given how the session had panned out so far we didn't hold out much hope for the end result; so much so in fact, that we didn't take the recording of it that seriously at all. G-Man threw some samples at it, Stevie Boy funked up the bass, Fardy and I over-amped and over-effected the guitars and I topped it off with some very shaky rapping (for 'very shaky' read 'cringe inducingly awful'). Perversely it worked! It was by far the best sounding song from this session; the end result almost sounded how 'indie powercore' should! Depending on where you were coming from it was either: Jesus Jones on steroids or Jesus Jones with haemorrhoids. 'Overdose' became a regular feature on the live set list after this.

Luckily 'Schooosh' was still getting us gig bookings, as not one of us wanted to use '152 or Faster' as a promo tape, which had been the original reason for recording it. After a lot of arguing and sulking (it's shit – yes, but we need to recoup the cost – but it's shit – yes, but we need to recoup the cost – but it's shit - ad infinitum) we decided to sell it through Our Price. With G-Man in the band we could now legitimately sell in Our Price throughout the Midlands and no longer had to reverse-shoplift them. To our surprise it was a gamble that paid off, the MTF t-shirt wearing public lapped it up and we sold out of the four hundred copies we'd had run off very quickly

217

(we didn't go for a second batch). In the Dudley branch it even made number six in the singles chart and helped earn enough money to venture into the studio again. We should have had enough money from playing live, but it always seemed to disappear on petrol / diesel, beer (lots of beer) and take-away food (lots and lots of take-away food), leaving just enough to cover a week's rehearsal room cost.

"Alright, boys," oh dear, not a good start, the last bloke called us boys. "I shall be your sound engineer for the duration," said The Tempest. He looked like he should be in Faith No More, and had a laid back way of speaking that sounded something like how a Californian would sound, if California was part of Birmingham's commuter belt. We'd booked into The Workshop in Redditch. It was going to cost us, yet we hadn't even done a pre-booking recce here. If it was good enough for The Wonder Stuff to record their early B-sides here (I still hadn't fully shaken that man crush), it would be good enough for us; even though we weren't purely The Wonder Stuff influenced these days, of course. Ocean Colour Scene and Ned's Atomic Dustbin were also clients of The Workshop, which further increased our pre-recording no-recce nonchalance.

"Alright, mate. Errr," I was slightly disappointed that it wasn't going to be David Morris. He'd done The Wonder Stuff's sound on the fore mentioned B-sides. "Errr, no Dave?" I asked hopefully.

"Nah, he only does the bigger names," The Tempest replied. Honest, but uncalled for. We've got, errr, I've got a fragile artiste's ego you know. He must've sensed the rapid deflation of my ego. "Don't worry, boys, I'm pretty good too." Well, we have heard that before, and with the use of 'boys'.

"Errr, OK. Let's do this thing," I said with somewhat limited enthusiasm. I was going to attribute this to one of the others, but unfortunately it was me who uttered it; too many mafia movies I guess. The next three hours flew by. The Tempest was something of an audio genius and quite the diplomat too; there was hardly any arguing or sulking during the mixing process at all. The suggestions he made, none of which included adding accordions or trumpets, also contributed to really help bring out the best in the songs. We'd finally captured the real MTF on tape. If it hadn't have been for my bad back I'd have been digging the foundations for that guitar shaped swimming pool myself.

Sleeve Notes: 'Où Est Le Canard?'

One of Plum Fingers' mates always used to shout 'Where's the duck?' at us when we played live. I was never one hundred percent sure why, but it stuck. We even had MTF t-shirts printed with it emblazoned on the sleeve. Why we chose to translate it into French? Once more my memory eludes me. Unfortunately Veiny was not a French speaker either and was quite probably away with the reggae fairies again when he did the artwork. The title appeared as 'Où Est Le Carnard?' on the final sleeve. Not one of us spotted the error until several months after release, and only when somebody asked what on earth 'carnard' meant. Oops.

Track 1. 'Colonel Clutz' 148BPM

A couple of days after I'd come out of hospital the aerial bombardment of Iraq, as part of Operation Desert Storm, began. I liked a good war film, but this was very real and, through my pain killer cocktail induced haze, I became morbidly fascinated with the twenty four hour news coverage. I didn't sleep during the first three days of the air war. This wasn't an anti-war song, I don't do politics (and certainly not if they're going to take my guitar away I don't), and it wasn't meant to glorify it either. You can read what you want into the lyric *'the planes fly overhead, killing zone destination, laser guided death, kill without deliberation'*. I loved Fardy's guitar work on this. Whilst my experiences of the battlefield are slightly limited: 'Platoon', 'Full Metal Jacket', 'Apocalypse Now', 'Hamburger Hill' and Wolves v Millwall / West Brom / Sheffield United, I reckon his riffing managed to capture the true ebb and flow of the battlefield.

Track 2. 'Mania Maniac' 148BPM

Let's talk about drugs, baby. More specifically, sex and drugs and rock 'n' roll. While there was a lot of rock 'n' roll in MTF, we didn't really do the drugs, apart from the occasional conjugal visit with the reggae fairies at Me Brother's house. Students, eh? We much preferred to poison our bodies with fags and booze. The amount of booze we got through (actually, combine that with the clinging odour that comes from living in the back of a van for weeks on end subsisting on nothing but doner kebabs, fish and chips, and curry) usually meant that there wasn't much sex either. At the time I was reading Huxley's 'The Doors of Perception' and downing prescription pain killers for my back injury; through that prescribed heady mixture I decided I wanted to explore 'chemical thought' in song[4]. I must've got my foot in the door as I was pretty pleased with the lyrics on this one, but for some reason I wasn't very perceptive (prescription pain killers and alcohol, possibly?) and I veered away from applying my song writing formula; there were two different changey / interludey bits and three verses. Appropriately, half way through recording it, a stranger appeared in the studio (G-Man and I must've forgotten to lock the door properly when we'd been outside for a fag) and beckoned me outside. He was a big fellow, so I wasn't going to argue and also hoped that the others would follow me out as back up. They didn't.

"Do you want to buy some drugs, mate?" he asked, once we were outside and looked around furtively. "You name it, I've got it." I bet you haven't got Tanya Donelly's phone number, have you?

"Errr, you got any Special Brew? I'm an alcoholic, mate, not a fuckin' junkie," I replied. There was an awkward silence as he stared at me menacingly. "Errr, sorry," I added sheepishly, my bravado appeared to be faster than Linford Christie and was galloping headlong down the street. At length he slapped me on the back, laughed a sinister laugh and disappeared into the night. I hope he didn't catch up with my bravado. Phew, though! That'd teach me for being a smart arse.

'Mania' was a bit slow and coming in at four minutes fifteen seconds, way too long for my liking. With hindsight I reckon it was at least one changey / interludey bit and a verse too long. We should've saved this one for when we became a stadium band and added a third changey / interludey bit and then a fourth verse with a double chorus, repeated four times to allow ten thousand people to get their lighters out. Sounds pretty good through the head phones, Stevie Boy reckons.

Track 3. 'Beautifully Absurd' 152BPM

Stevie Boy's favourite and possibly Fardy's favourite song (still unsure from his email). It was a simple, pure and perfect two minutes twenty-eight seconds of unadulterated 'indie powercore'. Not my greatest lyrical moment mind, but it was our: 'I love Rock 'n' Roll' (Joan Jett), our 'For Those About to Rock' (AC/DC), our 'Rock You Like a Hurricane' (The Scorpions), our 'Rock 'n' Roll' (Led Zeppelin), our 'Let's get Rocked' (Def Leppard), errr, you get the picture, but without actually using the word 'rock' anywhere in it at all. It was beautifully absurd. Nice reverse tape stop by The Tempest before the final double chorus end too.

Now we had something to send out to the record companies. We didn't elicit much response from the major labels, and if we did it was usually along the lines of 'this is a poorly photocopied generic letter to say we couldn't be arsed to listen to your tape'. One major did come back with a hand written letter that asked us to send her our next recording: promising. However, at least three of the minor labels came back with positive responses: 'Liked the tape, guys. Let us know when you are next playing in London, we'll meet up for a chat.' Never mind the guitar shaped swimming pool, I was digging the foundations for the faux seventeenth century country manor house now.

'Où Est Le Canard?' absolutely flew out of Our Price, so much so that we had to have another pressing made (do you have pressings made of cassettes?). It went straight in at number three in the cassette singles chart and stayed there for four weeks. It must've helped boost t-shirt sales too; on checking the bank balance a month or so after the release of 'Où Est...' we had more than enough wedge to book another session with The Tempest, and it would still leave enough for a curry and a few pints on the way home. With the interest we were now receiving from labels and press alike we decided to strike while the iron was hot. We booked in at The Workshop and specifically requested The Tempest. Who needed David Morris to make you sound like The Wonder Stuff, when you had The Tempest to make you sound like MTF?

Sleeve Notes: 'The Cogwinder'

Stevie Boy named this one. It came from a bloke he worked with who used to say 'I wuz gonna give 'um a roight cogwinder' whenever he was telling a tale about visiting a difficult customer. The sentiment fitted really well. Everything had come together perfectly, including the tongue in cheek cover version, and we were going to give everybody a right cogwinder with this one. Veiny's depiction of a Michelin Man wearing a gas mask as Da Vinci's 'Vitruvian Man' on the cover artwork was sublime. This, for me, was our finest ever eight minutes fifty-seven seconds captured on tape.

Track 1. 'Michelin Man' 168BPM

The fastest ever MTF song, and my personal favourite. *'You've reached the spreading age, now your body and muscles have all given up'*. I'd just turned twenty-four and, still being as vain as when I was the specky kid at school, I was very worried about the size of my ever burgeoning waist line. I decided to come out and tell everybody about it, in song, before I went past ten and a half stone! I hadn't even considered how much I might have spread by the time I reached forty-four. It was no surprise really though, the last twelve months had been spent devouring an inordinate amount of alcohol and a fast food mountain that could have solved the food crisis in any number of the smaller African republics. *'A martyr to the cholesterol motel, the take-away and fast food hotel'*; Stevie Boy and I tried to

222

make amends by playing table tennis once a week, before we went down the pub for Sunday lunch.

Track 2. 'Cynicism' 148BPM

Not the fastest and not my outright favourite, yet I reckon it was the best song I ever wrote that we recorded. There was another that would've taken the 'best song I ever wrote' title: 'Psychotic Fool'; but that was never immortalised on tape. 'Cynicism' told the tale of a group of hard working Black Country lads (you can hardly call picking the phone up in the morning to make sure someone was driving my van hard work, but I'm sure the other three worked very hard) and the dissatisfaction of trying to get by in the world while others seemed to have everything handed to them on a plate. Fardy considered the frustration in the lyrics to be palpable; I think that was more likely by accident rather than design, with me trying to hit the high notes, yet it did add to the feel. It was a good 'stage diver' this one. Sounds a bit political now I listen back and think about it; I don't do politics.

Track 3. 'Bitter End' 156BPM

This was G-Mans favourite song and we all believed it merited a second chance in the studio, as did 'Shot Down, Big Sky' for that matter. After a protracted rehearsal room debate, no rehearsal lots of debate, 'Bitter End' made the squad.

"Accordions and trumpets?" The Tempest asked incredulously. Fardy loved telling of the 'accordions and trumpets' advice. "Was he on crack?"

"No, mate, not crack, he was a fucking clown," Fardy added.

The ghost of Sound Engineer Guy was well and truly laid to rest as we tweaked the BPM up from 152 to 156. The Tempest suggested doing the opening split riff with acoustic guitars before reverting back to the electrics to explode into the main riff and verse. Some nice panned cymbals in the changey / interludey bit too. We were really pleased with the final result; it was how it should've sounded on '152 or Faster'.

Track 4. 'One for the Disco Kids' 148BPM

Given my abhorrence of doing cover versions, it was actually me who instigated including one, just the one mind, in our live set. On seeing The Family Cat do Dee-Lite's 'Groove is in The Heart' I had changed my mind and we had a go at 'Theme from S'Express'. It stayed on the live set for a while, until Fardy and I were looking for a new one to do and started messing about with Madonna's 'Get Into The Groove'; which is what 'One for the Disco Kids' is. I was almost certainly wondering if Madonna's phone number was easier to come by than Tanya Donnelly's, and whether recording this would be my in (to her lawyers most likely). To put her lawyers off the scent we labelled it as 'OFTDK', which came from a gig in Stratford-Upon-Avon. A rather too trendy looking audience had not taken much notice of us until we played this; it changed the whole complexion of the gig. Called back for a very unexpected encore it was the obvious choice to play again. Pop song as game changer! Obviously I'm biased, nevertheless, our version is way better than Madonna's original; the original had keyboards in it. We cynically included it on 'The Cogwinder' to widen our appeal.

Now we really had something to send out to the record companies! And to point out to them that we really did, we included a hand written note that said 'send us a poorly photocopied generic letter to say that you couldn't be arsed to listen to this tape at your peril'.

.....Thunderbird; lots of Thunderbird. Sound check at The Hummingbird in Birmingham; Stevie Boy getting carried away again, jumping up and getting concussion after hitting his head on the stage lights. The show must go on and he soldiered through the live set; he should've probably gone to hospital. Rock 'n' roll. Being interviewed by The Express and Star. Re-enacting the night patrol scene from 'Platoon' on the Stourbridge to The Lye train tracks with G-Man. So drunk. Bill posting with a couple of MTF t-shirt wearers,

cheers boys; we'd been nicked a couple of times, now we drove the volunteers around and told them where to post, while we stayed in the relative safety of the van around the corner. Flaming Drambuies; lots and lots of Flaming Drambuies. Leaving G-Man's drums outside a venue and not finding out until the following day; unsurprisingly they weren't there when we returned. Minor record label interest; they never call back. Turning up at my parents' house at three in the morning after a JB's gig totally naked (the trail of clothes my Dad retrieved began at the top of the village); I think this is when I learnt that the yellow ones didn't sit too well with alcohol. Major music press coverage; we even had an inch in the NME! Those fuckers never call back either. A girl from 'oop north. Living at Me Brother's house in London; I moved there for a while after the 'turning up naked' incident. Stevie Boy being debagged on stage by the bass guitarist of Strawberry Love Truncheon (he'd tried me first but I was wearing a belt!). Major record label interest; some other fuckers who never call back. Re-enacting the night patrol scene from 'Platoon' with Stevie Boy near a village in the middle of nowhere and then pulling a couple of sorts. So, so drunk. A girl from Finland. Management company interest; they never call back either. Playing gigs with Jain Faith. Veiny shouting 'rock 'n' roll' down a Burger King mike somewhere in central London. G-Man and I going toe to toe with some townies in a chippy in The Lye; it was our fault 'cos we had long hair apparently (we didn't come off so well in this one, luckily I had the pink, blue and yellow ones for after). Stevie Boy Yoko'd again. Stevie Boy and me at Mr Daves in The Lye, wooing the ladies with a couple of bottles of Thunderbird; smooth operators. Me, Yoko'd briefly (I anticipated and finished the break up song well before the end). Whole band vindaloo challenges. Fardy and his über dry sense of humour. Sound Engineer Guy; who was that fucking clown? Flaming Drambuies; yet more Flaming Drambuies. Re-enacting the night patrol scene from 'Platoon' with Veiny in Isleworth. Stevie Boy back on the team; excellent! The Tempest; you rocked dude. Going to buy a new amp in Birmingham; 'for a Wonder Stuff sound you do this, mate'. I've said it before, but you just don't twiddle with another man's knob; ever. Not being allowed into a venue in Oxford by the bouncer; the very same bouncer who had opened up to let us in to sound check about two hours earlier, bloody clipboard carriers. London; I loved London. More Thunderbird; way too much Thunderbird. The late night garage in Isleworth; don't suppose you've got these in a size ten? Playing gigs with Fretblanket. The girls from Stratford-Upon-Avon; now they liked a bit of it. Rock 'n' roll. G-Man and I doing a phal challenge in The Lye the whole kitchen staff cheering us on; it was hot, mentally and physically bum-burningly hot (I had to use the public toilets in Stourbridge's Rye Market the next morning, that is how ill I was). A girl from Buckinghamshire. Fanzine interviews, lots and lots of fanzine interviews; the good, the bad and the extremely ugly. Following the pretty lights. London again, we loved London; well, I know I did. A strange bloke in a German helmet and SS greatcoat; Fardy with a knife under his pillow (not sure Fardy loved London much after that). Selling out two pressings of 'Où Est Le Canard?'; mais bien sûr, mes amis. Major record label interest, again; the fuckers still never call back. Having a tramp steal my right trainer as I slept on a park bench somewhere in London; I'd misplaced the band again and, as I knew I wasn't in either Isleworth or Camberwell, decided to sleep on it until the newsagents opened up in the morning (I woke up in time to stop the theft of the left one, but was way too drunk to chase him down). Radio interviews; take your pick, I was either funnier or drunker than The Beatles (don't kid yourself, they drank; anyone who could write 'The Frog Song' knew their way around the optics). Hospital again, several times; epidurals are not nice, but did provide for an extra supply of the yellow ones and a new rather potent red one. Signing autographs for random kids in Birmingham; now that was weird, but I could get used to it. Fardy and his transcendent guitar work, Stevie Boy chugging the bass, G-Man thrashing the drums (when we hadn't left them outside a venue, that is). Interviewed and photographed by Sounds[(5)]; finally, some fuckers who called back. Almost getting to meet Mariella Fostrup (she hosted an arts programme on TV at Zero

Dark Ridiculous in the morning); television wankers, 'yeah I know, you'll call us back, right?'. 'The Cogwinder' with The Tempest; could we ever forget The Tempest? You rocked 'The Cogwinder', dude; large. A girl from Guildford. Strange phone calls; 'U-wan-doo TV Japan?'. Veiny, in full combat gear and gas mask; he danced a freaky Bez on stage and then dropped his bags for the full, full moon. Rock 'n' roll. Hungover, very, very hungover indeed; a lot. Errr, hang on, you want us to appear on Japanese TV? I'll get my passport ready, mate.....

1991 was all so beautifully, beautifully absurd. And it wasn't even over yet!

[1] Annus Mirabilis: Latin for 'wonderful year'. The first known written usage of the phrase is as the title of a poem composed by English poet John Dryden about the events of 1666. There was a fire in London and we beat the Dutch navy. He really should've waited until 1966, now that was a rather wonderful year.

[2] It was in the local papers, but it was a wave and we were going to ride it.

[3] Dexy's Midnight Runners song 'C'mon Eileen' used an accordion and trumpets. Sound Engineer Guy may even have been involved with the original session. Or was he really just a clown?

[4] How pretentious can a twenty three year old be? And the answer is, for those who are still unsure: very, very, very.

[5] Sounds, a music paper that had been running since 1970, folded in 1991. About two weeks after our interview. It was never published. I could've sworn it was Steve Lamacq (now a BBC radio DJ) who did the interview. I met him in a student union bar several years later; he had no recollection of ever coming to Dudley, let alone MTF. To be honest, he didn't look like the bloke who'd interviewed us. It must've been another Steve.

14. Better to Burn Out Than Fade Away

"Dream in a pragmatic way."
Aldous Huxley

We should've looked up 'pragmatic' back then; it was one of those words, along with sobriety, that didn't exist in MTF's vocabulary. After several calls with TV Executive-San we ascertained that we had to audition for the show first. This didn't dampen our enthusiasm, neither did the revelation that the audition was to be held in London and we wouldn't be flown out to Japan; in our minds we'd already sold out five nights at the Budokan and were downing sake on the eleventh floor of the Tokyo Hilton with an eager horde of geisha groupies.

"Look at this lot, did they know we were coming?" Stevie Boy said, as we pulled through the gates of a north London studio complex, narrowly missing several of the thirty or so teenage girls who were trying to peer into the depths of our van.

"They must have. Have you seen the graffiti, Matt?" asked Fardy. 'I Love Matt' was scrawled all over the gates and nearby walls.

"It's me, I'm Matt, hello," I shouted and waved to them, as I stuck my head out of the van window. They stared back bemused. "But I'm Matt, you love me." I obviously wasn't the Matt of their affections. Had I read the other graffiti on the gates, it would have been a slight a clue that we had just driven through a throng of gospel loving girls; it proclaimed their love for Luke too. Mark and John weren't getting a look in with this lot. We parked up and made our way to reception, watched by a sea of mystified teenage faces. G-Man turned and waved.

"You made it through the gates then?" asked the receptionist. "We've got Bros in recording their next album at the moment, but they're not even here today." Ah, Matt and Luke Goss, of course. That explained the graffiti then.

"Bros? Fucking clowns," Fardy whispered under his breath. We were told to wait and someone would come and get us when they were ready. Settling down into the luxurious sofas of the reception area we looked around at the numerous photographs and gold discs on the walls. We'd never been in a studio with gold discs on the walls. Heroes from childhood, Metallica, Black Sabbath and Judas Priest were among them, as were Duran Duran (who were not one of my childhood heroes but Stevie Boy was quite impressed) and Cliff Richard. I wondered if he recorded 'Devil Woman' here. I was trying to spot a gold disc by The Wombles when a clipboard carrying TV type approached us; he didn't look very Japanese. He introduced himself as TV Executive-San, the one and very same with whom I'd been talking on the phone for the last couple of weeks. I had thought it was a bit strange that a Japanese person would have a slight southern English accent. He was taller than I thought he might be, too.

With Stevie Boy humming the tune to 'When Will I Be Famous?'[1] TV Executive-San led us down a plush carpeted corridor, yet more photographs and gold discs adorned the walls, to a decent sized sound stage room. Hang on. This was unlike any rehearsal room we'd ever been in before. Where was the battered old drum kit? The over flowing ashtrays? The beer stained and decrepit amplification (of varying vintages and all of questionable serviceability)? If I had a pound for every time I've had a minor electric shock in a rehearsal room, I'd be about fifty quid richer. There wasn't even the cloying smell of a blocked toilet or rising damp. In fact, it smelt as though someone had given it a decent going over with the Shake 'n' Vac and Mr Sheen that very morning. It was fully kitted out too; on top of a small stage area (a stage area! And, it wasn't even that small) was a state of art PA system as well as the following luxuries: shiny Premier drums, Zildjian cymbals and a pristine looking, full Marshall back line set up. I could get used to this; I began to hum 'When Will I Be Famous?' too. The room even came with its very own sound engineer. TV Executive-San left us with him to set up.

"What are you called, lads?" he asked, as he set about the task of stripping the drum kit down to cater for G-Man's minimalistic set up.

"MTF," I replied before anyone could utter the full version.

"MTF? Isn't that short for 'male to female transfer'?" he asked, with somewhat of a smirk on his face. Can it really mean that? I'd rather have not known this; I should've used the full version after all. If only we hadn't just had another batch of two hundred odd t-shirts printed with MTF (in the MTV logo) as bold as you like across the front, I might've pushed for a name change there and then.

We were half way into a run through of 'Cynicism' when TV Executive-San returned with five other TV Executive-Sans in tow. They were most definitely all Japanese; two had cameras slung around their necks, another two held camcorders and the fifth was carrying the ubiquitous TV Type's clipboard. Three of them had even flown in from Tokyo especially for the auditions. There followed a lot of head bowing, smiling and muted hellos as we were introduced to the entourage. I was asked to state the band's name and the title of the song we were going to play in front of the camcorder.

"Errr, we are, errr, Mercenary Tree Freaks," I mumbled unenthusiastically, I'd gone right off MTF, and then with regained enthusiasm, "this is 'Beautifully Absurd'. 1, 2, 3, 4." Except I didn't need to do the '1, 2, 3, 4,' as the drum machine always clicked us in. I hadn't needed to do the '1, 2, 3, 4,' for ages. Audition nerves, I guess. So with a '1, 2, 3, 4, click, click, click, click' we launched into 'Beautifully Absurd'. It was good, it felt good. The sound in the room was fantastic, probably better than most of the venues we'd ever played at. Approaching the second verse, out of the corner of my eye, I could see Stevie Boy doing his bouncy thing when suddenly a very loud pop emanated from the bass amp. The bass went quiet and the rest of us petered out to leave just the drum machine pulsing away maniacally before G-Man killed it. Stevie Boy looked at his bass in confusion. We all looked at Stevie Boy in, errr, I'm not sure of the adjective that applied to the way we were looking at him. Six TV Executive-Sans all looked at us. I'm not sure of the adjective that applied to the way they were looking at us either. Very inscrutable, the Japanese.

"You've trodden on your lead, mate." I'd spotted the reason for bass failure: the lead had left the amplifier. Only a size thirteen monkey boot could've done that.

"They're gonna think we're a bunch of fucking clowns," Fardy whispered.

"Right, errr, can we go again?" I asked the TV Executive-Sans.

"No, that's ok. Just do your next song," replied the non-Japanese TV Executive-San. OK, I got it; we don't call you, you call us, right?

"Errr, right," I looked into the camcorder. "Errr, this is 'Cynicism'. 1, 2, 3, 4." Except I didn't need to do the '1, 2, 3, 4,' here either. I usually started this one off alone, and then sustained a power chord into screeching feedback before G-Man unleashed the drum machine. Except where was the feedback? I couldn't get my guitar to screech at all (stupid top class equipment in a quality rehearsal room). Stevie Boy and Fardy looked at me nervously. I turned towards the amp and thrust my guitar towards the speakers hoping to coax some feedback, any feedback out of the damn thing; nothing. I moved even closer; nothing, still nothing. The power chord had nearly faded to nothing too. They must've thought we were auditioning through the medium of mime. G-Man looked at me anxiously. He mouthed 'when?' and added a questioning gesture of the shoulders. Not going well at all! I began to panic.

"Oh fuck it, NOW," I shouted at G-Man in sheer distress. I didn't need to shout because my guitar was nearly silent. I also shouldn't have shouted because I was very close to the microphones that covered the drums. These highly sensitive pieces of equipment picked up 'oh fuck it, NOW,' and launched it around the room. Realising my mistake I span around to mouth 'sorry' at the assembled TV Executive-Sans. In doing so I inadvertently caught my guitar neck on a microphone stand. I fumbled the neck. A loud and very un-tuneful 'gggrrrwanng' erupted from my amp before salvation came with the opening 'click, click, click, click' of the drum machine. Finally! We launched into 'Cynicism'. We rocked the 'indie powercore' from there on. How that audition video has never made You've Been Framed or YouTube I have no idea. And, just like I hadn't been able to get any feedback out of my guitar, we didn't get any feedback out of the TV Executive-Sans at the end either. They remained as inscrutable as ever. All we received were a few polite bows and curt nods of head as they left the room, no doubt on their way to put a big red cross against MTF on both of their clipboards. The only feedback that did come our way came from the sound engineer.

"Loved that, lads. Fackin' loved it. MTF, eh?" he grinned, as we trudged out of the room. It looked like we'd just committed musical seppuku[(2)] and could kiss goodbye to five nights at the Budokan, as well as forget the eager hordes of geisha groupies. We waved goodbye to the less eager horde of Brosettes as we left the complex. Oh well, I suppose we could always buy some sake from Tesco on the way home.

We got the gig! Three days later TV Executive-San called to give us the good news. The contingent from Tokyo appeared to have had the casting vote and, while they had totally misconstrued our inept audition as part of the performance, saw us as fitting into some sort of avant-garde rock movement. Apparently, they like that type of thing in Japan. I wasn't sure we would be able to replicate that level of avant-garde ineptitude even if we tried, but we weren't going to argue; Japan here we come! I started to draw up plans for the parental annex on my faux seventeenth century country manor house before the foundation work went too far.

.....The lights went down. A cheer went up from the crowd, etc, etc. Yeah, OK, we all get the picture by now. The elevated drum riser was no longer bare. Three guitar wielding heroes emerged through the whirling dry ice, a fourth figure climbed on to the drum riser. The singer-guitarist swaggered towards the microphone.

"KONICHIWA TOKYO! Are you ready to rock through the medium of mime?".....

The devil, as always, was in the detail. Japan, denied! We weren't going to Japan, we were going back to London; filming would take

233

place at Limehouse Television Studios in Wembley. Appearing on Japanese TV in London wasn't that huge a disappointment mind (I'm not the most relaxed flyer for a start), as I was more than happy and slightly awestruck that Blur and James were going to be on the same show. They were real, like very real, like proper bands. Before we all became totally mesmerised we had to go to London, yet again, to record the backing tracks; we'd be miming, except for me who would have to sing live. Star Search probably had an audience of less than half a million (not too shabby, especially when you're used to playing in front of two to three hundred or so); the Japanese show had an anticipated viewing audience somewhere in the twenty million[3] bracket (and they would be the rock music buying public of Japan, not the UK's Saturday night fish and chip crowd in search of some light entertainment). That Blur and James would also be appearing in front of twenty million on the same show did nothing to alleviate my nerves.

"How long?" It was a collective groan and from more than just MTF members. The news that the sessions were now running even further behind schedule than they had been three hours ago hadn't gone down well at all. We were scheduled as the last band of the day to record and had turned up at Olympic Studios an hour early for our 4PM slot. The recording studio was in Barnes, south-west London, and, while it didn't have as many photographs or gold discs adorning the walls as the audition studios, it had a rock pedigree just as rich, if not richer: The Beatles, Jimi Hendrix, The Rolling Stones, The Who, Led Zeppelin and Queen had all recorded there. It might have slipped somewhat recently mind; it was rumoured that Chris de Burgh was currently laying some tracks down there. As well as a rich rock heritage it also had a rather well appointed rest area (we hadn't had sight of the recording rooms yet). In fact, it was more of a very large lounge than a rest area. It had sofas (all immaculate leather), a snooker table (without a single tear or beer stain on the baize), a grand piano (a real grand piano!) and a large screen television that was tuned permanently to MTV (this was in the days when MTV actually broadcast music videos).

It had just turned 7PM and there were still two bands to record before us. An hour and a half had been allotted to each session to get two songs down for the show. With the delay this meant that even if the next band went in at 8PM, we weren't going to be called until at least 11PM. The bands earlier in the day must've been even worse arguers and sulkers than MTF and Incee Wincee Spider combined.

At around eight o'clock a news flash interrupted, what felt like, the umpteenth showing of Roxette's 'Joyride' video to announce that Freddie Mercury had died. None of us were big Queen fans (or even little fans for that matter) but the other bands waiting seemed to be genuinely upset and gathered around the television to stare in mournful silence as the 'Bohemian Rhapsody' video replaced Roxette on a seemingly continual loop. Fardy moved towards the grand piano and sat on the stool in front of it. We looked on intrigued; we didn't know that Fardy had any inclination towards the piano. He lifted the keyboard cover, flexed his fingers, cracked his knuckles and then began to play along to the start of 'Bohemian Rhapsody', absolutely note perfect, except, at the end of each phrase he purposely put in a bum note, just like a vintage Les Dawson piano sketch. We rolled around in tears; not so the Mercury mourners gathered around the television. Any way the wind blows?

"Do you mind, that's so disrespectful," protested one of them. Fardy stopped abruptly. We stopped laughing and looked at each other, as though we'd just been told off by a teacher.

"Miserable fucking clowns," Fardy muttered under his breath. We burst out laughing again, to a tirade of tutting and several derisive looks. I'm sure Freddie would've seen the funny side, darlings.

We finally went in to record with the clock approaching midnight. We were too tired to be overawed by the recording facilities, amazing as they were. The sound engineer was too tired to be bothered to answer the 'did Jimi really record here?' and 'where did he sit?' questions for the twentieth time that day. He wasn't weary enough to mention that 'before you ask, yes, I know that Freddie

Mercury has died'. TV Executive-San was also tired, but nowhere near sufficiently fatigued to be unconcerned about the massive over spend on recording. Our budget allocation for artistic integrity got slashed and they rushed us through in less than forty-five minutes. It was an MTF record for getting two songs down in the studio, but the end result was a somewhat weaker sound than we would have got from The Tempest. In all, it was a very long day indeed for less than forty-five minutes in a studio; we eventually got back home just in time for me to phone and check that I had a driver in my van that day and for the others to get an hour's sleep before work.

We spent the next couple of weeks, whilst we waited for the actual show recording to come around, gigging and prepping the promotional material to go with 'The Cogwinder'. We wanted to try and hit the record companies with it before the television show was recorded, and therefore hopefully get any interested parties into the television studios. It worked! The minor record labels, who'd been interested in 'Où Est...' yet had gone very quiet ever since, once again renewed their interest (with hindsight they were probably only really interested in blagging a plus one or two on the guest list). From the major labels we still received several poorly photocopied generic letters to say they couldn't be arsed to listen, but we now had three (THREE!) who were making some positive noises; including A&R Girl again (the one who had asked us to send our next tape after 'Où Est...'). This time her response was even more intriguing: 'LOVED IT! Don't talk to anyone else until you've spoken to me first'. We put the minors down for a plus one and the majors for a plus two. I pondered whether to order a Ferrari or a Lamborghini? Why not both?

"Look, this is where they record The Word," said Stevie Boy, and pointed to a photograph of The Word's presenting team on the wall.

"Really?" I asked, as we walked through Limehouse Television Studios towards our allotted dressing room. I started to peer into every dressing room we passed, hoping to catch a glimpse of Dani Behr. Unfortunately Japanese television shows were recorded on

Wednesday, and not Friday when The Word was recorded. We were old hands at this television game now; it was just another day at the office. In make-up, we didn't even bother voicing our usual protestations and there were only a few lame jokes about men wearing make-up.

......*"Men wearin' mare-cup? Men wearin' fuckin' mare-cup? Bay no fuckin' jokin' motter, eh Ted?"*

"Arr, yam not fuckin' wrung, Bazza. Eh, med yow fuckin' loff tho', day it, when Bela Lugosi cum to werk n' did sum fuckin' weldin'?".....

Surprisingly, for a high profile MTF performance, the recording passed off without incident; as we were miming there were no guitar leads to unplug, the stage lights were high enough for Stevie Boy not to get concussion, and I tamed my nerves and managed to sing in tune. The resulting VT (as we in the trade call 'video tape') showed, depending on your point of view, either: a very polished performance from an 'indie powercore' band, or, four lads from the Black Country suffering from a communal and rather bad case of St Vitus Dance[4]. Either way, it was just another day at the office.

We got to meet Blur and James, but only briefly and usually in the gents. The rest of the time they locked themselves away in their dressing rooms, way too aloof to mix with the hoi polloi. At the after show party we had hoped to have a word with the assembled A&R Men, especially the two who had shown an interest in 'The Cogwinder', but they were all way too busy lining up to have a crack at the red-headed girl who sang in one of the other bands, rather than show any interest in doing their actual job. Blur and James didn't show their faces here either, as they had long since disappeared, chauffeured off into the pretty lights of the London night. We did manage to grab A&R Girl for a few seconds though.

"Hey, guys. Nice show, yeah?" she said. "I think we can possibly get you an opening slot on one of our band's tours, yeah?" 'Possibly', eh? Sounded promising. "I'll call you, yeah?" Ah, 'I'll call you' less so. We were getting quite used to the actual meaning of a music industry 'I'll call you' by now. And with that she disappeared to fight her way through the feeding frenzy with the other music industry freeloaders at the buffet table. If you can't beat them? We waded into the melee before all that was left were the salmon mousse vol-au-vents.

The following month was something of an anti-climax as we waited for the phone to ring. It never did. G-Man and I even went down to London and walked (more like sneaked) into one of the A&R Men's office (the label we would have liked to sign for) to try and gee him along. He was too busy in a meeting with three colleagues to sit down and talk with us, but said that he would call us. From what we could see, the meeting seemed to involve nothing more than throwing screwed up paper balls through a basket ball hoop on the wall (nice work if you can get it). We then tried to see A&R Girl at her place of work but their security was way tighter than at the first record company and we never even made it past the front door.

'The Cogwinder' was officially released with a gig in a small upstairs room of a pub in Stourbridge in March 1992. We followed this 'warm up' a few days later with another at JB's. Within a couple of weeks it was riding higher in Our Price's cassette singles chart (in the Black Country, not nationwide) than James' 'Born of Frustration' (a song they'd played on the TV show) and The Wonder Stuff's 'Welcome to the Cheap Seats'! We couldn't knock 'Bohemian Rhapsody', which had finally replaced Bryan Adams' 'Everything I Do', off the number one spot though. At one point we even had both 'The Cogwinder' and 'Où Est...' in the top ten.

While we waited for the call that would propel us further into the realms of our rock 'n' roll fantasy adventure, we settled back into our usual routine of gigging two or three times a week, and eating and drinking all of our tape and t-shirt profits. I was back in the zone, song writing wise, and we were also planning our next recording sessions. We knew where this one would be. I'd also, at long last, been signed fit for work and had returned to the day to day toil of driving up and down the UK's motorway network. Not brilliant for sitting around all day writing less than three minute slices of pure 'indie powercore' but probably came at the right time for my knees. All those happy little jigs of joy had begun to take quite a toll on them.

We waited. I worked.

We waited some more. I worked some more.

We'd just about given up hope.

And then....

The phone rang.

"Hi, Matt. TV Executive-San here. The show has been broadcast in Japan and has generated a lot of interest in MTF. A Japanese record company are very interested and are going to call you." Yeah, right, heard it all before, mate. "I've also got some fan mail for you, I'll post it on." It was a bag full of fan mail (thirty letters counted as a mail bag full in our books). 'The Cogwinder' was shipped off to Japan in the ~~thousands,~~ ~~hundreds,~~ twenty or so's. At the very least.

The phone rang again.

"Hi, Matt," it was A&R Girl. "We are very interested in MTF." I know, you keep telling us that. "There is no deal on the table at the moment, though." Surprise, surprise. "But we would like to pay for you to go into the studio with a producer and also put you on a university tour, see how you get on." We'll have some of that, darlin'.

The phone rang yet again.

"Hi, I represent Well Known Management Company. We've heard the buzz and are very interested in signing MTF to our company." You've changed your tune from a couple of months ago.

The phone kept ringing.

"TV Executive-San again, Matt, I forgot to mention that we'd like you back on the show." I'll just have to check our schedule first, mate.

And ringing.

"The producer of The Word here. Would you be interested in appearing on the show?" As long as Dani interviews us, we're in.

And ringing.

"Matt," oh, I knew that voice. "Can you a do an early morning delivery into Sheffield for us tomorrow?" The prospect of another day at the proper office bought me straight back down to earth. Lucky you called mind, I might be a bit busy next week.

I pulled into Sheffield very early the following morning to make the delivery. Once I'd unloaded and had all the paperwork signed, I jumped off the loading bay. CRACK. White searing lights flashed before my eyes. An agonising pain shot down my legs and through my lower back. I might've uttered the 'F' word; more than once. Oh dear, that didn't feel too good, I thought. I tried to climb back into the cab. No chance, I could hardly walk, let alone climb. I tried using a mind over matter technique in an attempt to mask the pain (the rubbish that I'd been told to try the last time my back had gone). That didn't work at all. I added an extravagant amount of swear words to my technique. That just about got me into the cab. A further tirade of invective eventually had me sat behind the wheel. I was in absolute face grimacing, eye watering agony. I should've saved some of the yellow ones, I thought. And then, why did I lay off my driver last week? Quickly followed by, how am I going to get down the pub tonight? Never mind the pub, how on earth was I going to get back home from Sheffield first? Sensibly, rather than waste time and effort on calling for an ambulance, I decided to drive myself back.

Five hours later, having broken the World Record for swearing in an hour five times on the bounce, I made it home. It should've only taken two but I'd had to pull over, for fear of passing out with the pain, on several occasions. Within two hours of arriving home I was lying on freshly starched sheets in a private medical facility in Birmingham, being soothed into a pain free delirium by one of the amino ester family (I don't remember which one, it definitely ended in 'caine' though) as it dripped into me intravenously. If I had been compos mentis I'd have congratulated myself, again, on taking out the private medical insurance that I'd been very reluctant to take out when I'd set up as an owner driver. And there I stayed for another week, although they took me off the 'caine' drip after three days;

some dispute over what and how much my insurance actually covered I think.

It was almost four months before I could move about again without any pain. Apparently, four months is a very long time in the music industry. I didn't realise it at the time, yet we had reached the beginning of the end; to be honest, depending on whereabouts I was in the pain relief cycle, I was either, way too giggly and smiley, or totally zoned out to realise anything at all. We'd had to cancel forty or so gigs; the television appearances also got cancelled, as did the recording session A&R Girl had set up, and her tour offer went the same way. Note 'cancelled' and not postponed. The musical landscape had shifted yet again. 'Madchester' and 'indie powercore' were deemed to be antediluvian by the music press. They were now hailing 'grunge' and 'Britpop' as this week's big thing. Even The Stone Roses were getting slated in the NME! That's how quickly the tide had turned.

I'd only just mastered 'indie powercore'. I didn't want to change direction so soon, and without a radical change in lyrical direction we would have had no chance with 'Britpop' whatsoever; we didn't have any jolly songs about quirky Cockneys living (extra)ordinary lives in leafy suburbia, and we certainly didn't have any about snorting Class A pharmaceuticals in run down squats on dilapidated northern council estates. Hang on. I could've had a go at writing about a strange bloke who wears a German helmet and SS greatcoat and lives in the 'burbs of not very leafy west London; that would fit the quirky, but wouldn't sound that jolly though.

It looked like we were about to miss the boat.

A&R Girl stopped calling.

The management company stopped calling.

The television executives stopped calling.

We rang them instead.

A&R Girl told me she'd call us. Then she stopped telling me she'd call us and then she stopped taking our calls altogether.

The management company just stopped taking our calls. They'd changed their tune from a couple of months ago. Again!

241

The television executives offered us a spot on Keith Chegwin's Star Search; we stopped calling them.

We were missing the boat.

The only positive that came out of this dark, dark period, apart from some rather strong dark yellow ones, came from fledging Spanish label Elefant Records. They obviously hadn't got a 'Britpop' movement in Spain and have you ever heard 'Spanpop'? Beyond awful! I'm not one hundred percent sure how they had picked up on us; we'd never played in Spain and I don't believe that Japanese TV gets transmitted in Spain either. Their main man and founder liked MTF though and offered us a one off single deal. He thought he was being commercially astute and had wanted to use 'OFTDK'. I told him no problem, as long as we were granted total immunity from any legal battle with the Queen of Pop's lawyers. He said he hadn't thought of that. Instead, 'Michelin Man' became the only ever vinyl release by MTF (Elefant Records ER-102, it comes up on eBay every now and again). Then, after a while, Elefant Records stopped calling too. It must've sold a few copies though; I used to receive a royalty cheque once a year, the last one came in 2004 for £1.75 (I've never cashed it). The rest of them combined would've only just about covered the cost of six tiles in a guitar shaped swimming pool.

We'd well and truly missed the boat.

I cancelled all work on the faux seventeenth century country manor house and gave up all hope of ever getting Tanya Donelly's phone number. This rock 'n' roll thing was way harder to do than it had appeared a couple of months ago. And, if something is difficult to do?

At our next rehearsal I dropped the bombshell that was the answer to that particular question.

"I'm leaving the band," I said. It was better to burn out than fade away. I wasn't going to blow my brains out though, or overdose on a speedball cocktail, or crash my car into a tree while having an hallucinogen induced episode, and I certainly wasn't going to 'accidently' hang myself with my trousers and pants around my ankles with an orange crammed in my mouth. I'd always thought that

I'd burn out like Bon Scott of AC/DC. Instead, I was going to burn out in academia. Mind you, I probably came quite close to doing a Bon Scott a couple of times at university (it usually involved tequila).

"Leaving? Errr, right. Why?" they asked in surprised unison. I could've ranted here about my disillusionment with the music industry. While partly true it would've only hidden the realisation that while we had made it out of rock's Vauxhall Conference, quite an achievement in itself, serious injury had meant that we'd fluffed our one and only chance at promotion to Division Three (League One in today's money). I really didn't want to spend the next couple of years in the lower reaches of Division Four (League Two today) before relegation back to the Conference and finally succumbing to playing cover versions in the Sunday leagues. And, if we were going to be totally pragmatic; I really needed a proper job.

"I'm going to university," I replied. I needed to widen my future employment prospects. There had to be another way to finance that guitar shaped swimming pool. I'd never liked going up the ladders and now, thanks to two impacted lower vertebrae, I could no longer drive or do any sort of lifting for a living. After a brief meeting with the Careers Service, I figured a middle management career in the transport and logistics industry might just be that way. Now that sounded like an interesting and rewarding career. No it didn't. 'Minimum effort, maximum sloth' prevailed yet again; I'd discovered that a degree in transport management was the easiest and quickest route into university. As I had industry experience (I drove a van; I doubt that would have landed me an Oxbridge interview) I might get accepted onto the course without having to spend a year or two taking 'A' levels (without any guarantee that I'd get the required grades). Industry experience meant I could start opening up the future employment horizon right away. I got accepted! This meant that I could spend the next four years doing happy little jigs of non-working joy (as long as my knees held out) in a student bar. Whether I made the move into middle management after that? Pffft, who knew? That would be four years down the line.

"University?" asked Fardy, and then muttered under his breath, "students, pffft, fucking clowns."

We didn't bother rehearsing after I'd broken the news; we'd ticked all the rock 'n' roll fantasy boxes we were ever going to tick. The electric guitar daydream quest was over. Instead we packed up solemnly, went down the pub and held a wake, while we reminisced over several beers (that turned into several, several more and then a curry) about the MTF years.

.....Franco whizzed past me, pedalling like fury. He was on a bike. He was on a bike? Yes, it was a bike. A full carbon framed racer. Cool. In the full and lurid lycra get up too. His tail, protruding through his salmon pink lycra shorts, trailed in his slip stream, ram rod straight as he flew away into the distance.

"FRANCO," I shouted. "Slow down, mate. I'm not as fit as you are." I tried to increase my speed. I was on a bike too. Except, mine appeared to have square wheels and a frame made of concrete.

"C'mon, Fat Boy," he shouted over his shoulder at me, one ear poking through a vent in his helmet. "Eammon Holmes is getting away."......

[1] 'When Will I Be Famous?' was a big hit for Bros in 1987. The album they were recording at the studio was 'Changing Faces' and released at the end of 1991. They split up shortly after that.

[2] 'Seppuku' translates as 'stomach cutting' and was a form of ritual suicide originally reserved only for samurai. It is also known as 'harakiri'.

[3] Japan's population at the time was estimated at around 124 million. The TV company estimate of twenty million viewers (16% of population) seems rather high to me for a rock music programme.

[4] Type 'Mercenary Tree Freaks' into YouTube. There are our two songs from this show and a couple of other live clips from MTF gigs that G-Man has posted. 'Michelin Man' is available on iTunes too.

Encore: Of Our Elaborate Plans

"At the end of a dream, if you know what I mean"
'Long Live Rock 'n' Roll' by Rainbow
(Lyric by Ronnie James Dio)

We were at the end of our dream. I started university in the north of England and we gradually lost touch. I haven't seen Stevie Boy or Fardy in twenty-one years. Like me, neither did much musically post MTF. It was thirteen years before I saw G-Man again. He carried the torch for the quest in a couple of bands after MTF's demise and has also dabbled with dance music. Since moving back to the Midlands we've had a couple of jam sessions and we keep talking about starting a band again. These days, we usually just end up going for a curry.

That was it; off I went to university (now there is probably another book here). I tried out with a couple of bands, but they never generated the same vibe that MTF had done and totally failed to captivate my interest. The only use my guitar got was for late night and very drunken sing songs back at our house; knowledge of 'Wild Rover', 'What Shall We Do With The Drunken Sailor' and the complete works of The Beatles came in very useful here, particularly if it was a 'non-indie powercore' crowd. By the third year my gear had almost totally disappeared as it was sold off, piece by piece, to fund those student essentials: beer, some more beer and Mad Dog 20/20. At the end of my final year, all I had left was an acoustic guitar; although I didn't play it much, I just couldn't bring myself to sell it. I loved university though. You could take 'minimum effort, maximum sloth' to previously unheard of, and totally unbelievable, levels. How I managed a 2:1 with honours ought to be the subject of a standalone degree course.

By the time I was two years into a middle management career in the transport and logistics industry I'd also sold the acoustic. Yes, it was as interesting and rewarding as I'd initially feared it might have been (there would probably be a book here too, except Ricky Gervais got there first with 'The Office' and might accuse me of plagiarising his characters).

245

Five years later I went out and bought a Gibson SG and Marshall amp. A decent Christmas bonus the following year had the SG joined by a Gibson Les Paul (I'd never owned two guitars at the same time before). I would've bought a Gibson Flying V, just like Wellington Womble's, but my local shop in Colchester didn't have one in stock. I even toyed with the idea of starting up a new band. Unfortunately, as I never knew where I'd be from week to week work wise, I could never fully commit to anything. The only use the guitars ever got were rocking out AC/DC's greatest in front of the bedroom mirror when Practice Wife wasn't around (she wouldn't have understood why I was standing in front of the mirror dressed in a short trousered school uniform complete with cap; I didn't want to explain).

Ten years in transport and logistics management was long enough for me; it's long enough for anyone in my opinion. I spent a year with the Police before I became a bohemian, free spirited, guitar strumming, traveller again (there was definitely a book here; I've already written it). I spent a couple of years travelling; I even ventured back into Portugal, but totally fell in love with Spain and spent most of my time there murdering yet another language.

And, after that? Well, to paraphrase my former man crush 'I'm still acting out that epilogue'.

Oh, yeah. One last thing: the significance of a talking cat? Eammon Holmes? Not a Scooby Doo.

.....The ageing rock singer-guitarist swaggered towards the microphone with a slight limp. He knew he shouldn't have taken part in that corporate golf event the day before a big gig. Or had the prawn and red pepper focaccia at lunch for that matter; it was repeating on him something rotten.

"WOLVERHAMPTON!" he screamed, through the crescendo of noise that was building to form the final power chord finish. "THANK YOU AND GOODNIGHT."......

Production Credits

Matt would like to thank the following people, without whom, etc, etc:

Proper Wife: for the support, encouragement, criticism, constructive criticism, patience, belief and, above all, the eye rolling. I knew I'd got it just how I wanted if a passage received an eye roll.

Stevie Boy, Fardy and G-Man: for the anecdotes, detail and ultimate inspiration; without you, there wouldn't have been MTF. Without MTF, there wouldn't have been those beautifully absurd three years. And without those beautifully absurd three years, there wouldn't have been this book. It might not be exactly how you remember it, but if you can, man, then you weren't really there. Vindaloo challenge, anyone?

Me Brother: for the cover artwork and graphic design stuff. Usual payment terms I hope: don't bother buying me anything for birthday or Christmas, should cover it, yeah?

Ametralladora: for the usual guidance and extreme patience. You want the next chapter by when? Errr, can I have another extension please?

And a special, and very sincere, thank you to:

The Almost Four Thousand: for buying 'Drunk in Charge'. That's way more books than I ever sold tapes, t-shirts and records combine! You must know that you have only got yourselves to blame for me writing another one though.

Also by Matt Rothwell

Drunk in Charge of a Foreign Language
(The Diary of a Spanish Misadventure)

Well, what would you do if your wife asked you for a divorce thirty days into a three month camping tour of Spain?

Set fire to the car and fly home?

Stay and get drunk for a couple of months?

Learn to chat girls up in Spanish, German and Russian?

Welcome to Spain as seen through the author's vino tinto glasses. It's a Spain rarely seen on television and certainly never mentioned in glossy travel magazines.

Paperback published by Ametralladora
ISBN: 978-0-9555896-1-4

Available from all good book shops, online or in the high street, and also exclusively from Amazon as a Kindle download.

For more information about the author visit:
www.facebook.com/MattRothwellAuthor